Creative Regionalism

OJB Landscape Architecture designed the central court at the North American Toyota Headquarters in Plano, Texas. This image of the central courtyard shows a naturalistic water feature that catches and stores stormwater for irrigation, canopy trees that provide an abundance of shade, and native plant species and other natural materials that evoke the spirit of North Texas. The design ties together the geometry of the cluster of glass curtainwall buildings and provides both visual and immersive regional experiences for the thousands of workers at the Toyota Campus (2018). All photographs are by the author unless otherwise noted.

CREATIVE REGIONALISM

Renewing the Aesthetic Experience of Landscape in Environmental Design and Planning

David DuMez Hopman

with a foreword by Frederick R. Steiner

GEORGE F. THOMPSON PUBLISHING

IN ASSOCIATION WITH THE CENTER FOR THE STUDY OF PLACE

I believe that sustaining beauty has currency and should be added to the many tactics and techniques used by those who care about sustaining our cities, regions, and planet through ecological design and planning. And I hope it will be given greater credence by designers and planners who seek sustainability in metrics and data-driven criteria as well as by social scientists and natural scientists who discount the ethical agency of a designed landscape's aesthetics...So while I believe that design cannot change society, it can alter an individual's consciousness and, perhaps, assist in restructuring one's priorities and values.

—Elizabeth K. Meyer

...Vital products of art in our specialized culture are always born from an open confrontation between the universal and the unique, the individual and the collective, the traditional and the revolutionary...Architecture, like art, is simultaneously autonomous and culture-bound. It is culture bound in the sense that tradition, the cultural context, provides the basis for individual creativity, and it is autonomous in the sense that an authentic artistic expression is never an answer to prescribed expectation or definition.

—Juhani Pallasmaa

Geographers cheerfully accept and try to integrate the apparently bewildering variety of disparate phenomena that give areas their distinctive character. Geography is science, but it is also an art, because understanding the meaning of an area cannot be reduced to a formal process. The highest form of the geographer's art is providing good regional geography—evocative descriptions that facilitate an understanding and appreciation of places, areas, and regions.

—John Fraser Hart

Top: Taliesin West in Scottsdale, Arizona, was designed by Frank Lloyd Wright as his winter home and as a school of architecture, and built by apprentices under his direct guidance. The UNESCO World Heritage Site brings the desert experience into the buildings with walls crafted from local stone mixed with concrete called "desert masonry" (2014).

Bottom: Architects Anderson, Mason, Dale and landscape architects Wenk Associates have continued the modern regionalist traditions featured at Taliesin West in a more prosaic setting at the Southeast Wyoming Welcome Center and highway rest stop near Cheyenne. The building design celebrates the local geology and regional earth colors with engaging rammed-earth walls (2018). Image courtesy of Frank Ooms.

Contents

Bluebonnets, live oaks, and limestone, all native to Texas, are centerpiece features in this minimalist but regionally inspired landscape design in Austin (2015). Here, the local environment is a starting point for the creative transformation of a suburban enclave into something new but also reflective of place. Photograph by Frederick R. Steiner. Used by permission.

Foreword

by Frederick R. Steiner

A region is an extensive place with critical attributes that differentiate it from other places. These characteristics can be physical, biological, and/or human. When we understand regional processes, we often become better designers. Such knowledge can unleash our inventiveness. At the very least, we can limit poor design decisions. Doing no harm is a low bar, but look around and one sees Aldo Leopold's "wounds of the world" everywhere.[1] The reduction of harm and the repair of past injuries are necessary starting points.

Landscape architect and educator David Hopman lays out a more ambitious vision from deep in the heart of Texas. Having lived in Austin for 15 years, I feel the rhythms of that heart. This is a book both *of* and *beyond* Texas. Regionalism requires the grounding in places that Hopman provides. As another Texan, Lady Bird Johnson, noted: "Wherever I go in America, I like it when the land speaks its own language in its own regional accent."[2] Lady Bird Johnson saw the native wildflowers of a place as a gateway to protect the environment and to advance beauty.

Although Hopman generally avoids the subversive, the political, and the economic, focusing instead on the practical, it seems to me that "critical regionalism" is fundamental to any effort to decolonize landscape architecture and architecture. In addition, as regionalism in landscape design must depend on ecological principles, it is inherently "subversive," according to Paul Sears.[3] Likewise, being critical can be subversive. In any case, Hopman presents a pragmatic method and inspirational theory for landscape design. Nothing is as practical as a good theory, the German American psychologist Kurt Lewin declared.[4] Hopman provides evidence of this practicality and explores failures as well—designed places that disregard the deep structure of a region.

When a designer understands regional systems, constraints become evident. A plant may be unsuited because of climate patterns and soil conditions, among other factors, even though it has aesthetic appeal. Good design depends on constraints. Regional systems also provide opportunities. I recall when landscape architects Steve Martino and Christy Ten Eyck began using native Sonoran plants in the Phoenix metropolitan area. Suddenly, Palo verde appeared everywhere. Authenticity elevates creativity.

Of course, regionalism has a long tradition in landscape design and planning. Patrick Geddes (1854–1932), Ian McHarg (1920–2001), Kenneth Frampton, Anne W. Spirn, and others have laid out strong cases for the values and benefits of regional thinking. Hopman is respectful of these regionalist voices, but he deftly lays out his own message based on his various experiences and thorough understanding of ecological design.

In his enterprising and spirited book, Hopman seeks to renew the aesthetics of landscape design through critical regionalism. Although Leopold is better known for his advocacy of a land ethic, he also championed land aesthetics and observed, for example, that every farm is a portrait of the farmer.[5] By extension, all built environments embody the values of those who inhabit them. Our ethics and values are displayed through how we organize our surroundings; that is, how we occupy the Earth. Regional sensibilities inform our values, which are reflected in the aesthetics of our designs and the aesthetics of our occupation.

As Hopman notes, critical regionalism is more of an approach than a style, and that approach is based on the essential natural and cultural elements that help define a region. When I think of Austin, in addition to barbeque, longhorns, and music, I see bluebonnets, live oaks, and limestone in my mind's eye (page 8). These elements can be mixed in a trite, superficial manner or engaged in ways that connect people to places through a variety of sensory experiences. In doing so, the transformative capacities of regions may be realized.[6]

David Hopman presents a broad, aspirational vision for landscape design and environmental planning grounded in critical regionalism. He understands that landscapes are cultural and natural artifacts of an ecosystem's dynamics and that ecosystems are characterized by flux and change. The promise of critical regionalism requires designers to "read landscapes," as J. B. Jackson implored more than seven decades ago when he founded *Landscape* magazine in 1951.[7] To do so, designers must get outside, look around, take in what they sense and see, dig deep into the characteristics of a place, read, talk to others, and act accordingly so that, as Hopman proclaims in his preface, regionally based designs can "improve people's lives." In *Creative Regionalism*, with its marvelous blend of theory and practice and compelling integration of text and illustrations, Hopman shows us the way.

Preface

The original impetus for this book was to study the relevance of critical regionalism theory and practice to rapidly developing areas of Texas. The problem for landscape architects and planners in rapidly developing areas such as North Texas, where I live and work, concerns where to look for a point of departure for a regional design when the immediate environmental context may have few prominent or easily identifiable regional elements. A notable example of this problem occurs in the Dallas-Fort Worth area, where designers are sometimes confronted with developments built in former agricultural fields with little or no existing native plants, topography, or easily perceptible regional design context, as seen in the photograph on page 14. Kenneth Frampton refers to these kinds of places as "critically resistant regions."[1] Ironically, the challenge of adopting a methodology for critical regionalism design in north-central Texas made the study of critical regionalism more interesting, challenging, and, ultimately, satisfying, and the lack of cultural integration in Texas created a parallel to, and sympathy for, the rapidly developing nations to which the theory was initially directed.

During the past several decades, it has become apparent that many prominent writers, scholars, and practitioners have strong opinions on the subject. Some posit that critical regionalism is but a First World theory that has been imposed, albeit with the best of intentions, on developing countries to which it was initially directed. In this book, I focus primarily on its application in the United States. In this context, I make less of a claim to the details of its global relevance and encourage readers and practitioners in other countries to apply the concepts of regionalism to their respective regions. Still, it is my hope that the relevance of critical regionalism will continue to be found worldwide, especially as I posit that the theory is, at its core, an aesthetic construct. The important global economic and political claims in its genesis are thus, for me, secondary considerations.

Another reaction I have received over the years is that a redefinition and updating of the term "critical regionalism" is somehow not permissible, that it has been defined to such a point that a new term should be chosen. It is my view, however, that critical regionalism has never been discussed in a comprehensive way, using the specific professional priorities that define the profession of landscape architecture and address directly the myriad issues of landscape design and building design. There is a great deal of overlap with the approaches of architectural regionalists, and this overlap is prominent throughout this research. Landscape architecture, however, also addresses issues that extend beyond architecture such as reconceptualizing natural systems and making use of both natural and cultural un-designed areas in ways that are not possible with built structures. Additionally, landscape architects often place a higher emphasis on experiential aesthetics as opposed to the formal visual aesthetics often prioritized by architects. The multivalent aesthetics of critical regionalism are a more comfortable fit within the mainstream priorities of landscape architecture. This fit is reflected in both the theory and the projects presented here.

In 2013, I had the opportunity to ask Kenneth Frampton, an early proponent of the concept who appears prominently in this research, why the ideas embodied in critical regionalism have not gained wider currency. He said it was a fair question and that, perhaps, people do not like the term "critical regionalism." I considered coming up with a new term, a new "ism" as is the norm for academics writing about a theory. I rejected this, as most of the ideas come directly from arguments proposed in writings about the term "critical regionalism," and it seems disingenuous to use these concepts and call it something else in order to propound a new minor school of regionalism.[2] I like the term "critical" with its emphasis on adding reflection and learning about a region to the sensuous pleasure that is frequently ascribed to successful landscape designs. A cadre of committed regionalists have had a long association with the term critical regionalism. For example, I discussed this work with Laurie Olin, FASLA, at a CELA meeting in Tucson in 2007, and he immediately interjected that "it is a subject near and dear to my heart." Finally, as a professor, I am committed to supporting the theory of critical regionalism and to educating new generations of landscape architects, architects, and planners on the tenets of the term and the many benefits the theory brings to a creative design process.

There is another school of thought that critical regionalism has been "debunked" as too open-ended to be meaningful, because it is a poorly defined theory of process full of inconsistencies and exceptions. I find it is more accurate to discuss the concepts in terms of ideology, as an array of unifying concepts and a frame of mind that shapes the priorities for the design process. Design can then move in widely divergent directions determined by the personal design aesthetics of the designers and their appropriate application in a given region or district, within the overall framework of critical regionalism.

There are people for whom critical regionalism is almost a spiritual concept that is too important and personal for any sort of comprehensive definition. While I feel some sympathy with this position, landscape architects and architects in both professional and academic practice must move forward with their designs and with the education of emerging professionals. The regionalist thinking that evolved to encompass the theory of critical regionalism should be an important component of that education and needs clarification. These issues and many more are discussed in much more detail as the research unfolds in this book. I ask readers who are familiar with the term and the concepts to approach the ideas presented in the spirit in which they are offered, as a sincere attempt to nurture and expand on this creative and productive tradition of regionalist design thinking.

The book begins with a comprehensive overview of the tenets of critical regionalism and why these tenets are important to the experience of place. Terms that are only briefly touched on in previous writings on the subject are explored along with their relevance to broad arenas of design and to the "life flourishing" of both people and communities.

This book's primary focus is on regionally inspired design at the level of human experience. The contention here is that there is a deep well of research and study available to people focused on the aesthetic experiences of landscapes at the level of site-specific design—research that is often not seen as a high priority by people more focused on the quantitative metrics of environmental performance and planning. Experiential aesthetics—that is, the aesthetic experience of landscape and of place—guides the exposition of all the ideas in this book in two ways: as they are explained and amplified into a comprehensive and practical contemporary definition of critical regionalism and as they inform and guide a creative regionalist design methodology that embraces relevant principles for regionalist designs intended to improve people's lives.

Plano, Texas, in 1998. This raw land was later developed, between 2014 and 2017, with the investment of more than three billion dollars as the mixed-use Legacy West Project, anchored by the North American headquarters of Toyota (see page 2).

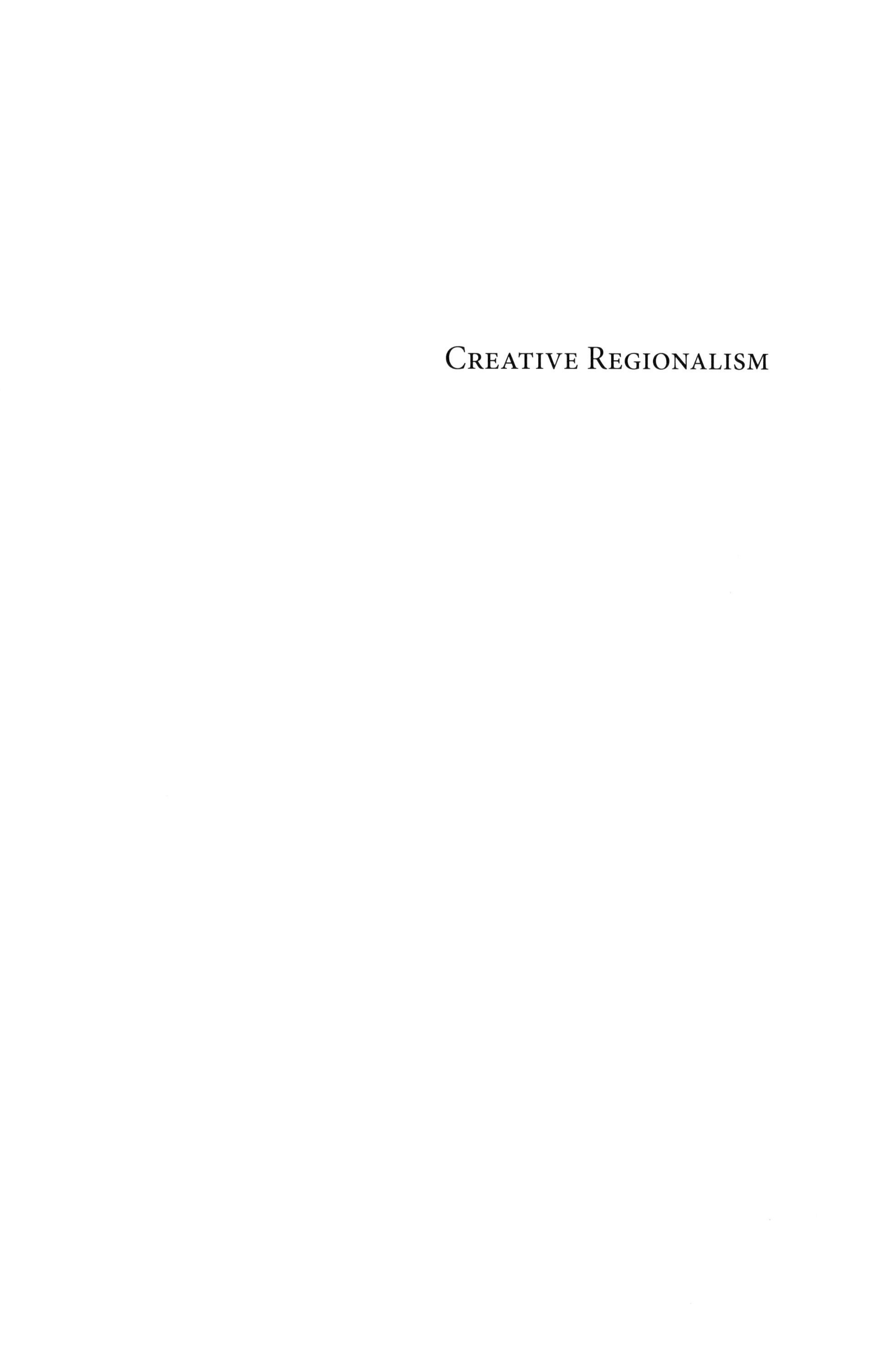

Creative Regionalism

Fig. I.1. This house, which was built on a limestone escarpment in Fort Worth, Texas, in 1994, is a compelling and instructive example of critical regionalism in Texas. The hacienda-style buildings and naturalistic landscape combine local forms and materials with the creativity of the architecture firm Lake/Flato and the landscape architects Rosa Finsley and David Andrews. The regional influences it demonstrates include historic Spanish missions in San Antonio, ancient temple gardens in Japan, local native plants, and the stratified limestone geology of the region. Photograph courtesy of Lake/Flato Architects (2020).

Introduction

During the mid-1990s, I was completing a Master of Landscape Architecture degree at the University of Texas at Arlington (UT-Arlington). We had a professor at the time, Richard Rome, who was working on his Ph.D. in aesthetics and the history of ideas at the University of Texas at Dallas. He brought many of the resources from his coursework to UT-Arlington by teaching summer classes in landscape aesthetics. These classes opened up for me a whole world of inquiry into how people experience space, beauty, and meaning in the landscape. It was then that I began a long process of questioning the values and design methodology used in landscape architecture and related design and planning professions.

In the aesthetics classes, we read terrific books by some of the best thinkers on how people experience landscapes and architecture. At the end of some of these books, a subject kept popping up as a conclusion and a way forward. The subject was *critical regionalism*. Steven Bourassa, in his seminal book, *The Aesthetics of Landscape* (1991), introduces his chapter on postmodernism by stating: "I shall compare two different types of postmodernism and advocate what has been called 'critical regionalism.'"[1] Chris Wilson, in his influential book, *The Myth of Santa Fe: Creating a Modern Regional Tradition* (1997), devotes a significant portion of his final chapter on "Modern Regionalism" to "speculations on a critical regionalism."[2] At that time, there was also an edited volume in print with published papers from a 1989 conference on critical regionalism held at California State Polytechnic University, Pomona, called *Critical Regionalism: The Pomona Meeting Proceedings*. This was the most extensive publication on the topic of critical regionalism and environmental design to that date (published in 1991).[3] The conference papers and books were written by academics and practitioners in the fields of architecture, planning, history, and cultural geography. The particular priorities and concerns of the profession of landscape architecture were difficult to find, except by extrapolation. The long-standing interest of landscape architects and planners in regional issues had not found an articulate expression in this important emerging theory.

I began to wonder how this intellectual stream of thinking could be applied to landscape architecture both to expand the study of landscapes generally and, most importantly, beyond theoretical debate to become part of a design and planning process. This inquiry happened while I was casting about for an important thesis topic that could potentially set a direction for the start of a career as a landscape architect. Being a career change student, after a 20-year career as a classical musician, it was perhaps inevitable to question not only how things are done in the practice of landscape architecture, but also why. I have observed in my present capacity as a professor in a graduate program that many students who are at some remove from their original college years tend to have a greater interest in the purpose and meaning of their newly chosen career path. This interest is what often leads to a pursuit of landscape architecture in the first place and was an important part of my personal decision to change careers as well.

I ended up spending three years, while working full time for a well-known regionalist landscape design-build company called Kings Creek Landscaping, in research and writing on the topic for a thesis titled *Towards a Critical Regionalism for Rapidly Developing Areas of Texas*.[4] After the completion of the coursework, the relevance of the topic to the profession was confirmed through nine years of working as a landscape architect with five very different types of firms. They included high-end design/build, a large engineering firm, a large primarily architecture-based firm, and the then-largest landscape architecture office in Texas. After I transitioned to a primarily academic practice, critical regionalism became one of the most important components of a graduate landscape architecture design studio that I taught from 2003 until 2021. It also informs all of the classes that I teach and provides a rationale and ideology for design decisions made by students.

In this book, I address a variety of questions that facilitate the understanding and adoption of critical regionalism principles into the design and planning professions of landscape architecture and architecture. What exactly is critical regionalism, and why do so many great thinkers and designers believe it is so important? How should the study of critical regionalism be approached? Is critical regionalism already prevalent in many regional works without the fancy intellectual label? Is it unrealistically utopian in the sense that many of the parameters discussed in critical regionalism theory rarely find full expression in any one work? Is it what the philosopher John Dewey calls "the possibility that is impossible?"[5] Addressing these questions, plus many more, is the subject of this book. It is also an attempt to understand the important question of how the theory can be disseminated most productively to practitioners and students. Designers and planners are often overwhelmed with an ever-increasing volume of information that can affect design and planning decisions. This book is my attempt to collate and synthesize a broad sweep of resources related to regionalist design and to make them accessible to thoughtful design and planning professionals, academics, developers, and students.

Critical regionalism can be summarized into a few concepts that offer profound insights when their ramifications are applied to the design, planning, and development of regional projects. (Fig. I.1) These ideas include an embrace of contemporary world culture as an indispensable part of an expressive regionalist design and planning process, a desire to provoke *both* intellectual (critical thinking) and sensual reactions to design by the end user and a broadening of the experiences intended by design to promote the importance of non-visual design cues.

As with many design ideas, works executed by artists are often inspirational exemplars that clarify the concepts. For example, some of the glass creations of Dale Chihuly are a microcosm of many of the issues surrounding critical regionalism. Especially notable is work by Chihuly from a series titled

Fig. 1.2. Baskets and original glass work by Dale Chihuly, from the *Baskets, Cylinders, and Soft Cylinders* collection at the Chihuly Museum in Seattle, Washington (2019).

Baskets, Cylinders, and Soft Cylinders that he started in 1977 (Fig. I.2). It was inspired by a collection of baskets made by U.S. Northwest Coast Native Americans at the historical museum in his hometown of Tacoma, Washington. Chihuly sought to replicate the effects of weight, gravity, and time in his glass creations in addition to some of the colors in the original basket weavings. The abstraction and transformation of the baskets into a new medium, as well as the artist's use of the best available technology from Italy for the glass creation, marks these as a type of critical regionalism. Artistic transformations of local/regional culture and their creative combination with modern technology and world culture can be seen in other creative arenas as well such as in film, literature, and music.

Many more elements have been introduced into the theory since its origin as a term in 1981, and the nine chapters in this book reflect the broad scope of issues that must be addressed in contemporary critical regionalism and design methodology. In that sense, the topics covered are broad in scope and not as comprehensive as they would be in a book with a narrower focus. There is a great deal of philosophical inquiry and reflection, grounded in a comprehensive literature review, interviews with dozens of active practitioners, and visits to projects throughout the United States, Canada, Europe, and

Asia. Trips to visit landscapes and designers in and near San Antonio, Austin, Philadelphia, Denver, San Francisco, Los Angeles, Seattle, Portland, Phoenix, Maastricht, Berlin, Stockholm, Victoria, Vancouver, Beijing, and Tianjin were made possible by the generous support of UT-Arlington. Many other locations featured in this work came from making travel a personal priority as an invaluable addition to my personal regionalist ideology.

The many projects and illustrations used to illustrate the theory are not primarily intended to show the latest "cutting edge" or most famous and highly celebrated examples of critical regionalism; rather, the projects are intended to amplify the theory by triggering associations for a wide variety of readers in a wide range of locations. I personally find theory *without* exemplars intellectually stimulating, as it triggers thoughts about my personal design aesthetic and my many experiences visiting a wide variety of landscapes in diverse locations. I highly recommend an old classic—John Dewey's *Art as Experience* (1934)—featured prominently throughout this book, for this very reason.[6]

In order to adapt the theories of critical regionalism to the priorities of landscape and building architects, planners, and environmental design and planning in general, it is first necessary to understand what those priorities are. In Chapter 1, I explain the varied theories of critical regionalism. The principles are taken from a wide variety of sources over a long period ranging from the 1920s to contemporary sources. The three best-known advocates of critical regionalism come from varied disciplines that color their definitions and approaches to the topic but nonetheless work to establish a grounded understanding of the value of critical regionalism to design. Alexander Tzonis and Liane Lefaivre have been writing about critical regionalism since introducing the term in 1981. Their books, *Critical Regionalism: Architecture and Identity in a Globalized World* (2002) and *Architecture of Regionalism in the Age of Globalization: Peaks and Valleys in the Flat World* (2012), justify the theory with references to built work from the ancient classical period to the modern in keeping with their academic credentials in architectural history and theory. Of particular interest is an alternate history of modernism and regionalism from the 1920s and 1930s to the 1970s—the era that is most often identified with the International style of architecture. The other person most often cited in early critical regionalism theory is Kenneth Frampton, a well-known and respected writer and professor (now emeritus) of architecture. Frampton presents an impassioned exposition on critical regionalism that reflects his aesthetic priorities as an architect and provides strong political and economic critiques of contemporary styles of architecture.

The theory presented in this book is not just the result of asking the question "What is critical regionalism?" but also asking why the components of the theory are important in terms of landscape architecture and planning. How do they relate to the experience of landscape, the design process, and the development of society and culture? The definitions of "critical," "universal civilization," "defamiliarization," and "resistance" that are key components of the theory are carefully defined with these criteria in mind. Critical regionalism is compared with other postmodern styles by using both theory and built projects to illustrate the issues. A discussion of commercial regionalism demonstrates how rigor, or a lack thereof, can move a romantic regional design toward the direction of critical regionalism or leave the design firmly in the populist commercial arena. Recent research on the value of nostalgia as a psychological resource is also proposed as an important consideration for regional design.

In Chapter 2, I explore the crisis of modernism that led to the development of the theory of critical regionalism. Some of the best writers on the relationship of modernism to postmodernism and regionalism are introduced. These sources are primarily from the twentieth century—the period when the excesses of modernism and the International style were first becoming apparent. The postmodern experiments in art-based design, pure academic form-based design, and the commercial regionalism of consumer culture are shown to be limited in their ability to be creative, expressive, and culturally integrative. The origins of critical regionalism are explained in the context of an historic regionalist ideology that never died out completely during the height of the International style following World War II. Regional cultural and natural elements and the contemporary thinking and technology that move cultures and regions forward coalesced into a new and evolving theory of critical regionalism.

Critical regionalism is presented in this book as an experiential aesthetic construct; therefore, the aesthetics of landscape are used to place the theory within the contemporary priorities of landscape architects. In Chapter 3, I present an introduction to four-part aesthetics and explain how the four aesthetic areas relate to the experience of landscape and help to define the profession of landscape architecture. These four parts—natural laws (environmental psychology), cultural rules, personal strategies (creativity and personal design aesthetics), and environmental imperatives—are shown to be integral to a comprehensive experiential landscape aesthetic. I argue that the four areas must be addressed in any design philosophy that embraces contemporary thinking such as critical regionalism. Additionally, these four areas are shown to be an effective way to position members of a design and planning team into the roles that are the most intellectually stimulating and productive for them. The result will be more successful designs that rigorously address the four aesthetic areas without placing the entire burden of research and creativity onto one individual.

In Chapter 4, I discuss the evaluation of critical regionalism designs. How can we tell if a landscape is a good or bad example of critical regionalism and thus serves as a successful exemplar? Rigor, authenticity, and appropriateness are shown to be criteria subject to critical judgment. These criteria and the definitions of critical regionalism are then applied to Denver Northside Park by Bill Wenk, FASLA. The park is proposed as a successful example of a landscape design that exhibits the characteristics of both critical regionalism and four-part aesthetics. Of particular note is the conscious defamiliarization by Wenk of the industrial infrastructure (a decommissioned sewage treatment plant) that was the basis for a "design by subtraction" method. The result is a convincing example of a "hushed reverberation" of region, heavily influenced by the creativity of the designer. A list of elements of four-part aesthetics and critical regionalism is presented and subsequently used to evaluate the park design for elements of critical regionalism.

In Chapter 5, I ask the key questions: What is regionalism and how is it related to place? Various regionally defining parameters are explained, including an extensive discussion of bioregionalism. In order for landscape architects and planners to bring their unique professional perspectives to critical regionalism, they must understand and apply a balance of cultural, physical, and ecological parameters. The resulting understanding of the geography of a region, as it best applies to a particular project at a particular scale, begins the creative process that moves a design in the direction of critical regionalism. Vernacular influences are explored as prototypical regionally defining parameters that can be creatively transformed for critical regionalism. An extensive discussion follows of the Solana corporate campus project in North Texas and its complicated relationship to regionalism in that area. The large-scale regional ambitions of the team of consultants that designed Solana raised important questions about the approach to regionalism at the transnational scale versus the district and the site scale where a region is experienced by local users of buildings and landscapes.

In Chapter 6, I delineate examples of regional elements that can be explored with an artistic eye and a rigorous and sincere search for regional inspirations. I refer to the artistic eye as creative seeing, a key element in experientially based regional aesthetics. Appropriate artistically qualified regional elements are shown to be location specific, time specific, and related to the stage of cultural development of an area. The importance of transcending personal biases with a flexible and situational design aesthetic is proposed as a key to developing the sensitivity to see a variety of regions with creative vision. An understanding of the insider and the outsider perspectives is described as another key component of the design process and an important reason to hire professional design consultants. Outsiders are people who do not live in an area or who are not stakeholders in a particular design project. Most landscape architects and planners are outsiders in relation to their design work and perceive landscapes more easily as aesthetic artifacts, while insiders tend to see them in terms of their practical importance or function.

Many regionally defining parameters cannot be readily observed in the landscape. In Chapter 7, I introduce these non-visual regional and district-defining parameters. Some parameters involve other senses such as sound, touch, and evocative regional scents. Other non-visual regional influences arise from the relationships that develop in an area between the various players in the development process. Beck Park in Dallas, Texas, for example, is a project that derived its form and materials largely from such a technological network. This network can also include land-use policies, such as form-based codes, that set new regional design responses to codified constraints in motion. Other projects are heavily influenced by a process involving the public. This important determinant is particularly important for areas with shifting populations that can change the character of regional design in an area. Hastings Park in Vancouver, British Columbia, is as an example of how the desires of a new Italian population influenced the new creative regional design of a park's renovation.

In Chapter 8, I discuss the relationship of critical regionalism to plants and natural systems. Critical regionalism is shown as a viable starting point for rethinking the concept of nature and its relationship to ecological performance in dense cultural environments. The chapter begins with a discussion of the benefit of using the inherent forms of regional native plants as opposed to trained forms that treat plants in a structural or "architectural" sense. A detailed discussion is presented that outlines a reconceptualization of native prairies into a form that is compatible with human use, the evolution of culture, and the important parameters of environmental and ecological performance that are frequently missing from contemporary projects. Various design and planning methods are then explored for provoking critical thinking with plants and natural systems such as rigorously designing nature/culture transitions, using a garden narrative that unfolds over time along a carefully designed path to intensify the experience of a series of natural features, and placing site-specific art in the garden that relates to the native plant forms of an area. Agricultural influences are briefly addressed to show their relevance both to critical regionalism and to the early stages of cultural development. Finally, a brief discussion of critical regionalism and garden styles is presented with the hope that more landscape architects will take advantage of the medium of regional plant forms and plant communities to create expressive, creative, and future viable designs.

In the Conclusion, I begin with a discussion of the problems associated with creating a systematic methodological approach to critical regionalism. An ideology of critical regionalism that loosely points the designer and planner in creative and culturally integrative directions is offered as an alternative to a proscriptive methodological approach. The design is then consummated using the personal creative process that the designer finds most compelling at various stages throughout a design career. The design and planning process is kept fresh by a perpetual process of reinvention using continually renewing regional and universal (global) design influences. The chapter concludes with a personal statement on the value of critical regionalism as an ideology both as an element of design thinking into the future and as an influence on new design methodologies and new 'isms' that will evolve and transform over time.

Fig. 1.1. View of Tianjin, China, near the bullet train station, showing a layered history of Western design domination (2017).

Chapter 1:
Defining Critical Regionalism

> History is not ended with our historian's "periods"; the world is ever beginning anew, each community with it, each town and quarter. . . . How then shall we continue the past tradition into the opening future?
>
> —Patrick Geddes[1]

As an alternative to "the stylistic postmodernism of reaction," Steven Bourassa proposes a postmodernism of *resistance* referred to by Kenneth Frampton as "critical regionalism."[2] The contemporary use of the term "critical regionalism" with regard to architecture and planning, however, was first introduced in 1981 by Alexander Tzonis and Liane Lefaivre in their chapter, "The Grid and the Pathway," in the book *Architecture in Greece.*[3] Since that time, the term "critical regionalism" has emerged as a significant, though never dominant topic in contemporary architectural and landscape architectural theoretical discourse worldwide that merits closer attention.

Critical regionalism grew out of the need to find a way for rooted, regional cultures in developing countries to adapt to rapid economic progress and the resulting foreign, social, and technological influences without dissipating "the cultural resources which have made the great civilizations of the past."[4] Despite the long history of discourse on the importance of nurturing regional identity, we still see developing countries making the same mistakes that led to the theories of critical regionalism in the first place. One of the most compelling examples is contemporary China where the search for international relevance and the imperatives of economic development have resulted in a devaluing of traditional Chinese typologies in favor of international design influences (Fig. 1.1).

Contemporary Beijing features thousands of examples of placeless academicism and eclecticism in a rapidly growing city of about 22 million people.[5] In Figs. 1.2 and 1.3, one sees two celebrated examples built since 2000 by highly acclaimed architects from developed countries. These examples typify the desire of China to gain world relevance by appropriating the styles of the featured architects without reference to the cultural and natural history of their location in China. China has spent huge amounts of money hiring architects for signature buildings—enough money that they could have asked for regionalist thinking as part of the design process. Instead, they chose the route of cosmopolitan glamour.

More recent theory applies the ideology of critical regionalism to a wider variety of geographical areas, especially areas in advanced nations that have also become culturally dissipated. Rather than preserving a rooted culture, the problem in some developed countries is to mitigate the sense of cultural

Fig. 1.2 (top). China Central Television (CCTV) Tower completed in 2012. Designed by Rem Koolhaas and Ole Scheeren of OMA architects. Commonly referred to in Beijing as "the big pants building" (2017).

Fig. 1.3 (bottom). The Beijing mixed-use office and retail project called Galaxy SOHO, designed by architect Saha Hadid, 2009–2012 (2017).

Fig. 1.4. The unique Museum of Chinese Gardens and Landscape Architecture (MCGALA), designed by the Beijing Institute of Architectural Design and the Beijing Shanshui Xinyuan Landscape Design Institute Co., Ltd., opened in Beijing in 2013 (2017).

estrangement engendered by the homogenous and "placeless" megalopolitan developments associated with modernism and the International style, functionalism, and the excesses of consumer culture. Melvin Webber calls this "community without propinquity" (kinship) or the non-place urban realm.[6] The influential twentieth-century philosopher Paul Ricoeur summed up the problem succinctly: "There is the paradox: how to become modern and return to sources; how to revive an old dormant civilization and take part in universal civilization."[7]

In Fig. 1.4, one sees a recent effort in China to celebrate both the traditional building forms in China and the long history of naturalistic stonework in a modern context at the Museum of Chinese Gardens and Landscape Architecture in Beijing, which opened in 2013. The museum, and many similar ones throughout China, brings worldwide city and garden forms to the people of China as design and planning exhibitions for learning. They are designed to accelerate the education of the population, necessary to sustain the extremely rapid pace of development there.[8]

The people thinking and writing about these regional questions and issues have concluded that we "can no longer practice the dogmatism of a single truth."[9] Hence, the dialectical premise of critical regionalism seeks to mediate the ideologies, personal design aesthetics, and exigencies of professional design and planning practices with the equally important cultural and ecological anchors of region.

Another important impetus for critical regionalism is to imbue romantic regionalism with elements of personal creativity, contemporary technology, and critical thinking. Without a methodology for critical regionalism, a rigorous creative design solution can be overwhelmed by the overpowering influence of a strong romantic regional context.[10]

The theories of critical regionalism have been emerging and transforming since their inception in a reconceptualization process that is a hallmark of the theory itself. Even as writings on the subject of critical regionalism have shown a great diversity of opinion as to what elements constitute a critical regionalist design, the following factors tie these diverse opinions together:

1. A critique of the perceived excesses of modernism, functionalism, and enlightenment rationality.
2. A critique of the romantic, picturesque, and commercial approaches to regionalism.
3. An embrace of the postmodern emphasis on place, rather than primarily on forms and space.
4. An embrace of regionally defining physical, tactile, environmental, ecological, social and cultural elements and personal creativity.
5. A desire to create designs and plans that balance a celebration of regional character with the influences of world culture.
6. A striving to make a landscape an object for intellectual contemplation as well as sensual pleasure.
7. A distrust of grand design solutions and an embrace of incrementalism.
8. A desire to create an imageable *bounded* place where the excesses of endless megalopolitan development and a consumer-driven culture are resisted.

Much of the early thrust of writing on critical regionalism was aimed at political and economic questions or concerns. My research, however, focuses on the theory most relevant to landscape architects, architects, and planners and steers free of the Marxist criticism that is such an important component of Frampton's early ideas on the subject. Design and criticism theory is most useful to practitioners if it deals with development conditions as they actually are. If the theory is to be relevant in the United States, it must be in concert with both its democratic and social institutions and its capitalist system of landscape development. The focus on aesthetic experience puts the rationale for critical regionalism into a proper context for working designers and planners. The theory is not necessarily subversive, political, or even economic but rather a practical way to encourage the creation of landscape designs and plans that are creative and expressive and advance regional culture and identity.

The definition and ideology of critical regionalism should not be confused with a simple definition of a term. Critical regionalism has a wide variety of meanings and is not a simple singular proposition or even a readily definable dialectic. Additionally, critical regionalism is a continually regenerating aesthetic proposition. With it, creative designers and planners will always find new perspectives on the ever-changing kaleidoscope of regional influences and one's cultural heritage will not "soon be exhausted, burnt out . . . with a cannibalized lexicon of historical references . . . and free floating commodities and images."[11] Designers and planners are presented with an approach that offers something fresh, generative, and ever-evolving.

The various characterizations of critical regionalism reflect the particular profession and the ideology of the person describing the approach. Landscape architects, architects, and planners will interpret critical regionalism by using the parameters most relevant to their professions. For example, Tzonis and Lefaivre have approached the subject of critical regionalism from a historical perspective in their books *Critical Regionalism* and *Architecture and Regionalism in the Age of Globalization.*[12] Their discussion covers regional trends and reactions to them, ranging from pre-Roman times to the post-World War II era. Of particular note to landscape architects is the discussion of the work of J. B. (John Brinkerhoff) Jackson (1909–1996) during the rapid development immediately following World War II. Jackson was a key figure in the development of landscape studies as an academic field, and Lefaivre describes him as "the most single-minded, consistent, articulate and polemical regionalist around."[13] His magazine *Landscape*, which he founded in 1951 and published until 1969, is credited with celebrating the "lure of the local" with a "particular sensitivity for vernacular architecture, geography, topography and lifestyle of the southwest."[14] Jackson offered a compelling expansion of the commodity, firmness, and delight construct that is outlined in Chapter Three with his essay, "The Imitation of Nature" (1970). The excerpt below from the essay is highly resonant with this research and has been a touchstone of well-known practitioners of regionalism such as Richard Haag and Laurie Olin:

> As a manmade environment, every city has three functions to fulfill: it must be a just and efficient social institution; it must be a biologically wholesome habitat; and it must be a continuously satisfying aesthetic-sensory experience. Up to the present we have given all thought to the first of these. There are signs that the second will receive its due attention before long; for it is already outside the city gates. But the third will be realized only when we learn once again to see nature in its entirety; not as a remote object to be worshipped or ignored as it suits us, but as a part of ourselves.[15]

The historical perspective in regionalism, going back to the nineteenth century and earlier, is both interesting and highly relevant but is not the primary focus of this research. The concern here is how critical regionalism affects the experience of landscape and how critical regionalism can be useful to a contemporary and creative regionalist design ideology for active practitioners.

Defining "Critical"

Diverse writers on postmodernism have imbued the word "critical" with the aesthetic, cultural, and political values they find most important. Tzonis and Lefaivre are interested in critical thought and turning buildings into objects that provoke thinking by the user. Critical in this sense does not mean adversarial, but rather refers to a regionalism that is self-examining and self-questioning. Tzonis and Lefaivre distrust the sentimental "embracing" between buildings and their consumers and instead advocate "pricking their conscience . . . [The] critical approach reintroduces 'meaning' in addition to 'feeling' in the view of the man-made world."[16] They recommend an investigation of the unique, critical character of a region as opposed to purely romantic regionalism, which they criticize as being "chauvinistic, atavistic and sentimentally hallucinationist."[17] Implicit in this approach is a critical rethinking of "the very thoughts which lead to . . . design and through which people use and appreciate . . . buildings."[18] Critical regionalism adds the significant overlay of an educated architect's reactions to and interpretations of a region to the desire to provoke both intellectual and experiential reactions to the design by the end user. The perception of the design by the end user then results from a dialogue between the landscape architect's mind and experiences, the user's mind and experience, and the cultural and physical features of place that have impressed themselves on both to form a common, perceptual regional language.

French Philosopher Paul Ricoeur (1913–2005) was very influential in the formulation of critical regionalism as a viable theory. He stressed how important the development of a personal design aesthetic is to the imaginative perception of varied cultures: "In order to confront a self, other than one's own self, one must first have a self."[19] His belief that "we do not possess a philosophy . . . which is able to resolve the problems of coexistence" is a principal reason for the evolving theory of critical regionalism.[20] Professor of architecture and author Richard Ingersoll addresses the problem of coexistence by setting up a dialectic between the embracing of regional elements and the distance required for critical reinterpretation of those elements created through education, travel, and professional experience:

> [The] necessarily negative side of critical culture is captured in Nietzsche's dictum: 'a great truth wants to be criticized, not idolized.' It accounts for much of the misunderstanding about critical regionalism: If it is to be 'critical,' it must be both accepted and rejected. The best analogy to explain this difficult and seemingly contradictory condition is the concept of Brechtian theater in which the actor is constantly reminding the audience that he is both a fictional character and a real actor. This kind of awareness creates a critical distance from reality while remaining a part of reality.[21]

The critical culture described by Ingersoll creates an important separation between educated regionalist designers and vernacular designers who may have tremendous artistic skill but lack the self-awareness that comes from critical distance. If a sincere striving towards critical self-awareness is undertaken, it can be a lifelong pursuit that will deepen as it informs the design process throughout a long career in the design and planning professions.

Universal Civilization

A more pervasive meaning of the word "critical," in critical regionalism, is Frampton's use of the term to denote the mediation "of the impact of universal civilization with elements derived indirectly from the peculiarities of a particular place."[22] Ricoeur, however, describes universal civilization as both the scientific thinking that will lead people with similar intellectual backgrounds to the same conclusions and to technical expertise that diffuses continually throughout the world to all people and to all places:

> Mankind as a whole is on the brink of a single world civilization representing at once a gigantic progress for everyone and an overwhelming task of survival and adapting our cultural heritage to this new setting. To some extent, and in varying ways, everyone experiences the tension between the necessity for the free access to progress and, on the other hand, the exigency of safeguarding our heritage.[23]

Places are moving towards a universal economy and common way of living, involving such items as transportation, human relationships, comfort, leisure, and news programming. Ricoeur warned that the world is approaching "*en masse*" the same basic consumer culture with "the same bad movie, the same slot machines, the same plastic or aluminum atrocities."[24] Designers and planners have an opportunity to bring lessons learned from the excesses of consumer culture in developed economies to developing areas. One of these lessons is the imperative to celebrate the vastness and richness of cultural diversity that enhances human existence by pushing back hard against cultural homogenization.

The American historian, sociologist, philosopher of technology, and literary critic Lewis Mumford (1895–1990) was equally influential in the development of a regionalist theory. He believed that we should never consider regional ideas without mentally "adding to it the idea of the universal."[25] The universal is seen as an indispensable background tool for regionalist thinking in order to gain the perspective necessary to understand the best ideas that will help a region celebrate itself. As Mumford has declared:

> As with a human being, every culture must both be itself and transcend itself: it must make the most of its limitations and must pass beyond them: it must be open to fresh experience and yet it must maintain its integrity. In no other art is that process more sharply defined than in architecture.[26]

Mumford believed that it was impossible to produce a design that was in tune with the needs of its time by exaggerating "the local at the expense of the universal."[27] He stressed that it was more important to study and learn the ideas and conditions that were the genesis for historical forms than merely to imitate those forms. This understanding can lead to new creative design and planning solutions that address and contribute to continually evolving contemporary conditions.

In the practice of critical regionalism, technology is not seen primarily as an alien force proceeding without our control or something that is being done to us; rather, it is a continually transforming design parameter, based on the ethos of the day, that provides an important global experiential frame of reference for travelers and migrants, that unites all people on the planet. At the same time, the most important theorists of critical regionalism recognize that significant opportunities for regional expression are frequently lost when technology (universal civilization) replaces older regional responses to building techniques, climate control, and expressions of local ecology, among other issues.[28]

In Figs. 1.5 and 1.6, I offer a simple example of how the regionalist architecture firm Lake/Flato responds to the mild San Antonio weather at the Government Canyon State Natural Area near San Antonio, Texas. The project combines a contemporary design style and modern materials with a strong response to the site and climate. The "barn" doors of the classroom open to a view of the prairie and aid with climate control made possible by the prevailing breezes. Lake/Flato is internationally renowned for the development of a regionalist design methodology that is carefully calibrated to function in the climates where buildings are built, as opposed to some of their many imitators who capture the regional forms but not necessarily the climatic functions of the buildings that helped in the creation of those forms.

Many design theorists have reinforced and amplified the competing demands articulated by Lewis Mumford at the beginning of the emerging era of the International style. Nikos Kalogeras also defines "critical" in terms of the desire to deal with new opportunities offered by contemporary technology that are balanced by a respect for the lessons of the past: "The study of vernacular architecture as a link to the history and the local culture provides design guidelines and the confidence to approach spatial solutions that address the future while respecting the past."[29] For the architect and professor Kenza Boussora, "critical" describes an examination of existing design precedents that will then be fused with modern technology and contemporary needs. [30]

One of the difficulties in defining modern technology in terms of landscape design is that the most advanced and forward-thinking technical solutions can turn out to be a return to the natural

Figs. 1.5 (top) and 1.6 (bottom). The Government Canyon State Natural Area classroom and meeting space in San Antonio, Texas, designed by Lake/Flato, Architects (2007).

FIG. 1.7. Traditional farming methods are used at the Tra Que organic herb farm in Quảng Nam, Vietnam (2016).

systems that were in place before they were replaced by "modern" mechanical systems. For example, a concrete culvert might be removed and replaced with "softer" vegetative erosion and flood-control measures, or bioremediation could replace a complex mechanical system of sewage treatment in the search for future viable design and infrastructure solutions. Another example is ethnobotanists who study historical agricultural practices that created productive farms without irrigation in areas such as Spain with very low rainfall or organic farms such as the one in Vietnam shown in Figure 1.7. The forms and techniques of these vernacular technical solutions can then become "contemporary technology" as sustainable responses to the imperative to reduce the carbon footprint of agriculture and address changing rainfall patterns caused by global warming and the climate crisis.

Judith Chafee, an architect and educator deeply influenced by desert environments, expands the definition of universal civilization to all the past experiences, influences, and sources of information that affect thinking and perception. She calls this the "baggage of the brain" and uses critical regionalism as a means of discovering new architectural forms that combine understanding of place with these elements of universal civilization.[31] This broad definition is most in concert with this research. Personal experience (personal strategies) is balanced with the other three aesthetic areas outlined in Chapter 3. The aesthetic and cultural impact of a broad definition of universal civilization is always enhanced by diverse experiences gained from education, travel, professional practice, philosophical inquiry, and critical thinking. Additionally, the creativity that is amplified by teams of individuals with diverse backgrounds and skill sets is taken advantage of to create resonant and informed regional designs and plans.

Defamiliarization

For a landscape to provoke critical thinking, it must first be noticed. Designers using critical regionalism methods and principles strive to create thought-provoking perceptions of and reflections about landscapes through a heightened or altered psychological sensibility in a process called defamiliarization. The term is borrowed from the study of structures of consciousness as experienced from the first-person point of view called phenomenology. In phenomenology, as in critical regionalism, attention is directed toward some object experienced by virtue of its content or meaning (which represents the object).[32] As John Dewey has posited:

> Any product that is not of the very "easy" sort exhibits dislocations and dissociations of what is usually connected . . . It brings to definite perception values that are concealed in ordinary experience because of habituation. Ordinary prepossession must be broken through if the degree of energy required for an esthetic experience is to be evoked.[33]

From a phenomenological perspective, defamiliarization is a way of breaking through what is referred to as "natural attitude"—the unnoticed and unquestioned acceptance of the things and experiences of daily living. The landscape becomes, through defamiliarization, a focus of attention and an object for reflective analysis.[34]

Natural attitude will vary according to the experience and concerns of an observer. For example, someone driving down a scenic road could be focused on how to get through traffic and be ignoring the rest of the environment entirely whereas an engineer might be thinking about the quality of the paving surface, a planner about the volume of traffic and the housing and workplace patterns that led to the traffic, and a musician about the sounds in the car. The critical regionalist designer will attempt to draw the attention of the driver to the features intended by the road design and away from these "natural" modes of thinking that tend to ignore the immediate experience of landscape, albeit through a car windshield.

The role of defamiliarization in design—seeing the world in new and unforeseen ways through a renewal of conscious perception—has been considered by a wide variety of writers as they address the topic of critical regionalism. Fredric Jameson, the American literary critic and Marxist theorist advocates using defamiliarization as "a way of restoring conscious experience, of breaking through deadening and mechanical habits of conduct, and allowing us to be reborn to the world in its existential freshness and horror."[35] Does this mean that a landscape design based on critical regionalism needs to be extreme enough to provoke the existential "horror" of human existence as Jameson suggests? Landscape architects addressing the four-part aesthetics outlined in Chapter 3 will instead strive to create defamiliarized elements within regional contexts and established neighborhood patterns and not primarily to make the project stand out for purely artistic or philosophical reasons that are overly idiosyncratic to the designer.

Georges Descombes, the Swiss landscape architect and professor, writes about revealing "a site, a history, a place, or an idea . . . [by] generating a feeling of oddness, creating a source of different attention, a different vision, a different emotion."[36] Defamiliarization has been compared to the techniques of the Russian formalist writers of the 1920s whose literature did not reflect reality but constituted an interpretation of it. This concept further distances critical regionalism from vernacular design by creating a renewal of perception that draws the viewer into reflection about the interpretation of region intended by the designer. The process begins by taking the responsibility to thoroughly understand regionally defining elements and then "incorporates them 'strangely,' rather than familiarly . . . [to make] them appear strange, distant, difficult, even disturbing."[37]

If a landscape is a creative act of making—an original landscape—it will be noticed, experienced, and understood on its own terms in the present rather than evoking a past experience—that has been mentally processed to the point that it is no longer a subject of attention or of interest for critical reflection. By consciously making a landscape perceptible through defamiliarization, critical regionalism allows the imagination unique to every person to be brought to bear on the design. The echoes of past personal experiences are thus blended with immediate sensual perception. This past experience is, by definition, imaginative and personal because it is only in the mind's eye and not part of the current scene.

An element of incomprehension may even be present in a defamiliarized landscape in the same way that part of a sublime aesthetic experience at a place such as the Grand Canyon is due to the almost incomprehensible sense of scale and time engendered by the experience of the place. Works from impressionistic poetry to contemporary classical music and jazz have proven over time that the aesthetic enhancement created by incomprehension is both real and widely shared. This incomprehension, however, may lead to one of the dangers of defamiliarization as designers may believe that their work must be an isolated means of *self*-expression. This can lead to eccentric, highly personal aesthetic decisions that may alienate the experience of the work from the general population and be *creative* for the designer but not *expressive* in the sense that it is expressing discernible and transferable design elements (Fig, 1.8). Colin Rowe and Fred Koetter address this in their book, *Collage City*:

Fig. 1.8. The metal arbor at Pacific Plaza in Dallas, Texas, designed by HKS Architects. The punched metal canopy represents a morse-code pattern derived from a code used by the Pacific Railroad to identify stops between New Orleans and El Paso. The design is creative but so abstract as to not be expressive to the park users, even if they are informed about the regional connection with signage (2020).

> We may receive strength from the novelty of prophetic declamation; but the degree of this potency must be strictly related to the known, perhaps mundane and, necessarily, memory laden context from which it emerges.[38]

A creative and idiosyncratic personal aesthetic is a valid point of view for an artist because the general population can choose whether or not to engage with an art object. Landscape architecture and architecture, however, require that a person "dwell" in a space and lead their complex lives both apart from as well as in concert with the intended artistic effect of the design. By mitigating personal aesthetics with contemporary cultural modifiers, designers can help to avoid growing too aesthetically distant from the users of landscapes—users who are not as perennially focused on design trends and design thinking. The designers will not become marginalized by their inability to create perceptibly expressive designs in the same way that some avant-garde artists are. On the other hand, if a landscape or building is *too* easy to digest experientially, it soon disappears as an aesthetic object that

FIG. 1.9. Detail of a water feature from the Palisades urban parklet in Vancouver, British Columbia, designed by Chris Phillips, FCSLA, in 1996 (2008).

provokes original critical thinking as part of the experience. The relative degree of defamiliarization required to make a design expressive but not overly eccentric (and hence alienating) or, alternatively, to remove the design from perception by not including enough unique aesthetic components, is entirely dependent on the local context. There is no inherent amount that is generally applicable, and it is always contextual and relative.

In Fig. 1.9, one sees an example of a landscape that is defamiliarized by the juxtaposition of minimalist modern columns under a tall modernist building and a water feature that uses local stone from the Vancouver area in a naturalistic way. The stone would be unremarkable in a naturalistic setting and a minimalist architectonic expression for the water would be equally unremarkable among the many water features in modern Vancouver. The pairing of the two materials seems ideal from the standpoint of both defamiliarizing them and provoking critical thinking into the nature of both. This thinking is in concert with the theme of the project: rivers, the passing of time, and the need to be mentally "present."

The design creativity furthered by the use of a defamiliarization strategy can encourage the tendencies of some landscape architects to believe that in order for landscape architecture to be viewed as a proper profession with a status and intrinsic value equal to other professions such as engineering, law, and medicine, it must rise above popular regional concerns and preferences rather than using cultural modifiers in original creative ways. Evidence for this position can be seen by the writing of well-known formalist landscape architects, among them Peter Walker, who has focused his writing on critical discourse as it is defined by "the media of the intelligentsia," without giving at least equal weight to experiential aesthetics and other important regional issues.[39]Another example is Harlequin Plaza in Greenwood Village, Colorado, which was certainly a well defamiliarized landscape that was bestowed design awards and credibility by its affiliation with art and not through any direct connection to the office workers who used it or to the Denver region. In an otherwise thoughtful essay that addresses both the problems and the promise of Harlequin Plaza, outlined in Chapter 2, Laurie Olin writes: ". . . regardless of one's personal pleasures and aesthetic preferences, this is an effective and moving work."[40] This kind of approbation for design intent unrelated to the actual aesthetics of the space is slowly giving way to more inclusive criteria as the profession of landscape architecture matures.

Overly personal and academic form-driven designs and artistic statements exacerbate the natural tendency of any profession to grow away from the sensibility and experience of the *lay*person—the end user of the landscape. A good example of this problem outside the world of architecture is in academic music composition. There are more than 2,000 music programs in the United States at colleges and universities where people study music theory and composition. The music that students and professors produce tends to be very academic and personal, with difficult harmonies or atonality. The result has been that new classical music has found little acceptance in the general population, even within the 8.8% of people who have attended a classical music concert during the past 12 months.[41] The same can be said for almost any fine art where the participant must become educated in order to understand and appreciate fully the intent of the artist. Similarly, academic and highly personal designs run the risk of separating the subject (the local population) from the object (the landscape or building). The designer can move the local cultural preferences but cannot get so far ahead that the design creates the overarching alienating incomprehension mentioned above. This is one of the strengths of addressing a design problem using a four-part aesthetics approach as outlined in Chapter 3 and critical regionalism. The personal design aesthetic of the landscape architect will be grounded by addressing cultural rules, environmental psychology, and regional ecological aesthetics.

Consider Fig. 1.10 of the Jefferson County Government Center in Colorado as an example of a simple defamiliarized landscape. The landscape design is by Todd Johnson, FASLA, then with the landscape architecture firm Civitas in Denver.[42] The heroically scaled slabs of Colorado Buff Sandstone are placed at increasingly improbable angles in the traffic circle by the main entrance. The stones transmit

FIG. 1.10. Expression of tectonic forces at the entrance of the Jefferson County (Colorado) Government Center (2006).

a palpable sense of tectonic forces and gravity, if the viewer is receptive to it, in a way that is hard to glean from the photo. With reflection, these forces are imaginatively tied into the *un*imaginable stresses involved in the creation of the surrounding Rocky Mountains and, in particular, the Flatirons near Boulder. The viewer is also drawn into the time and materials of the stones creation by an interpretive sign. Part of the sign reads:

> These rock stone slabs represent sandstone deposits from the Permian period (245–280 million years ago), and are known as the Lyons sandstone. This rock formation has produced the tracks of pre-dinosaurian, mammal like reptiles, spiders and insects that lived in the desert . . . They are the oldest tracks known from eastern Colorado.[43]

The landscape is both effectively defamiliarized with an original creative artifact and tied into both the site and the region with interpretation and, potentially, the experiences of the local population with the surrounding mountain landforms that it evokes.

Both the overall form of a design and the details of a more complex design can command a deeper and more prolonged period of aesthetic engagement after being noticed through defamiliarization. This is one of the attractions of naturalistic form systems and natural materials. Stone, for example, can be viewed for the form of the design from a distance. The infinitely detailed variations in each stone are a continuing source for artistic reflection at much closer range. These multiple levels of detail and meaning are largely missing from manufactured materials such as plastics, metals or concrete. For the author, the most effective landscape materials for creating continuing variety and the ensuing aesthetic engagement are plants. With a thorough knowledge of plants native to a region, the landscape architect has the opportunity to create a continually unfolding experience that keeps the landscape aesthetically fresh and keeps the user engaged and *present*. In Chapter 8, I develop this theme with a discussion of the expressive qualities of regional plants, plant communities, and their urban corollaries.

It is also possible to defamiliarize a landscape within an un-designed natural environment. Critical thinking can be provoked by changing the frame of reference. On Bainbridge Island near Seattle, Washington, there is a very forward-thinking and influential environmental education center called IslandWood, dedicated to creating a place where students from urban environments can explore the natural world, experience the joy of learning outdoors, and discover their own capacity to change the world around them. According to IslandWood's Website:

> The mission of IslandWood is to provide exceptional learning experiences and to inspire lifelong environmental and community stewardship . . . We envision a future in which all people view themselves as lifelong learners, and share an extraordinary bond of stewardship for the environment, for their communities and for each other.[44]

IslandWood is arguably one of the most successful environmental learning centers in the U.S. and has found many innovative ways for young people and others to experience the landscape. Examples include:

1. A suspension bridge that takes the visitor about 60 feet into the mid-level tree canopy;
2. A treehouse built over 30 feet up into a tree;
3. A 130-foot fire tower with views of the tops of the tallest tree canopies; and
4. A floating classroom that is pulled out into a pond with winches attached to ropes.

Each element encourages the visitor to see nature in new ways and provokes inquiry into both the experiential qualities of natural systems and the essence of human/nature interactions. The small, densely populated and "vertical" city/state of Singapore has adopted a similar approach with its "Skyrise Greenery" project that has created multilevel walkways through an urban tree canopy.[45] The defamiliarized landscapes at IslandWood are not examples of critical regionalism, although the treehouse could be considered a type of critical regionalism (Fig. 1.11). It is an adaptation of the Ewok huts from the third *Star Wars* movie (universal civilization) placed firmly in the aesthetic realm of the Northwest's woodlands.

Fig. 1.11. The treehouse at IslandWood on Bainbridge Island, Washington, is inspired by the Ewok treehouses in *Star Wars*. Designed and built by The Treehouse Workshop (Jake Jacob and Peter Nelson) in 2002 (2008).

Defamiliarization has been shown to be a useful concept for expressing creativity in a landscape design in a manner that will give the landscape a better chance of enhancing an intensification of experience to the users. Defamiliarization is also useful for the designer and for the project owner in terms of recognition, personal satisfaction, and career or commercial advancement. It separates a project from the vast, often-undifferentiated agglomeration of artifacts in metropolitan areas and creates a strong mental image, or brand, for the project, the district, and the region. The most important advantages, however, accrue to the end users, particularly in landscapes intended for large numbers of people in the public realm. One important advantage is the way defamiliarization directs attention to the here and now and encourages the user to be "present" in the landscape. The *intensification* and *enhancement* of experience that results can thus reinforce positive psychology or what Tal Ben-Shahar calls "life flourishing."

In the spring of 2005, Tal Ben-Shahar offered a class at Harvard University on the subjects of positive psychology and well-being. The class was an immediate hit with more than 380 students enrolled. By the spring of 2006, the popularity of the class had risen to 855 students, and it became the most popular class at Harvard.[46] This class started with a survey of scientific literature on the study of happiness that goes back to the mid-nineteenth century. The latter part of the class was taken up by discussions about specific issues raised by the students.

Ben-Shahar discussed the class on the *Diane Rehm Show* aired on National Public Radio.[47] He related the importance of a study by Nobel Prize-winning psychologist Daniel Kahneman called "A Survey Method for Characterizing Daily Life Experience: The Day Reconstruction Method."[48] In this survey, Kahneman et al. studied how people experience the settings and activities of their lives. The study is intended to provide "quantitative information about time use and the frequency and intensity of stress, enjoyment, and other affective states [that] is potentially useful to . . . anyone who wishes to measure the well-being of society."[49] The study asked more than 1,000 women to keep a log of their daily activities. The next day they were asked to document how they felt during those activities. Options ranged from happy, competent/capable, and warm/friendly to frustrated/annoyed, depressed/blue, and criticized/put down.

Some of the responses were expected. The three most positive activities were intimate relations, socializing, and relaxing, and the three most negative were commuting, working, and housework. One surprising finding, however, was that "taking care of my children" was rated as among the least positive activities even though children were rated high as interaction partners and further study revealed that most women loved their children and indicated they were the most meaningful part of their lives. According to Ben-Shahar, Kahneman discovered that the reason for the dissatisfaction was that, when the women were with their children, they were not really with them in the sense of being "present" mentally; rather, they were thinking about their work or future home activities, talking on the phone, answering e-mail, and so on. The quote below is from John Evans, the songwriter and member of the pop group "The Box Tops," who wrote a song that expressed this issue during the 1960s. The song is an example of how being present has been a cultural issue beyond the academy for many years:

I'm happy, but I'm blue, 'cause I'm here with you, but you couldn't make it here with me.[50]

The Ben-Shahar study showed that a greater focus on *individual* activities, with a simplified lifestyle, is a strong predictor of positive psychology or happiness. Ben-Shahar uses the analogy of two favorite pieces of music to make his case. If two pieces of music are rated #1 (best) on a scale of one to ten, then listening to both at the same time does not give twice the pleasure; rather, the effect can be an annoying noise. The continuing escalation of electronic chatter, the 'buzz of civilization,' makes the ability of defamiliarized landscapes to bring us into the present more important than ever. As Deepak Chopra has stated, if "life can be a series of surprises, that is the most joyful experience you can have."[51]

The philosopher Friedrich Nietzsche and other influential pre-modernist thinkers promoted a minimalism that was influential in the evolution of modernism and the International style as an antidote to what they perceived as overly chaotic cities at the turn of the twentieth century. They saw the need for an architecture that minimizes distractions by the senses and encourages people to turn inward for reflection and happiness.[52] The emphasis here on the *intensification* of experience through defamiliarization turns this idea on its head with more recent research findings based on environmental psychology and happiness studies.

Defamiliarization is one of the tenets of critical regionalism that is now perceived as more important and more mainstream than it was in the theory's early evolution. The current "buzzword" related to the concept is *mindfulness*, which has been touted for such positive therapeutic outcomes as a reduction of stress and anxiety, improved immune function, enhanced compassion, better sleep, lower blood pressure, better heart health, and, especially, better attention. This is sometimes achieved through meditation techniques derived from Buddhist principles. As with defamiliarization, the goal is to be "present" and not to be constantly distracted beyond the task at hand. The contemporary mindfulness movement has been championed by such luminaries as Arianna Huffington and the late Steve Jobs. It has also been popularized since 2012 by Andy Puddicombe, who developed a smartphone app called "Headspace" that translates Buddhist teaching into short lessons that are accessible to hard-charging professionals. The app has been downloaded more than 70 million times since 2012.[53]

New Cultural Rules

An additional important benefit from defamiliarization to the users of a landscape is the potential to develop new cultural rules. Regional elements are often only dimly perceptible to the user of a landscape or building. We live in a jumble of design influences and travel and move across great distances on a regular basis. The meaning that derives from the combination of artifacts that comprise a designed landscape is strictly what the observer perceives. Thus, the emotional reaction to the landscape is an inseparable combination of what we perceive and the emotional experience that the perception provokes. As Jacqueline M. Stavros and Cheri B. Torres write:

> We see what we look for and we miss much of what we are not looking for even though it is there . . . Our experience of the world is heavily influenced by where we place our attention.[54]

The most intense reactions will engage both the present through the senses and the past through shared experiences. Shared regional experiences can thus become an integral part of the identity of a particular population in a particular place. Critical regionalism is a tool that allows us to create these shared experiences by breaking through the habits of indifference and engaging the mind and senses in memorable ways.

Without a designer's artistic eye and conscious effort to extract, celebrate, and defamiliarize the regional context, there is no reason to expect that any but the most superficial regional features will become part of the perceptual identity of many people. This regional design "education" is perhaps most important for areas where there are large influxes of people from diverse areas, as is the case in the American Southwest where populations, who often immigrate to the area for economic reasons, need to become "anchored in" to both the social/cultural ethos and the natural forms and systems of their new home. The landscape, through a critical interpretation of regional elements, thus becomes a didactic device in the creation of what Richard Weller refers to as a "reciprocal 'fitting' of organism to environment."[55] The defamiliarized and newly noticed elements can slowly and even subconsciously educate a population about the cultural, environmental, and ecological potential of their own region, to the point that they begin to perceive it through the designed landscape in a more meaningful and less environmentally destructive way.

Meaning is the key word and is very different from a quantitative or scientific description of a region. The vast majority of information that is researched and disseminated about metropolitan areas is quantitative, and we are getting better and better at measuring such issues as economics, the environment, and transportation. The qualitative imperatives of the evolution of region are slowly becoming a higher priority as a later stage of development in the relatively new burgeoning cities of the Southwest such as Las Vegas and Phoenix. Critical regionalism offers a positive push in this direction that can apply at any stage of development.

Defamiliarized regional designs are also a tremendous asset for designers who may notice the new designs and subsequently incorporate them into their regional design vocabulary. Critical regionalism can help to intensify the image of a neighborhood, community, district, or region by the accumulation of aesthetic potential, an intensified experience of landscape, aided by the impact of each regionally designed landscape. The attention of the viewer may then drift back and forth from each individual landscape design to the greater regional scale that informed the designs and back to the individual small details that determine the sensual experience of the landscape (see Figure 6.6). Through multiple iterations of critical regionalism designs, a cumulative aesthetic of the region is built up in the mind of the local population. This is parallel to the way we observe any landscape by experiencing it serially and assembling it in our mind as a unified whole. If the landscape has both a rich sensual and a rich critical content, the experience of the site and the region will intensify and deepen over time. The landscape will help users to evolve beyond the limitations of superficial popular taste as exemplified by consumer culture and romantic regionalism.

As critical regionalists transform regional precedents through professional design training and experience, the precedents can become more universal and expressive to a wider audience. In this sense, the landscape becomes a mode of artistic expression through the unique aesthetic experiences that it invokes and rises above the functions ascribed to it. The poetics of a new landscape design, aided by critical regionalism, can transcend the historical and/or practical meanings of the site to become a *new* addition to the worldwide language of landscape. This creative new addition to the evolution of world culture can then be part of a design process that readapts the new ideas regionally in order to make them resonate anywhere in the world. Critical regionalism teaches us about the region and also about ourselves not by the reductive process of science or history but by the "clarified, coherent, and intensified or impassioned" *experience* of a region.[56]

Designers who have a critical regionalism ideology take their role seriously as an important element of region and, most importantly, as potential regional innovators. They make perceptible to the multitudes that lack the same discerning eye the life-affirming elements that are of passionate concern to the regionalist designer. The changes that flow from creative designers to become cultural norms do not flow in an even stream any more than evolutionary changes do in biological species. There can be incremental regional change or "punctuated equilibrium" that produces what may at first be perceived as a radical departure but may be seen in time as a logical series of regional transformations that are triggered, redirected, or aided by the designer. Chris Reed, an educator, researcher, landscape architect, and the director of the firm Stoss Landscape Urbanism, applies these concepts to adaptability by writing that ". . . the designer becomes a producer or curator of effects, dynamics, and of a whole range of socio-environmental and urban conditions."[57]

Defamiliarized regional elements can lead to both a new concept of history and a subjective vision of a contemporary regional context. The designer who embraces critical regionalism understands, as John Dewey did, "that every past was once the imminent future of its past and is now past, not absolutely, but of the change which constitutes the present."[58] In this view, historic elements are reinterpreted according to the contemporary vision of the designer in such a way as to "break with the dominant artistic canon of the generation immediately preceding."[59]

Any defamiliarized element can be disconcerting upon first experience and it may take time to determine if it has high aesthetic value or if it is too personal to the designer and of little consequence. Dewey divides artistic innovation into three stages:

1. Experimentation that is generally condemned by the public. Ricoeur (1965) describes this initial stage as bringing forth "something which will be shocking and bewildering at first";[60]
2. The new style is used to modify previous styles and so is given a "classical" validity; and
3. "Technique is borrowed without the urgent experience that at first evoked it. The academic and the eclectic result."[61]

The third stage above is the one that is most relevant to the "constant reinvention" that is a salient component of critical regionalism. This reinvention is as important to the original innovators as it is to the designers under their sphere of influence or to the culture that stays vital because it is in a constant process of renewal. The continued flood of new ideas created by a sensitized experience of region and the transformation of regional influences into creative design solutions helps prevent the designer from repetition and becoming creatively "switched off." Every design becomes an adventure, and the restless spirit of the designer is never quite consummated through a process of "generation, improvisation and expression."[62] To quote Bob Dylan: "As long as the artist does not feel that he has arrived someplace but is always in the process of becoming, he is pretty much alright."[63] Defamiliarization is the mechanism for communicating this *becoming* to users who experience a landscape.

Resistance

Bourassa refers to critical regionalism as the "postmodern of resistance" as opposed to the "postmodern of reaction."[64] The idea of resistance is useful and appealing to landscape architects and architects who must deal with a variety of influences that come between the first flash of design inspiration and the final completion of construction that realizes that inspiration. Resistance is an important element of a rigorous design and planning process that will help prevent a design from devolving into something trivial or merely functional.

Resistance is a well-established tenet of postmodern environmental design thinking. The resistance that is a characteristic of critical regionalism is in concert with a growing trend that seeks to mitigate the excesses of technologically enabled cultural globalism. Spanish sociologist Manuel Castells describes a variety of groups that are pushing back by championing a particular value such as "religion, state, region, neighborhood, tribe, family, sexual orientation and environment."[65] Resistance is as important a component of the identity of groups as it is for a designer who practices with a critical regionalism ideology. The resistance advocated here is not necessarily radical or heroic with "bellicose visual rhetoric"; rather, it is a resistance that is appropriate to a particular region at a certain point in time and against specific problematic influences.[66] An area with a rich, thriving regional tradition would be more amenable to a peaceful resistance that leads by example. The greater the "alien" forces who try to impose their will, usually commercial in today's development ethos, the more important and stronger the resistance against "cultural entropy, cultural trivialization and cultural homogenization" would then become.[67] In recent years there has also been increasing resistance against both governments and NGOs in an effort to balance new uses and designs with the established regional landscapes and buildings that have traditionally been part of a regional cultural fabric.[68]

Kenneth Frampton offers a comprehensive description of resistance that encapsulates both critical regionalism and the ethos of postmodernism:

> Resistance against the domination of positivistic technology and its involvement in the maximization of production and consumption, wherein the dominant attitude towards nature is always violent and exploitive . . . , the resistance of locally grounded cultural form as opposed to the phenomenon of universal technology, . . . the way in which bounded form can be brought to resist the space endlessness of megalopolitan development, . . . a resistance to an emphasis on the visual experience of place over the senses of hearing, touch and smell . . . and the establishment of bounded domains and tactile presences with which to resist the dissolution of the late-modern world.[69]

The path to direct experience afforded by all the senses (tactile presence = experiential aesthetics) and not just vision will also help resist the focus on information over experience that is a feature of formalist designs.

Chris Wilson writes of a resistance to "the tendency to turn culture and the environment into exploitable commodities," a corollary to preconceived or overly sentimental thinking as is found in romantic regionalism.[70] This resistance encourages the designer to rethink past regional experiences, without dismissing them, in order to imagine the landscape in new ways. The result can be a new creative design that will not be purely personal, academic, or derivative but rather an honest creative expression of the sensibilities of the designer linked to a creative expression of the regional context. The conscious blending of regional elements with a personal design aesthetic also sets up a resistance to subconscious design that may or may not address the regional context. This resistance encourages the designer to be self-aware, to utilize curiosity, and to take considerate care with the aesthetic decisions in a regionalist design process.

Landscape architects Michel Desvigne and Christine Dalnoky write eloquently of a resistance to "top down" design that denies the special local features of a landscape and imposes overly personal and idiosyncratic "narcissistic formulas" for design as opposed to a "bottom up" design that draws creative inspiration and celebrates existing physical, social, and cultural conditions.[71] As Desvigne and Dalnoky write:

> . . . we dream of cities rooted to their landscape, cities where one can feel the slope of a hill, sense the freshness of valleys, follow the flow of water and the cycle of the seasons, …in which night truly falls, in which time is inscribed on the earth, on the skin of the landscape. To get back its dignity, landscape architecture must learn to fight back, to hide out in the hills and struggle.[72]

Lawrence Speck, a professor of architecture, echoes a similar sentiment by bemoaning the emphasis on abstract design theories at the expense of "a world full of living breathing physical environments that stand ready to deliver empirical inspirations for art and invention."[73] Bioregionalists also see natural features as resistant counterforces in the design process to the "easy communication and transportation, and general gregariousness of thought" that is relentlessly breaking down regional differences.[74] Jim Dodge writes of a resistance using bioregional forces representing "intelligence, excellence, and care" against the forces of greed that lead to the destruction of ecosystems.[75] Boussora adds the anti-regionalist forces of rapid "economic growth, the standardization of building elements and building systems, the rising cost of traditional materials, and . . . legal requirements" as forces to be resisted.[76] Finally, Brian Walker states that critical regionalism provides a valuable framework for resistance that facilitates "learning *how* to change in order not to *be* changed."[77]

Objections to Regionalism

The excesses of the scenographic, romantic approach to regionalism, outlined in Chapter 2, have led some architecture critics to denounce all forms of regionalism. Such criticisms are among the driving forces behind the developing theories of critical regionalism. The architecture critic John Pastier, writing in *Texas Journal* in 1985, denounced regionalism as a "flight from reality into myth-mongering" and "a form of economic elitism masquerading as a democratic common-sense style."[78] For Pastier, "reality" encompasses the aesthetics of the architect, the program of the client, and modern technology; it does not include the psychological or cultural anchors of region, which are more difficult to verify in a quantitative way as "reality."

The criticism that regionalism is elitist arises partly from the denigration of less-expensive modern materials by some regionalist designers. Ironically, the same regional materials that attained their regional status by virtue of their availability and practicality in a given area in a past epoch are now often out of reach to all but the wealthy. Architect and professor Doug Kelbaugh's statement that "Critical Regionalists keep on . . . insisting on real slate floors in their entrance foyers" is a statement that may be problematic to some economic classes due to the current high cost of the "regional" and "authentic" material of slate. [79] We will review in upcoming chapters a much broader range of regional design influences that make regionalism accessible to a wider range of economic classes.

This research is not focused on the important arenas of economics or social justice but on the aesthetics and ecological principles that must be designed into every successful project. Critical regionalism may always be viewed as elitist in the United States because only the wealthy use designers interested and capable of making use of it. Even public places are designed differently in advantaged areas because of the combined public/private funding sources. For example, the 85-million-dollar, five-acre Klyde Warren Park in downtown Dallas (named after the nine-year-old son of a key benefactor) would not have been possible without $50 million-plus in private donations. The park, completed in 2012, delineates the edges between Dallas's Arts District and the burgeoning development of Dallas's Uptown District. The park never would have received the large donations required to build it in its present form in an economically disadvantaged area. Similarly, the World Trade Center Memorial in Lower Manhattan would not have been built in its present configuration in other boroughs of New York City. Economic elitism is not a reason to dismiss critical regionalism as a theory; rather it is a reason to question the theory's ability to solve social and economic problems that it is ill-equipped to handle.

Another critique of regionalism is that it can lead to the same sort of homogenization as the "International style," except that the similar designs are in the style of a particular area.[80] In an essay criticizing critical regionalism, the writer and architectural historian Keith Eggener asks the profound question: Whose regional vision is the normative regional orthodoxy for a given area? Is it Tadao Ando for Japan, Oscar Niemeyer for Brazil, Charles Correa for India, or Luis Barragan for Mexico? The answer could be a resistance to schools of regionalist design that are simply borrowed and not reconceptualized, even if the end product is highly successful. If Barragan's style, for example, "began . . . as an architecture of resistance, it might very well be seen today to be an architecture to resist."[81] The style would then become another regional parameter to use for a creative regionalist design process but not one to be copied without transformation in the way that designers using historicism methodology do with historical styles. Writers sometimes falsely conflate regionalism with historicism, which they criticize for not responding to contemporary conditions. Lewis Mumford contrasts the meaning of contemporary regionalist practice with historicism and formalist design:

> Focused in the region, sharpened for the more definite enhancement of life, every activity, cultural or practical, menial or liberal, becomes necessary and significant; divorced from this context, and dedicated to archaic or abstract schemes of salvation and happiness, even the finest activities seem futile and meaningless.[82]

Critical Regionalism versus Provincialism

Critical regionalism is not provincialism. Provincials "do not know what they don't know" and lack the same degree of understanding of universal civilization.[83] Wendell Berry, writing before critical regionalism became part of the mainstream intellectual debate, defined a critical regional sensibility as "local life aware of itself."[84] In this construct, knowledge of particular places supplants the "myths and stereotypes" of provincialism or romantic regionalism. A provincial will misunderstand a rigorous regionalist design *process* as opposed to the readily perceptible *products* of regionalism (the *way*, not the *what*) and fall into the trap of what Frank Welch calls "artificial scenography, as when adults played cowboys after five by donning boots and big hats to go to Billy Bob's or Gilley's."[85] Billy Bob's and Gilley's are two huge country and western saloons that were popular in North Texas during the 1980s when the television show *Dallas* presented to a national audience a romantic, stylized, "Hollywood" regional vision of Texas. Critical regionalism's dialectical premises are an aid to avoiding provincial thinking by encouraging confrontations of the "universal and the unique, the individual and the collective, the traditional and the revolutionary."[86]

Fig. 1.12. San Antonio-Provincialism/Vernacular design is seen at King Willie's Barbeque, now closed (2007).

Another objection to regionalism is that it is sometimes understood as a style that is less creative and original than a more personal expression. In critical regionalism, however, any imitation or reproduction of regional elements is always developed and transformed by the educated sensibility of the designer. The result may be good or bad but will rarely be a direct copy of the original instance. Even the most ubiquitous and hackneyed commercial establishments can be brought into a regional context if there is the societal commitment and recognition of their value. Many travelers have a vivid memory of their first experience seeing a McDonald's hamburger restaurant near the Spanish steps in Rome as I did on a visit in 1994. The restaurant was fully integrated into the historic context and even featured regional cuisine in addition to the usual American fast-food fare.[87]

Contrasting Critical Regionalism and Romantic Regionalism

Frampton in an early exposition of critical regionalism writes that it "distances itself equally from the Enlightenment myth of progress and from the reactionary, unrealistic impulse to return to architectonic forms of the past."[88] He contrasts critical regionalism with "the simplistic evocation of a sentimental or ironic vernacular currently being conceived as an overdue return to the ethos of a popular culture" and continues:

> . . . for unless such a distinction is made one will end by confusing the resistant capacities of Regionalism with the demagogic tendencies of Populism. In contradistinction to Regionalism, the primary goal of Populism is to serve as a communicative or instrumental sign. Such a sign seeks to evoke not a critical perception of reality, but rather the sublimation of a desire for direct experience through the provision of information. Its tactical aim is to attain, as economically as possible, a preconceived level of gratification in behavioristic terms.[89]

American architect, author, and educator Michael Sorkin criticizes the semiotics (signs as elements of communication) of regionalism by lamenting the disconnect between the artificial "urbane disguises" of preserved cities and the people who inhabit them. He notes that such design is based on the same calculus as advertising (or commercial/romantic regionalism), the idea of pure imageability, which may not attend to the real needs and traditions of the people who currently dwell in an area.[90]

Understanding the differences between critical regionalism and romantic regionalism (the regionalism of reaction) is key to the development of a personal design aesthetic that uses critical regionalism. Romantic regionalism appeals to the most superficial appreciation of both the decorative details (the sensuous qualities) and the regional expressiveness of a new design as attempts are made to evoke the appeal and emotions of landscape elements that are recreated. Dewey reminds us that true *aesthetic* perception of an object as opposed to the *recognition* of the object requires both time and reflection,

Fig. 1.13. The "Palo Duro Canyon" exhibit at the Gaylord Texan (2008).

two elements that are often at odds with the commercial imperatives of romantic regionalism. A critical regionalist design may not be as readily accessible to the masses in the same way that a romantic regional design is. This expressiveness will rather appear when an astute observer seeks out the design or notices it. The instant recognition created with romantic regionalism places us at a psychological remove from the *experience* of the new design as it quickly triggers the stored emotional responses that the landscape evokes. The romantic regional element referenced *is* the design, and, therefore, the design itself is a semiotic device for a remembered and transferred experience or a mythical vision of a region that only exists in the public's imagination. This places the observer in a mentally distant frame of mind and impedes one's ability to experience the new design on its own terms in a transcendental way. A sincere perception of the landscape is impossible due to the overwhelming meaning attributed to the artifact. The unique qualities of the landscape cannot be experienced and, instead, are perceived and processed as a universal or at least a readily recognizable archetype.

Transference of regional experience can be seen in the design of theme parks, restaurants, resorts, banks, and many other types of commercial development. For example, in Grapevine, Texas, near Fort Worth, there is a resort and convention center called the Gaylord Texan. This Texas-themed development was built by the same company that created Opryland in Nashville, Tennessee. The development was recognized by the *Dallas Business Journal* in 2005 as the "Best New Development" in the retail/hospitality category. The Texan features a 4.5-acre interior courtyard with reproductions of both the Alamo and Mission San Fernando from San Antonio (to scale), a miniature version of the San Antonio River Walk (complete with "floating" barge), a scale model of Palo Duro Canyon (Fig. 1.13), complete with

Fig. 1.14. A miniature train environment is recreated as a Texas landscape inside an enclosed and climate-controlled "landscape" at the Gaylord Texan (2008).

a miniature covered wagon and a ceiling support shaped like an oil derrick, among other decorative items of "Texana." Everywhere one looks there is a signifier intended to transport the viewer mentally to a common, well-understood distant landscape. In Fig. 1.14, one sees a mind-bending level of forced artificiality. People are watching a model train set of a miniature Texas landscape surrounded by artificial copies of famous Texas landscapes, all inside a climate-controlled structure that makes the entire "landscape" a simulated one. The designers and developers have carefully crafted the populist experience of the place and made it very successful commercially in the same way that designers in Las Vegas and Disney properties do. They have not, however, attended to any critical thinking in the design that goes beyond the most obvious and simplistic or one that could contribute to the evolution of culture in the North Texas region.

The regional elements that are uncovered and used in a critical regionalism design are the *vocabulary* but not the design itself; they are not merely "decorative" but form the raw material for a creative reinterpretation of a region where the elements are an intrinsic new creative regional expression. The design is experienced on its own terms in a unique way with each individual. In critical regionalism, the familiar regional context may be the first and most easily accessible perceived element of a design. It can be a way to draw an observer in aesthetically and a way to help create an integrative cultural environment. The starting point for the theme of the design can even be the mythological regional constructs used to create simulacra.[91] This ease of perception will, however, make this aspect of the landscape the first to disappear from perception as it is absorbed back into the phenomenological "natural attitude."

On the other hand, a design based on critical regionalism may not be perceived by all or even most observers as an example of regionalism. It could devolve into romantic regionalism if it follows such a hard-lined and literal transference of regional experience. A more descriptive and flexible term is *regionalist design*, which denotes that the landscape may be more or less regional depending on the intentions of the designer and the regional sensitivity of the user. The critical regionalism aspect of the design may require more time and reflection to be consummated aesthetically.[92]

Naturalistic design, if it is used as a style and not as a functioning ecological landscape, is another type of regional project type that is common to landscape architects and is a type of romantic regionalism. Naturalistic design's aim is often to make it appear to the viewer that the idealized natural forms constructed are preexisting idyllic natural features of the site. In Fig. 1.15, one sees the courtyard outside

Fig. 1.15. A stacked Kansas limestone wall at the Hays Medical Center in Hays, Kansas (2015). Design and construction in 1997–1998 by David Hopman and Rosa Finsley, proprietor of Kings Creek Landscaping. Idealized and "hyper" nature brings psychological benefits, created by defamiliarization, into the hospital context.

FIG. 1.16. Austin, Texas's City Hall light well and stairs for an underground parking garage (2005). Seeping limestone wall creates an abstracted hill country "cave" experience.

of the main atrium lobby of the Hays Medical Center in Hays, Kansas. The aim of the designers was to create the illusion that the hospital is built on top of existing weathered seams of the limestone that naturally underlies many areas of Kansas. The huge slabs that weigh as much as 20 tons each were trucked in from about 200 miles away, where they had been sitting in an abandoned limestone quarry for many years. Although this kind of project addresses many of the issues of the four-part aesthetic outlined in Chapter 2, it is not critical regionalism because it is *evoking* a familiar natural archetype and not transcending it to become an original design statement without the overriding reference to a familiar Kansas landscape.

Limestone is a ubiquitous feature of Texas buildings and landscapes as it is in Kansas. In Fig. 1.16, one sees the stairwell design for the entrance to the parking structure of City Hall in Austin, Texas. Here, the limestone is used in an architectonic way to create a feature that transforms the aesthetics of the otherwise prosaic concrete-and-steel construction. The stone is a water feature with continuously seeping water and evokes the experience of, but does not directly copy, the many limestone caves in the famous Texas Hill Country of Austin. Therefore, it can be classified as a simple example of critical regionalism rather than the naturalistically focused romantic regionalism of the project in Hays, Kansas.

Romantic Regionalism as Critical Regionalism

With the emergence of increasingly sophisticated theming and branding companies and the evolving skill of designers, can themed developments transcend their populist and commercial impetus and move towards critical regionalism? The Turkish architectural theorist Suha Özkan writes that neo-vernacularism (romantic regional design) can rise above the purely scenographic and commercial "depending on the sincerity of the designer-architect, on whether they simply wanted to design a stage set with pastiche or if they wished to create a genuine spatial and architectural experience."[93] The lines between rigorous original design and commercial-driven design are becoming increasingly blurred and difficult to quantify, particularly in the context of the development process in the United States, where the vast majority of private development is driven by the single-purpose goal of commerce and profit. How to consider these lines as a part of the design process is a key element for designers interested in the benefits of regional design influences. As with defamiliarization, the study of psychology can once again provide guidance and perspective within the four-part aesthetic construct. One of the most relevant areas of research revolves around nostalgia.

In my experience as both an academic and a professional designer, I have seen many designers describe the nostalgia associated with established regional cultural forms as regressive and stultifying to creativity and cultural evolution, but these same designers may be unaware of the role of nostalgia in their own professional lives. For example, nostalgia can elevate the importance of design thinking such as the tenets and ethos of modernism, for aging baby boomers who came of age as college students or as young design professionals at the height of the modernist period in the 1960s and 1970s. Recent psychological research has turned aversion to nostalgia on its head and demonstrated that nostalgia is not always the pathology commonly ascribed to it. Rather, it is a coping mechanism by populations of all ages and across the globe that "enhances psychological health and well-being, and . . . promotes adaptive psychological functioning among individuals at risk for poor mental health."[94]

Wildschut and colleagues used content analysis of essays written for the periodical *Nostalgia* to reveal that one of the most common subjects of nostalgia is life events, among them weddings, family gatherings, vacations, and events that are highly social in nature. The positive psychological value of thinking about these events and places accrues across all ages and cultures and is not unique to vulnerable populations. Researchers also found that an experimentally induced sense of meaninglessness also results in increased levels of nostalgia as a coping mechanism. The benefits of a feeling of nostalgia were found to include a heightening of positive mood, an increase in self-esteem, and stronger feelings of social connection. The social connection aspect is highly relevant to designers as the research shows that triggers for nostalgia "counter the deleterious effects of loneliness . . . and [soften] the blow of feeling alone."[95]

Feelings of nostalgia may be beneficial for mitigating a lack of meaning in life and for loneliness; they may also be a benefit of a regional style that has elements of romantic regionalism. It is logical to assume that nostalgia triggered by a place would have some of the benefits of other triggers that have been tested, such as favorite songs and the palliative effects of nostalgic reflections on aging populations. This is an area of design for which research can help designers to navigate between the "theater of memory" that triggers the benefits of nostalgia and the "theater of prophecy" that expresses the creativity of designers and moves culture forward.

> We may receive strength from the novelty of prophetic declamation; but the degree of this potency must be strictly related to the known, perhaps mundane and, necessarily, memory laden context from which it emerges.[96]

The value of creating social spaces in a culturally relevant and accessible way that can trigger nostalgia enhances well-being in at least two ways. First, it creates experiences that are intrinsically linked to feelings of connection and well-being. Second, these experiences provide a repository of memories that people can use "to meet belongingness needs, reassuring themselves that they are socially competent and that there are people in their lives who value them."[97] Research indicates that nostalgia triggers even stronger perceptions of meaning than thinking about a recent positive experience or a desired future experience. Nostalgia in the built environment can thus be a palliative for the stress experienced by people with meaning deficits, can improve well-being, and can help people cope with stressful experiences. These experiences include the transformation of their environment through development.

Nostalgia raises many questions that should be pursued by people interested in research related to regionalism and well-being in the built environment:

1. How effective is nostalgic place design as a trigger that lowers the risk of mental illness?
2. Can nostalgia be a palliative for the existential anxiety associated with environmental disruptions such as natural disasters and armed conflict?
3. Can design enhance the psychological well-being of older populations who already use nostalgia as a catalyst for successful aging?
4. Can nostalgia in the built environment be a resource that helps young people navigate the stressful transition to adulthood?
5. What are the best visual and other sensory experiences that creative regional designers can use to add nostalgia triggers to a design without resorting to hackneyed regional expressions?
6. Is the cycle of nostalgia within a human lifespan quickening along with the more rapid pace of cultural evolution?
7. What are the psychological effects of different proportions of preserved and created nostalgia triggers and new innovative designs?

Nostalgia as a tool for designing the built environment is another valuable element of design thinking that is addressed by critical regionalism through a balance of creative and expressive influences. Nostalgia is fraught with danger if it is motivated solely by the imperatives of commercial development. Nonetheless, as has been stated, rigor may be a better predictor of the effectiveness of a design as a regional statement rather than its intended use as a commercial venture with nostalgia overtones, as the following example indicates.

Phase one of the 58-acre Westminster Promenade in Boulder, Colorado, with landscape architecture by DHM, was completed in 2000. The landscape architects worked with a large team of consultants that included a theming company called Communication Arts. The company consulted on paving, lighting standards, seating areas, public signage, finishes and fixtures, the logo and associated artwork, and the project's marketing identity.[98]

The promenade was designed with a regional High Plains theme that features walkway paving evocative of the image of large agricultural fields viewed from a plane. Light fixtures and benches incorporate a grass pattern that references the grasses of the Colorado plains. The color palette of pale greens and tans evokes the colors of the prairie grasses and wheat fields nearby. The first inhabitants of the Westminster area, the Plains Nations such as the Arapaho, provide an educational resource through their symbols and artwork portrayed in educational panels and paving at the base of eight over-scaled light fixtures (Fig. 1.17). The promenade is intended to take visitors on a historical journey where they learn about First Nations, bison, mountain men, westward migration, and other facets of the Colorado High Plains life throughout the Westminster area.[99]

FIG. 1.17. Over-scaled light fixtures with interpretive panels and crop patterning with Native American motifs in paving at Westminster Promenade in Boulder, Colorado (2006).

The interpretive elements on the site relate an account of the history of the Denver area that provides some balance between a celebration of the white Colorado settlers and the plight of the indigenous people they displaced. For example, the abridged text below appears on the plaque on an oversized statue of Arapaho Chief Little Raven:

> Chief Little Raven…was the Arapaho leader during a different time when mountain men, settlers and gold-seekers flooded the Denver area in the late 1850's and early 1860's. During the 1850's, approximately 1,500 Arapahos were camped on the site that would eventually become Denver. Chief Little Raven was a warrior, diplomat, orator, and a leader who tried to achieve peace with the pale-faced new comers…The Fort Wise Treaty of 1861, which many Arapaho refused to sign, pushed them out of their homeland in the Cherry Creek and South Platte Valleys. Three years later, the Colorado Volunteers, led by Colonel John Shivington [sic], massacred many Arapaho at Sand Creek.[100]

When I first visited the Westminster Promenade, I expected my usual reaction to romantic, themed regional developments. What I found, however, was integrity in design that began to transcend the purely commercial aspirations of regionally themed projects such as the Gaylord Texan. This project is among a few others I have personally seen that have impressed upon me how integrity of purpose by the city, developer, and consultants makes it possible to overcome the single-minded commercial pressures of regionally themed developments and create a *unique* response to environment that can approach critical regionalism. The project interprets and transforms regional elements without literally copying them. They have created an accessible interpretation of Colorado that may be influential in moving commercial design further away from the pure populist imagery of places such as the Gaylord Texan. For example, there are no life-size copies of Native American dwellings or miniature versions of famous mountain scenery. Ultimately, whether the project seems creative or hackneyed will be in the eye of the beholder. Additionally, local observers will always be more critical of local regional themes since they have "seen it all" in terms of local regional expressions. For example, objectively, the shops at La Cantera in San Antonio are at least on the same level as the Westminster Promenade in terms of design integrity (Fig. 1.18). It is, however, more difficult for me, as a long-time Texas resident, to be objective and appreciate the creativity involved at La Cantera, since I take theming of my personal domain so seriously and personally.

FIG. 1.18. Rigorously designed and executed Texas commercial regionalism at shops at La Cantera in San Antonio, Texas (2007). Designed by landscape architect J. Robert Anderson, FASLA.

Conclusion

John Dewey describes aesthetic experience as a combination of desire and thought, the sensuous and the intellectual. The intellectual engenders a prolonged contemplation of the object, as the object triggers ideas that are beyond the landscape, or other design, that is readily perceptible, but the sensuous aspects facilitate an immediate and powerful emotional engagement and provide the benefits of bringing people into the present.[101] Regional elements that trigger emotional connections will fall into the sensuous, the intellectual, or even the subconscious categories of perception. This is a fair description of critical regionalism as it navigates through the easy sensuous appeal of romantic regionalism, the austere manipulations of pure academic form-driven design, the creative regional vision of the designer, and purely function driven design that tends to disappear from perception. Critical regionalism is an ideology that moves design thinking towards having "the substantial cake of reason while also enjoying the sensuous pleasure of eating it."[102] The theory and design tools of critical regionalism discussed above can be used to design what Anne Whiston Spirn refers to as the New Aesthetics "that encompasses both nature and culture, that embodies function, sensory perception, and symbolic meaning, and embraces both the making of things and places and sensing, using, and contemplating them."[103]

Chapter 2:
Critical Regionalism, Modernism, and Postmodernism

As noted in Chapter 1, the theory of critical regionalism as a term was first written about in 1981 as a postmodern critique of the excesses of post-World War II modernism. This makes a discussion of modernism and its relationship to regionalism central to an understanding of critical regionalism. Critical regionalism theory first gained prominence in architectural history and theory. Therefore, much of the discussion in this chapter will focus on the architects who were highly influential in its genesis.

Just as postmodernism is a reaction to the excesses of modernism, the modernists were reacting to the "heavily laden symbolism and decoration of Victorianism . . . [and] focused on space rather than style."[1] Their ideology, particularly with the advent of the International style, discounted the importance of historical and cultural influences and the fodder for design creativity found in the details of traditional architectural forms. Instead, their focus was primarily on the programmatic and structural elements that could be expressed *efficiently*, using contemporary forms and materials.[2] One of the most important tenets of modernism was the premise that social and design problems could be solved primarily through the use of a rational (scientific) process. In the areas of architecture and landscape architecture, modernists studied the same regional designs as the postmodern regionalists now do, but they derived very different lessons from the study. The intellectual filters of their enlightenment ideology and machine aesthetic confirmed for them the validity of their rational approach.

The modernists searched for universal and timeless ways of perfecting architecture without reference to the historic styles and symbols that had dominated Western architecture since antiquity. According to Lewis Mumford, in rejecting traditional architecture, they " . . . also rejected the human needs, interests, sentiments, and values that must be given full play in every complete structure."[3] For modernists, the authentic human *expression* found in traditional architectural styles was thought to be in the past or in more simple and exotic cultures.[4] The goal was to cast off ties to place whether at work, in leisure activities, or as part of a personal sense of identity. This identity would then be replaced by a placeless orientation to achievement or to a particular economic class (Figs. 2.1 and 2.2).[5]

The modernists were utopian and believed that their new "machines for living [set in] space, light and greenery" would emancipate the people that dwell in them from the bonds of the past and cultivate a "new universal man."[6] They endeavored to escape the "shackles" of tradition, history, and the drudgery of place-bound tyranny that they believed were pervasive elements of cultures around the world. They embraced technology as a means to quash social hierarchies and to mitigate perceived restrictions on freedom.[7] This evolved into a belief by many modernist architects that true aesthetic integrity could

Fig. 2.1. Vancouver Island in British Columbia showing the banal glass curtain wall that is associated with the International style architecture that is prevalent in the city (2011).

emerge only from a non-historic, process-based, methodological approach—an aesthetic style known as functionalism. As Steven Bourassa concludes, "Functionalism was an 'International style' that was appropriate universally, at all places and times, regardless of the cultural, historical, climatological, or topographic context."[8] Mumford criticized the functionalists for making engineering an end in itself rather than a foundation for a more humanized form by stating that "the brotherhood of the machine is not a substitute for the brotherhood of people."[9] The methods of functionalism arrived at a design solution based on scientific analysis of the design "problem" using a reductionist approach to each element of the design process. The regionalist professor of architecture, Douglas Kelbaugh, offers this summation:

> Refinement of technique . . . more scientific programming, better drafting tools, better simulation, critical path scheduling, quality control, more pre-fabrication, . . . post-occupancy evaluation, etcetera, became a preoccupation of the design and engineering professions and schools. It was all part of the positivistic attitude that a definite, correct solution could be found for every problem. This has since proven to be an overly optimistic inheritance from the Enlightenment.[10]

Landscape architects were not immune to the rational ethos of the age. The influential planner Ian McHarg wrote during the 1960s of a need for a "rational basis for human affairs" in order to assure"-survival and life." McHarg wrote brilliantly and very influentially on both the process and the value of applying a rational approach to large-scale ecological land planning. He also believed that the more

Fig. 2.2. Images of the evolving "Vancouver style" with its carefully controlled sightlines, building setbacks that bring the architecture down to a pedestrian scale, and its rich variety of shops, fountains, parks, and other pedestrian amenities. The landscape experience becomes the locus for the image of the districts and transcends and camouflages the placeless forms of much of the city's glass curtain wall architecture (2011).

qualitative and poetic aspects of design, which are the focus of this research, should be "left to their own devices, unaffected by the rut of men and simple rational laws."[11] McHarg acknowledged the importance of poetic and artistic interventions, but the lack of measurable scientific goals led to a distrust of the qualitative aspects of design—a denigration that persists today as the measurable rules of a planning scale are often elevated above the aesthetic and qualitative concerns at the level of human experience.[12]

International styles and the struggles of various cultures to respond to them have been a feature of design in time periods ranging from the Roman Empire with its classical international style to the contemporary single-family subdivision that has spread from the United States as far as China. The traditional historical impetus for the creation of regional schools of group identity, that push back against international styles, is an "aspiration of liberation from a power perceived as alien and illegitimate."[13] The power alien to the culture today in the United States, however, is more likely to be a national or transnational corporation geared toward commercial development and not a government imposing its nationalist architectural aesthetics on a "subjugated" region as in Roman times.

The American architect Ralph T. Walker, FAIA, writing at the height of the International style in 1948, questioned its ability to address the human needs associated with user aesthetics and the development of regional cultures with the observation that "in Rio the education ministry looks exactly like a building that was designed for a giraffe in the London zoo, . . . and exactly like the building that has been designed for the United Nations."[14] Ironically, this International style replaced the previous worldwide embrace of classical design that evolved from Greece to ancient Rome and its revival during the Renaissance. European modernism replaced the emptiness of the historical revivalism that preceded it with an equally empty aesthetic that Mumford called "covert imperialism" in which the few—the educated elite—decide for the many what design styles are most appropriate.[15] Commercial pressures and "irrelevant academic curricula" are often blamed for pushing designers in this direction.[16] During the height of the post-World War II modernist era, design academics often ignored the regional achievements of the past and focused on the formal characteristics of design, which were repeated "without hesitation as the only solution."[17]

The excesses of the International style are a ubiquitous feature of cities throughout the world. An early and celebrated example that can still be experienced is the campus of the Illinois Institute of Technology (IIT) in Chicago (Fig. 2.3). On a visit there in 2013, I had the feeling that I was visiting a preserved mausoleum to a failed and dehumanizing ideology. The campus has kept the *zeitgeist* of the time with the International style buildings by Mies van der Rohe and the severe featureless planes of landscape with very minimal poetic interventions and without reference to regional ecology designed by landscape architects Alfred Caldwell and Peter Lindsay Shaudt (Fig. 2.3).[18]

Van der Rohe neither anticipated nor was concerned about the negative long-term implications of the International style he so vociferously advocated. The style was adopted by the commercial building industry as well as the design-consultant establishment as the most cost-efficient building model and therefore the most preferred. New cities such as Dallas and Hong Kong that evolved into their present forms primarily during the post-World War II years, and cities with large redevelopment efforts during that time, were the ones most severely affected (Fig 2.4–2.6). The implications are especially dire in areas without strong regional landforms such as mountains or water bodies. Many areas in the vast and largely flat regions of the United States, such as Illinois and Texas, fall into this category. Dallas, Texas, is a well-known example (Fig. 2.5). The ubiquitous International style buildings built there from the 1960s to the 1980s led to the famous comment by the author Norman Mailer that the Dallas skyline looks like "a collection of Kleenex boxes standing on end."[19] The development industry in Dallas has slowly been reshaping the city back into a more humanized, livable, and imageable form since those characteristics became part of the contemporary ethos of design starting during the 1980s.

Another well-known example of the excesses of the International style is the city of Stockholm in Sweden. Stockholm is a very beautiful and livable city that was an early and enthusiastic adopter of many styles of modernism, including regionally constituted forms developed by Alvar Aalto and others. It is also a city that is almost completely historically intact, since it was never destroyed by World

FIG. 2.3 (TOP). Illinois Institute of Technology Campus, 1940–1960 (2012). The campus realized the "Gropius ideal of an anonymous impersonal architecture" with both the buildings and the landscape design. Quote from Liane Lefaivre and Alexander Tzonis, *Architecture of Regionalism in the Age of Globalization: Peaks and Valleys in the Flat World* (London, UK: Routledge, 2012), 126.

FIG. 2.4 (BOTTOM). The Air Force Academy in Colorado Springs, Colorado, also embodies the Gropius international modernist ideal (2012). The spectacular mountain setting, however, makes the landscape a dominant feature that complements and enhances the visual impact of the architecture. Design by Skidmore, Owings, & Merrill (SOM) led by then 34-year-old Walter Netsch.

FIG. 2.5. Dallas, Texas (2006). The critically resistant urban fabric was as featureless as the farmland seen on page 14.

War II as so many European cities were, yet it has continued its contemporary evolution. The residents and visitors to Stockholm have a unique setting where *both* its rich historic legacy and its new contemporary forms are available for historical education and appropriation. Substantial portions of the city, however, became a victim of overbuilding in the late twentieth century in the minimalist featureless International style.

The excesses of modernism in Stockholm are a very good example of the International style as a subset of modernism that "demands a global relevance for its existence."[20] Other more successful examples of modernism in Stockholm show that it has the tools and techniques to deal with regionalist issues and that there is no *inherent* contradiction between the aims of modernism and a regionally constituted design ethos.[21] Some early modern architects, before the advent of the International style, were actually very supportive of regionalism. Le Corbusier, the Swiss-French architect, designer, painter, urban planner, writer, and pioneer of what is now called modern architecture, was inspired by vernacular architecture because of its severely utilitarian nature in responding to climate and locally available materials.[22]

Fig. 2.6. The visually powerful regional setting of Hong Kong helps the city to transcend the severe utilitarian design of many of the buildings, such as the numerous, nearly identical high-rise public housing projects (2016).

Le Corbusier believed that modernism would always reflect the "climatic, geographic, topographic conditions, the currents of race and thousands of things today unknown" of individual regions.[23]

Stockholm, cited here for its excessive use of featureless International style buildings, is also home to alternative types of modernism that are allied with the contemporary theory of critical regionalism as presented in this book. An early example is Woodland Cemetery (Skogskyrkogården) designed by Gunnar Asplund and Sigurd Lewerentz (Figs. 2.7 and 2.8).[24] Asplund is considered by many to be the most important Swedish architect of the twentieth century. Woodland Cemetery is a good example of how he created a bridge between the allied austere formalities of classicism and modernism.

The powerful aesthetic effect of preserving and carefully integrating existing landforms and an old-growth Nordic forest for use as the cemetery experience at Woodland Cemetery had a large impact on cemetery development throughout the world. The influences of "high" formalist contemporary architecture and carefully controlled landscape design were balanced with the dominant experience of ancient and medieval Nordic burial archetypes that intimately tie the cemetery to the culture of Sweden. In 1994, Woodland Cemetery was recognized for its contributions and became one of the few works of twentieth-century architecture and landscape architecture to be placed on UNESCO's World Heritage List. The list was created to help protect the most significant sites throughout the world that celebrate natural conservation, cultural properties, and the interactions between the two.[25]

Hugh Morrison, another early modernist thinker and professor of art history at Dartmouth College from 1932 until 1978, wrote in 1940 that the copying of European modernism would be just the first phase of modernist design in the United States. He fully expected that the style would evolve through a commingling with American regional styles and eventually evolve into a full-blown American regional

FIG. 2.7 (TOP). The interior of the Holy Cross Chapel at the Woodland Crematorium at Skogskyrkogården was the last commission completed by Gunnar Asplund before his death in 1940 (2010). The classical allusions and modern materials that presage the International style are carefully balanced with features that anchor the building to the region such as rounded edges that evoke the landforms on the cemetery landscape and a dominant mural by Sven Erikson depicting Nordic burial themes that trace the ancient Nordic pagan origins of the cremation concept.

FIG 2.8 (BOTTOM). Careful integration of the graves within the ancient Nordic forest at Skogskyrkogården, without the rigid formality found in many cemeteries.

style with an ornamental vocabulary expressive of both local and national character.[26] International style modernism, however, never did divorce itself from the self-conscious style of an academic discipline or evolve into a regionalist movement.[27] Since the postmodern period began in the 1970s, many architects have developed strong regionalist practices in the United States; nonetheless, it is my view that until regionalism is a predominant component of both design studios within the academy and in professional practice, we will continue to see regionalism ignored stylistically and supervened functionally by the universal technology and building styles that are still used for most development.

The campus of IIT also illustrates the problematic future viability of international styles that do not follow the dictum that "form follows climate."[28] The formalist principles that informed the design are balanced with functional imperatives created by the program and the tectonic (structural) drivers of form. However, the cold non-temperate climate of Illinois is not addressed as an opportunity for a unique expression that is tied to the region. The architect and professor Kenza Boussora amplifies this critique of modernism in four areas from the standpoint of countries in the Middle East where early development of the theories of critical regionalism took place:

1. Many of the buildings are climatically inappropriate with wasteful and overly complicated energy systems.
2. Modern architecture contains spatial standards that are out of sync with the Middle East in areas such as sanitation, communal living, or assumptions about privacy.
4. Local resources are not taken into account in terms of material, labor, technology, or finance.
4. Modern architecture is seen as culturally destructive due to the ignoring of regional heritage.[29]

She points out that the four problems above are all solved through an embrace of regionalist design that will "put back into architecture what modern architecture has taken out."[30]

Postmodernism

Postmodernists believe that, while functionalism will always be an important element of design, it should not be the main expressive idea for all the reasons stated above. The fundamental aesthetic limitation of functionalism is that it expresses mainly the function and misses the myriad qualitative elements that imbue the design with broader meaning. One type of functionalism that is gaining increasing currency among landscape architects and architects is functionalism focused on environmental and ecological concerns. While these types of functions are critically important, they must be carefully integrated with the evolution of culture and the enhancement of aesthetics engendered by other important areas of design, as is discussed in Chapter 3.

If design comes down to a proscribed set of rules and "best practices," the profession of landscape architecture and other design professions may become prey to another kind of functionalism: algorithmic functionalism. A scientific approach to building or regenerative environmental design is increasingly being programmed into computers that have a cognitive intelligence that continues to grow at an exponential rate but is devoid of human poetics and experience. Affective, moral, and other kinds of *human* intelligence must remain fundamental in the design process whereby the computer remains an indispensable tool but not a vehicle used by programmers and the computer software companies to exert undue influence on design decisions.

Architects, more so than landscape architects, tend to be heavily influenced by the tools they use to produce their designs. There are many interesting examples of personal styles that are closely tied to the "making" that occurs when models are used in the design process. The New Mexico-based architect Antoine Predock uses clay models, and his buildings often look heavy and anchored to gravity and the earth. Another celebrated architect and educator, Frank Gehry, uses cut-and-bent pieces of paper in the design process. The resulting curved planes and gravity-defying poststructuralist personal expressions that he creates are strongly influenced by this method (see Fig. 5.4). Even architects who still work with balsa wood models are influenced towards platonic geometries such as rectangles and squares by the nature of the medium. There should be concern, therefore, that the parametric and other form-creating capabilities of computer software may become another impediment to humanized architecture.

Critical regionalism, as outlined in this research, is an ideology that is useful to focus design processes and allow the users of powerful and compelling computer software to transcend both the purely functional and the arbitrarily eccentric capabilities of this transformative technology. A critical regionalism ideology can help designers keep parametricism from becoming another universal and placeless machine aesthetic. This contemporary exigency was presciently articulated by Patrick Geddes (1854–1932) in 1915—a hero of Ian McHarg—when he related the persistence of culture to the ability of plants to survive through adversity from one growing season to another (perennation):

> Our record of local history and achievement is . . . a perpetual renewal of certain recognizable elements . . . It is of the very essence of our growing sociological re-interpretation of the past to see its essential life as continuous to the present . . . and so to maintain the perennation of culture, the immortality of the social soul.[31]

This "perennation of culture" gives agency to historic forms and ideas as drivers for solutions to both contemporary needs and for the projection of future needs that is a key imperative of every environmental design decision.

Modernist architects believed that a building or landscape should not only express its function, structure, and the nature of its materials, but also the spirit of the modern era which embodies a precision and efficiency that is contradicted by ornament and contextual evocation.[32] The postmodernists, by contrast, react to the estrangement they feel has occurred as a result of the excesses of functionalist design propagated by modernist ideology. Some early postmodernists attributed these excesses to the commoditization of the landscape in the capitalist world. They argued that the combined forces of a rational process that placed a singular focus on function and the economic imperatives of our capitalist system make it difficult for a design to rise above the most efficient and least expensive means to achieve the ends of the design program.

It should be noted that a high degree of economic development must occur in any society before the alienation caused by modernism becomes an important enough issue to compete with the economic imperatives of development. The Spanish architect, professor, and author Luis Fernandez-Galiano describes this dilemma in a critique of regionalist trends in architecture:

> The defense of the region in the international theater implies an element of denial. A black square of negative thinking on the white square of the global village. Being regional sounds parochial to the politicians aspiring to cosmopolitan glamour, suicidal to architects who cannot afford to narrow down their potential clientele.[33]

Critical regionalism was shown in Chapter 1 as a practical way around this and other objections to regionalism that can combine "cosmopolitan glamor" with expressive regional content and can absorb a wide range of client-driven design directions into a creative regionalist style.

More recent postmodernists are concerned with issues of authenticity and cultural meaning in architecture rather than as an economic ideological position. These writers argue that ordinary space should not be stripped of its cultural significance—what Juhani Pallasmaa, Dean of the Faculty of Architecture of the Helsinki Institute of Technology, called "a strengthened sense of causality and existence" that derives from regional, natural, and material conditions.[34] Beginning in the mid-1960s, the postmodernist architect and writer Robert Venturi became one of the most influential theorists to critique modernism. His writings changed the architectural paradigm toward one of developments that "embody the difficult unity of inclusion" and away from projects that feature an absence of more qualitative design components.[35] He was one of the early advocates of "bending the curve" away from the International style toward an architecture that not only addressed the program, structure, and formalist principles that were the primary focus of architecture at that time, but also celebrated the qualitative elements of expressive content and art. He famously showed his affinity for ornamentation by reinterpreting Mies van der Rohe's famous dictum that "less is more" to read "less is bore."[36] Steven Bourassa provides a good summation of the contrast of modernism and postmodernism:

> Modernism encompasses Enlightenment rationalism, denial of tradition, a universal functionalist style, prohibition of ornament and symbolism, a romantic individualism which valued buildings that stand out rather than fit in, and a penchant for grand, totalitarian solutions to

> urban problems. Postmodernism, by contrast, is characterized by skeptical distrust of human rational abilities, respect for tradition, an eclectic aesthetic, recognition of the importance of ornament and symbol, a contextualism that values buildings that attend to surroundings, and an incremental approach to the solution of urban problems.[37]

Implicit in Bourassa's summary is a support for a regionally sensitive postmodernism in which attentiveness to local culture and history mediates the modernist preoccupation with method and technique. The pairings below show various constituents of style that reflect the changing priorities from the International style to postmodernism:

Modernism/International Style	Postmodern Style
universal	situational
collective	individual
standardized	unique
conscious	subconscious
future oriented	history oriented
idealistic	realistic
structure oriented	form oriented
rational	emotional
absolutist	relativist
theoretical, orthodox	pragmatic
exclusive	inclusive[38]

Other design elements that illustrate the break between modernism and postmodernism (what Pallasmaa calls second modernism) are the postmodern embrace of symbolism, allusion, metaphor, memory, materiality, unfinishedness, imperfection, and stylistic borrowings that the modernists had largely rejected.

Regionally based postmodernism is only one of several possible alternatives to the modernist ideal. Architecture and interior design professor Ann Cline (1942–2001) divided the conservative and liberal wings of postmodernism. She described regionalist or critically regionalist postmodernists as the conservative wing and an alternative expression from whatever the source as the liberal wing.[39] One example of a non-regionalist, liberal postmodern design method is the art-based approach. In such a design process, abstract design systems are extracted from contemporary and historic art movements and reinterpreted into landscape designs.

FIG. 2.9. Harlequin Plaza in Englewood, Colorado, with the 'Mad Hatter' from *Alice in Wonderland* in the center (1995).

In Fig. 2.9, one sees Harlequin Plaza designed by George Hargreaves and completed in 1983. The plaza was highly celebrated for its iconic design that drew inspiration from Picasso's "Harlequin" paintings and the surrealist painters Giorgio de Chirico and Salvador Dali. It was a prime example of the largeness of artistic ambition and pursuit of novelty that is often recognized and rewarded in the design professions. Mark Johnson, then principal of the Denver-based landscape architecture firm Civitas, described the original design as "Crisp, dramatic, unyielding, and defiantly out of place; the project embodied and objectified the height of suburban detachment."[40] The plaza, however, was derided by those who worked in the office park for its lack of usable spaces and low-quality construction materials. When I visited the Plaza in 1995, these problems were very apparent. It felt more like a view garden for people in the buildings and ignored other important aesthetic criteria such as the prospect-refuge implications of its open spaces that are subject to the peering eyes from the surrounding glass buildings. The checkerboard paving was simple asphalt painted white to create the checkerboard pattern and, like the other materials, felt insubstantial and was not aging well.

This type of problem with materials is often found in designs where the artistic statement of the designer is placed above the aesthetics of the people who use the landscape to lead their lives instead of to view temporarily as one would an art exhibition (see Fig. 4.7). The prime objective of the designer of some art-based landscapes becomes to get the creative design built, and the limiting factor of budget often leads to low-quality materials. The ultimate life-cycle costs of inexpensive materials used for art-based designs rises substantially if they contribute to the perception by users that their needs and lifestyle have not been sufficiently considered and they subsequently demand another design solution. This is precisely what happened at Harlequin Plaza. In 1998, it was removed and replaced by a plaza with more people-friendly amenities designed by the Denver office of EDAW.[41]

Kenneth Frampton describes the two competing trends of postmodernism as the neo-Historicists and the neo-Avant-Gardists. The neo-Historicists believe that the excesses of the Avant-garde, exemplified above by Harlequin Plaza, have been so discredited that the only choice is to return to tradition. The neo-Avant-Gardists embrace the continuing evolution of modernism, which they see as both inevitable and as the best path forward for personal creativity.[42]

Bourassa provides a comprehensive exposition of some of the problematic aspects of the Avant-garde style of the postmodern movement, which he calls the "postmodern of reaction." The "postmodernism of reaction is strictly a matter of style in the narrow, mannerist sense of the word."[43] This style is exemplified by Michael Graves with his "grammar of ornament approach" and Robert Venturi with his idea of the building as a "decorated shed." [44] In both cases, historical references and ornament become highly desirable elements, and it is no longer necessary for architectural form to express primarily the functionalism and machine aesthetic of rationalism. John Dewey describes the architecture of reaction as "arbitrary conceit, fantasy, and stereotyped convention."[45] Bourassa criticizes this decorative approach as "an instrumental pastiche of pop- or pseudo-historical forms," "do-it-yourself history," "cardboard scenography," or an example of "precisely that avalanche of academicism, commercialism, and kitsch that is always ready to swamp our culture in the absence of a tradition vigorous enough to resist it.'"[46]

In Fig. 2.10, one sees *Your Move*, a collaborative work by Daniel Martinez, Renee Petropoulis, and Roger White consisting of oversized Monopoly, chess, domino, and other board game pieces added as decoration to the sparse and functional plaza design for the Municipal Services Building along John F. Kennedy Boulevard in Philadelphia, Pennsylvania. The use of surface elements of regional character (Monopoly was invented in Philadelphia) without the continuing evolution of authentic tradition can doom a design to be a "naively shallow architectural souvenir."[47] The approach has been compared to that of a pastry cook "employed to attach some trimmings within and without after the structure has been delivered to him by an engineer."[48] Another example familiar to landscape architects is when this approach is used to create design enhancements for functionalist and featureless bridges by applying decoration after the fact, rather than helping to design the form into the bridge itself (Fig. 2.11).[49]

Writer and architecture critic Ada Louise Huxtable summed up the problem by arguing that it "takes a creative act, not clever [historic] cannibalism, to turn a building into art."[50] Morrison describes this as being "creatively modern" whereby historic styles are not imitated but rather are studied for

Fig. 2.10. *Your Move,* art-based decoration as a postmodern landscape (2006) in Philadelphia, Pennsylvania.

their use of "materials and mass, adaptation to site, simplicity, informality, and all their other great qualities."[51] By contrast, what Huxtable called "historic cannibalism" substitutes the authenticity that results from designing with sensitivity to the *dwelling* practices of contemporary everyday life and the continuing evolution of culture developed by the ongoing creativity of designers with the belief that authenticity can be created through the mere superficial manipulation of appearance. Much of this type of design is the result of commercial pressures and is a type of commercial functionalism. Chris Wilson has written eloquently about this type of regionalism, which he refers to as "romantic regionalism."[52]

Romantic Regionalism

Romantic regionalism is one of the most pervasive elements of the continuing embrace of both the postmodernism of reaction and worldwide capitalist imperatives. Romantic regionalism grew out of the *picturesque* art tradition of the late nineteenth century. The term picturesque was first applied to landscape paintings, then romantic gardens, and finally to the architecture set in the picturesque landscapes.

FIG. 2.11. Decorative pastiche is applied to a bridge at a spectacular scale on the Dragon Bridge over the River Han in Da Nang, Vietnam, completed in 2013 (2016).

According to Chris Wilson, the architecture can be romantic in three ways: "First by its association with a bygone epoch or exotic land; second by its informal floor plan and asymmetrical facade composition; and third by its setting, whether by its use of local materials or its careful siting on the land."[53]

The early development of romantic regionalism was, like critical regionalism, partly a critique of the excesses of capitalism and industrial society. It was a reaction to the perceived evils of industrialization and a desire to return to what was considered the more humane and often regionally inspired work of artisans and craftsmen of the medieval period. This led to the popularity of the Gothic revival style and to the formation of utopian socialist communities that championed handcraftsmanship. It also contributed to the birth of the "Arts and Crafts" movement during the 1890s. The romantic regionalism tradition can be prominently seen today in the tourist industry where such interests as "unspoiled nature, ancient history, distant lands, and exotic peoples" have captured the public imagination and have been used as thematic lures for countless commercial projects.[54]

Many influential writers have addressed romantic regionalism as a pervasive component of contemporary culture. Tzonis and Lefaivre refer to this type of regionalism as Commercial Regionalism, which they criticize as "pornography of sorts," due to the emphasis on emotion over rationality and the ease with which one can become totally possessed by it in a purely sensual way. It is "the professional architecture of the *genius commercialii* of tourism and entertainment which . . . offers to alleviate the pain of atopy and anomy of contemporary life in as-if settings, simulacra of places, facades, masks of environments offering the illusion of participation, . . . of a feeling of 'being there.'"[55] The forced artificiality of romantic regionalism can make landscapes look like pretend creations. The writer, farmer, and teacher Wendell Berry calls it a "regionalism based on condescension, which specializes in the quaint and the eccentric and the picturesque."[56] Paul Ricoeur, professor and one of the most influential philosophers of the twentieth century, calls the spread of pure consumer culture and its manifestation in design as "absolute nihilism in the triumph of comfort." The whole of humankind becomes a kind of imaginary museum: Where shall we go this weekend—visit the Angkor ruins or take a stroll in the Tivoli of Copenhagen?[57] Pallasmaa echoes this sentiment by asking if the worldwide move to a consumerist culture is dooming our culture to "lose all its authenticity and turn into a planetary waxworks show...a naively shallow architectural souvenir."[58] He believes that authentic regionalism is only possible in areas not completely conquered by a consumerist society. The capitalist system of development in the United States receives the majority of the blame for the problems and excesses associated with romantic regionalism.

The Austin-based architect and professor Harwell Hamilton Harris, in an early description of romantic regionalism, refers to it as a "regionalism of restriction . . . anticosmopolitan and antiprogressive [which] becomes a cloak for misplaced pride of the region and serves to build in ignorance and inferiority."[59] He contrasts it with a "regionalism of liberation," which combines regional elements with contemporary thinking. The irony of commercially motivated romantic regionalism is that, while it purports to celebrate local regions, albeit in a very superficial and facile way, it may be in actuality one of the most powerful forces that devalue an authentic sense of place.[60]

As designers grapple with the issues that surround commercial regionalism on a regular basis, it always comes back to a balance of historical sources, creativity, and cultural progression. Good design should be applicable to any type of landscape and architecture, including commercially driven design, not just the boutique clients with the loftiest aesthetic aspirations. In Chapter 4, I show how the ideology, rigor, and creativity of design consultants are often better predictors of a design team's ability to transcend these problems, rather than just the fact that a project has a commercial imperative. Critical regionalism is a theory for the creation of a framework that enables designers to work through these contradictions and produce designs that meet both the commercial and the socio-cultural imperatives of development with appropriate rigor and integrity.

Conclusion

The discussions in this chapter of the problems with modernism, functionalism, the International style, and the machine aesthetic of the post-World War II period explain the historical rationale for the development of postmodernism. Once the International style was understood as a cultural "dead end" by observing its impact on the character of cities such as Dallas, decisions on design aesthetics in the postmodern era moved in a variety of directions. Some were eclectic and highly personal, such as art-based design, and some were driven by a desire to tap into the romantic regionalism desires of both tourists and local populations with regressive commercial regional expressions. The best designers, however, reignited the development of a tradition that never died out completely during the height of the International style. They started using *both* regional cultural and natural elements and the contemporary thinking and technology that move cultures and regions forward. This tradition, which has roots in regional modernist projects such as the architecture and landscape architecture of Skogskyrkogården, is critical regionalism.

Chapter 3:

Critical Regionalism and the Aesthetics of Landscape

As revealed in Chapters 1 and 2, the aesthetics of landscape are a principal reason for the evolving theories of critical regionalism. As such, it is important to outline the relevant theory that separates the approach to critical regionalism taken by landscape architects from the one taken by many writers from other disciplines who have outlined aesthetic principles in the past.

The architects who have written about critical regionalism over the years are in accord with many of the aesthetic priorities of landscape architects. There are, however, areas of contrast partly based on the design cultures of the two professions and partly based on the type of designs undertaken. For example, landscape architects have the opportunity to integrate the principles of critical regionalism with regenerative design and natural systems to an extent that is not possible when designing a structure. There is also less focus in landscape architecture on contemporary technology as a generator of form, particularly in the area of parametric computer-aided design. The deemphasizing of a primary focus on form generation elevates the importance of evidence-based environmental psychology, cultural rules, and natural systems relative to the importance of technological innovation and the resulting new building typologies. Another important difference is that the exploration of the theory of critical regionalism is combined here with a bridge to its practical application. The aesthetic theory proposed and explored may seem at first intentionally idealistic or utopian, but many ideas related to aesthetics come directly from observation of built works that are then used as exemplars for applying critical regionalism to future designs. This research is also grounded by dozens of relevant discussions with practicing regionalist designers and by experience as a landscape architecture practitioner. The research methodology is emblematic of the profession of landscape architecture, which tends towards an approach to theory and design that is derived from both observation and analysis of the built and natural environment and environmental research, sometimes referred to as a bottom-up approach. Architectural theory, by contrast, is often focused more on ideas that come from history and personal aesthetic inquiry and reflection associated with a top-down approach. Of course, many of the best architects and landscape architects think of design more holistically, and critical regionalism reinforces this positive design direction.

As I have traveled the United States talking to landscape architects, I found that many of the design firms where they worked have a design philosophy that can be summed up with a few interrelated ideas. The ideas are sometimes illustrated with Venn diagrams and referred to as a triple (or quadruple) bottom line. This concept can be traced at least as far back in history as the first century CE with Vitruvius's admonition to design for *firmitas, utilitas,* and *venustas,* strictly translated as structural stability, appropriate spatial function or program, and aesthetics but identified more commonly as commodity, firmness, and delight.[1] An example from the late eighteenth and early twentieth centuries comes from the landscape architect and planner Patrick Geddes, one of the celebrated founding fathers of the modern town planning movement, the inventor of "conservative surgery," (careful editing and adaptive reuse of historical districts) and the creator of the term "conurbation" (groups of cities now referred to as metropolitan areas). He used the tri-partite structure of place, work, and folk—the geographical, historical, and spiritual—to understand the evolution of cities.[2] Contemporary landscape architecture firms continue this tradition both in their marketing material and on their Websites. For example, the Colorado-based firm Design Workshop promotes a synthesis of community, art, environment, and economics. Nuszer Kopatz, another Colorado firm that is now part of Stanley Consultants, described its design process as a synthesis of beauty, livability, and functionality. Finally, the San Francisco-based firm Peter Walker and Partners (now PWP) advocated for many years a blending of art and culture. The four-part design aesthetics construct in this chapter is a subset that addresses many important parameters for a thriving and future viable human civilization leading to what Lewis Mumford has referred to as "biological prosperity, social cooperation, and spiritual stimulation."[3] I prefer the term "future viable" to the more commonly used "sustainable" as a clearer tie-in to the design professions which are frequently thinking forward in time to the needs of future generations.

Defining Aesthetics

It is not my intention here to discuss all the implications of aesthetic theory—a fascinating subject to which people devote entire academic careers. Rather, I offer the theory that is most relevant to an expanded definition of critical regionalism as it applies to landscape architecture.

The four-part aesthetic construct below, and subsequent theory on critical regionalism, is based on experiential models of landscape aesthetics. These theories are most relevant to a definition of landscape aesthetics, as defined by many landscape architects, since they involve the *experience* of landscape. John Dewey summarizes experiential aesthetics as the *enhancement* and *intensification* (emphasis mine) of everyday experience.[4] This broad and comprehensive definition is meant to encompass both sensory and intellectual components. The famed ecologist Aldo Leopold (1887–1948) also wrote poetically about the cerebral aspects of experiencing nature as part of what was then a revolutionary aesthetic construct. For him, the aesthetic experience of wildness had everything to do with the integrity of its evolutionary heritage and ecological processes and less to do with the landscape's picturesque qualities.[5] Information for the mind that addresses both cultural and natural systems is in contrast to the pictorial models of aesthetics that place us at a distance from experiencing the sensory richness of an actual place. The word "pictorial" is used here as shorthand for buildings and landscapes that have or suggest the visual appeal or imagery of a picture. This simple reference to the elevation of the visual over the more broadly experiential should not be confused with the definitions of the term "pictorial" as applied to historic photography from the nineteenth and twentieth century or to the long debate about the semantic content of pictorial representation that is a feature of contemporary aesthetics (see Figs. 3.1 and 3.2).

Pictorial models of aesthetics are often reinforced and are always with us due to their easy reproducibility by continually evolving technologies. Designers are encouraged to produce projects that photograph well in order to win awards and to develop their client base. Designers are also sometimes directed to create landscapes that are optimally viewed from a distance at the expense of direct experience in the landscape. The program for the design can call for a landscape that looks its best from certain levels of an office tower or from the windshield of a passing car. Owners, in turn, use the images of pictorially constituted landscapes to market their products and to provide a commercial imageability that differentiates their development, as was the case with Harlequin Plaza (see Fig. 2.9).

Although such pictorial approaches predominate in current design aesthetics, they are not the only way to have an aesthetic experience. It is certainly possible to have aesthetic experiences—enhancement and intensification—with pure thought, without either pictorial or other sensory augmentation. For example, we often hear about "beautiful" and "elegant" mathematical formulas. Additionally, we have all experienced the joy of "aha moments" that are not connected to any direct sensory stimulation. For example, the joy in a comedy may come from the internal comprehension of the inherent absurdity and contradiction between competing ideas, although the information from the ideas comes from the senses. In Chapter 1, I explored how these types of experiences are an integral component of an experientially based aesthetic that also embraces critical regionalism.

A comparison between the aesthetics of landscape architecture and architecture by Steven Bourassa helps to explain why the theory of critical regionalism as it is currently constituted does not reflect some of the issues most relevant to landscape architects:

> ". . . the aesthetic objects of architecture are individual buildings and other man-made elements, while the aesthetic object of landscape is defined holistically to include the entire scene, containing any number of buildings, artifacts and natural objects, including people."[6]

The emphasis by many architects on isolated buildings is exacerbated by the architectural press that still tends to present them as standalone objects without meaningful reference to the immediate

Fig. 3.1 (top). The large water features on the University of Texas at Dallas campus, created by PWP landscape architects, are designed for pictorial appeal and discourage immersive interactions (2020).

Fig. 3.2 (bottom). The fountain at the Winspear Opera House in Dallas, Texas by Michel Desvigne and Smith Group/JJR is also a minimalist reflective fountain that adds to the pictorial beauty of the Foster and Partners-designed building. The pictorial aspects invite engagement and the accessible water greatly enhances and intensifies the experience for both people and animals during special events (2009).

context and without people. They can then become purely sculptural objects. There are, of course, increasing numbers of architects who carefully consider context and I address their contributions in subsequent chapters. Landscape architects, however, tend to focus more on context and to include un-designed areas in their designs, from both natural and cultural environments, in a way that is rarely seen in architecture. It is true that many buildings are designed to be purely utilitarian and not aesthetic objects per se, but they are still created by the hand of man and not as a result of the relentless forces of natural systems or by the dereliction and decay of cultural artifacts.

Buildings, natural areas, people and cultural artifacts together contribute to a "sense of place." This is a term that is applied quite often by designers in many professions as an important criterion of beauty or aesthetics. Geographer John Agnew describes place as "the local structure of feeling" that pervades being in a particular place.[7] The structure of feeling is another way of describing the experiential aesthetic experience. Other people refer to it as the character of a place or even as the "vibe." Professor of architecture (now emeritus) Steven Moore proposed a conception of place as "a dynamic process that links humans and nonhumans in space at a variety of scales."[8] The scale that is most important to the ideas presented in this book is a small enough area that the human poetics of space are experienced directly.[9] More intense experiences result from combining thought with the *direct* information received from both our outward senses, such as hearing, smell and sight, and our inner senses, such as equilibrioception, chronoception, and thermoception. The scale of direct experience can reflect and trigger thinking about larger areas than those that are immediately perceptible. The *direct* everyday experience of a place, of a design, is the most important focus of this book.

So if the *enhancement* and *intensification* of everyday experience is the goal, what are the aesthetic components that cover the widest possible range of experiences and, simultaneously, facilitate a personal design aesthetic that is in concert with critical regionalism? The four areas that follow represent a comprehensive experiential aesthetic construct that covers the areas of concern to landscape architects for both the study of the experience of landscapes and as a framework for the development of a rigorous creative personal design aesthetic. The first three areas are taken from theories developed by such writers as John Dewey, Arnold Berleant, and Steven Bourassa. The fourth area is proposed as a vital component for designers of landscapes to address as part of a personal design aesthetic for practice and goes beyond what is required for an understanding of the experience of landscape. It is also a frequent topic for bio-regionalists such as Robert Thayer and Jim Doge and more recently by Tobias and Morrison with a broad multidisciplinary approach.[10] The four aesthetic areas are as follows:

1. Environmental Psychology (Natural Laws)
2. Cultural Rules
3. Personal Strategies (personal development and creativity)
4. Environmental Imperatives

Environmental Psychology

Bourassa defines the first of the four aesthetic areas as natural laws (environmental psychology) in keeping with Dewey's discussion of human nature. Environmental psychology represents those aesthetic responses that are innate in us as human animals and are hardwired into our brains. These responses involve the limbic and reptilian parts of the brain as well as the more developed neo-cortex. Numerous experiments using both laboratory animals and humans with diseased or injured brains have documented the affective (as opposed to cognitive) responses that remain from our evolutionary past, though to a lesser degree in humans than in other animals, or are learned precognitive responses such as those found in post-traumatic stress disorder (PTSD). The specific subconscious functions of many of these areas of the brain have been mapped using neurophysiological research, experimental psychology, and "blindsight" research.[11] Blindsight is the ability of people to react in scientifically measurable ways to visual stimuli without any consciousness of the stimulus. It has helped researchers separate the higher brain functions of consciousness from the subconscious responses triggered by the more primitive parts of the brain where precognitive environmental psychology responses dwell.

Natural laws are a separate aesthetic category from the psychology of forms and space that is part of the education of most architecture and landscape architecture students in the U.S. and is sometimes referred to as formalist or Gestalt theory. Formalist theories claim that most humans *develop* emotional responses to specific forms that are cultural determinants as defined by the design professions in specific times and places. *Gestalt* is a term in psychology that means "unified whole" and refers to theories of visual pattern recognition developed by German psychologists during the 1920s. Gestalt principles such as figure and ground, continuation, and similarity are useful organizing principles for design but do not explain the aesthetic purpose of these principles. The study of environmental psychology goes deeper to explain *why* traditional design rules and forms have aesthetic value across a wide range of cultures and personal tastes. The assumption is that innate human responses must have an evolutionary basis in order to persist. As Bourassa suggests, "It is hard to comprehend why [biological] preferences for specific types of environments would evolve unless inhabiting those environments would contribute to survival."[12] The examples below demonstrate the aesthetic value of survival mechanisms and how they must be addressed as part of a rigorous contemporary expression of critical regionalism.

Two widely disseminated examples of environmental psychology theory in this complex area are habitat theory and information processing theory. Habitat theory was first proposed by Jay Appleton in 1975 in his influential book, *The Experience of Landscape*, in which he postulates that, in order for a landscape to be aesthetically pleasing, it must be perceived to enhance our chances for survival. Proponents of this theory argue that, because people for most of their prehistoric existence were hunter/gatherers in savannah-like settings, these are landscapes deemed most pleasing. And humans need to be close to a body of water for survival, which might explain modern preferences to live in park-like

Fig. 3.3. Here is a good example of prospect-refuge at the Fair Park light-rail station in Dallas, Texas (2010). Fair Park was built for the 1936 Centennial Exposition and contains the largest collection of Art Deco exposition buildings in the world. Brad Goldberg, the station designer along with his wife, Diana, stated; "it was important that the design of the station be extremely sensitive to the historic context, the functional requirements of Fair Park, and the context of the surrounding neighborhood." The fluted limestone columns are inspired by the nearby Hall of State. Quote from Fair Park Station (May 26, 2019); https://www.dart.org/riding/stations/fairparkstation.asp.

settings and to live near lakes, rivers, and the ocean.[13] A relevant element of habitat theory for designers of the environment is called prospect-refuge theory. Prospect-refuge theory is premised on the need of early humans to see without being seen in order to hunt successfully while protecting themselves from other predators. Appleton applies this theory to the urban context by advocating that a well-designed urban area should afford "the observer the security of lateral cover until the moment when he is ready to concede the refuge as the price of achieving a wider prospect."[14] This transitional space, whether a vestibule in a building or a transitional area in a landscape, can be the difference between a comfortable and inviting passage between spaces and one that provokes anxiety or even a sense of danger (Fig. 3.3). A poorly-designed or inappropriate transitional space that does not account for prospect-refuge can overwhelm and negate the positive aesthetic response intended by the designer.

Another relevant example is information processing theory, developed over many years by the environmental psychology research team of Stephen Kaplan and Rachel Kaplan. They typically used photo-elicitation (the study of photographic preferences) by showing various groups of people photographs of both real-world landscapes and photographs of simplified models of proposed landscapes to study group preferences for a variety of both natural and cultural environments. Their studies showed that complexity, coherence, legibility, and mystery are the favored landscape characteristics.[15]

1. *Complexity* because it encourages further exploration;
2. *Coherence* because it enables understanding of the environment;
3. *Legibility* because it helps an individual get oriented; and
4. *Mystery* because it holds forth the promise of new information.

Balancing the competing claims of these four elements is both a normative part of the thinking of landscape architecture practitioners and an important element of critical regionalism. Designing landscapes that are interesting enough to be noticed and provoke critical thinking (complexity and mystery) and also coherent enough to express regional cultural integration (coherence and legibility) is a key concern.

A foundational principle of critical regionalism related to critical thinking and environmental psychology is defamiliarization. The strategy of defamiliarizing a design to provoke critical thinking was written about by Kenneth Frampton and others as the theory first evolved during the 1980s. Another principle revealed by more recent environmental psychology research is the benefit of nostalgia as an adaptive psychological mechanism to mitigate stress, including the stress of ever-accelerating changes in the built environment. It turns out that surprisingly, and somewhat counterintuitively, nostalgia may actually support the public acceptance of creative contemporary regional designs. Research shows that "nostalgia triggers" derided by many designers actually help people become more receptive and more psychologically resilient to new design forms and experiences, becoming an "arsenal of psychological mechanisms that enables people to use the past to fight the future."[16] In Chapter 1, I discussed how defamiliarization and nostalgia relate to the design thinking that is key to an understanding of critical regionalism.

The study of innate human behavior is a fruitful academic discipline with research results that are continually working their way into the design professions and improving the way designers create positive aesthetic experiences. Many studies have been undertaken since Appleton and the Kaplans released their groundbreaking work. Every area of direct sensory input and its effect on the enhancement and intensification of the landscape experience is being explored. How we respond to sound (both musical and otherwise), microclimates, levels of enclosure, boundaries and transitions, texture, movement (kinesthetic and haptic sensory input), color, scent, and more are all subjects for research and scholarly publications.[17] These studies, both empirical and scientific, are appearing in literature aimed at designers. Two important examples are *People Places* (1998) by Clare Cooper Marcus and Carolyn Francis and *Therapeutic Landscapes* (2014) by Clare Cooper Marcus and Marni Barnes.[18] Marcus states with reference to therapeutic gardens that "these [research] sources have been barely tapped by the design professions and their application to the designed landscape is negligible. This is a serious oversight in the effort to create spaces that are as beneficial as possible."[19]

It is rather surprising that so little effort is made to understand the impact of environmental psychology on built form considering the long history of the topic. As early as 1923, architect Walter Gropius (1883–1969) addressed the issue in an exhibition entitled *Art and Technics in New Unity*.[20] Even earlier, the philosopher David Hume (1711–1776), quoted below, wrote in the eighteenth century about a universal genesis of design thinking that transcends cultural biases.

> It appears then, that, amidst all the variety and caprice of taste, there are certain general principles of approbation or blame, whose influence a careful eye may trace in all operations to the mind. [21]

While most landscape designs can benefit by using elements of environmental psychology, it will be a higher priority criterion in some types of projects than in others. Landscapes designed for children, the elderly, dementia patients, hospitals, nursing homes, and prisons are some of the special conditions that favor a design approach that focuses on this area. Places where large groups of people are intended to congregate such as parks, streets, and shopping districts are other areas that can most benefit by applying the latest knowledge of how people respond to space on an innate subconscious level.

A few years ago, a candidate for a faculty position in landscape architecture visited the University of Texas at Arlington (UT Arlington) campus as part of the application process. This candidate was completing a Ph.D. that had environmental psychology as its principal area of focus. It was fascinating to hear her reactions to the campus landscapes. Every design was described and evaluated by how it responded to the rules of environmental psychology rather than more typical responses such as personal preferences or comments based on meaning, formal characteristics, or environmental and ecological issues. This attitude is indicative of the divide between some academics and practitioners of landscape architecture. Academics can benefit from a definition of aesthetics that is more inclusive of design influences beyond their area of specialization, and practitioners can improve their designs by engaging and using environmental psychology research. Few designers, however, will want to treat this important area as a proscriptive set of rules and use them as the basis for a design, unless it is for a highly specialized landscape for special populations, such as a garden for dementia patients. Design has many qualitative components related to culture and personal creativity that cannot be explained using the scientific process that led to an understanding of natural laws. The second aesthetic area, cultural rules, begins to broaden the possibilities for creating more meaningful and intensified landscape experiences.

Cultural Rules

Bourassa defines cultural rules as "those bases of behavior that are transmitted socially rather than genetically."[22] They are referred to as rules, rather than laws, because they are in a constant state of evolution, concentration, and dissipation as opposed to the natural laws of psychology that are more immutable.

Cultural rules are the subjective *collective* values that population groups assign to landscapes rather than inherent characteristics that are experienced on a subconscious psychological level. They have many societal and personal implications for landscape design. From a societal standpoint, they determine if the design is culturally *integrative* or culturally *dis-integrative*. As Albert Meyer asks, does the work "contribute and enhance the excellence-vitality-organic order . . . or is it detrimental to it?"[23] Our economic system and development process encourage a tendency to minimize the cultural differences in the built environment. There is a large economy of scale in using the same building materials and even the same designs across regions or continents regardless of site or conditions. It is usually less expensive to repeat a well-resolved design, complete with construction details, than it is to address the actual site and environment and tailor the design accordingly. Cultural differences reinforce the special sense of a particular place that help make the landscape and the buildings suitable for appropriation as a part of our identity. We need only consider other cultural arenas, such as music, food preferences, clothing styles, and leisure activities, to see the differences possible across populations and geographical areas.

The rapid pace and scale of development in the U.S. makes it imperative that designers develop a "social imagination" that reflects and enhances the societal values of the regions and districts in their designs.[24] Aldo van Eyck suggests that architects are "pathologically addicted to change" with the result "that the present is rendered emotionally inaccessible."[25] Users of the environment, however, are not always ready to abandon the past, and they can feel disoriented by the pace of change. To keep this from happening, the transformation of regions and places that is part of every dynamic society must proceed at a pace that can be absorbed by the local population. As Lester Rowntree reflects:

> In an era of rapid environmental change, visual biases and aesthetic traditions are used to slow landscape transformation . . . Landscape tastes, it would seem, reflect the biases of a people toward the artifacts of their occupancy by giving cultures a sense of historical perspective and identity through their surroundings.[26]

The theme of rootedness and connection has been written about consistently since the early twentieth century. Lewis Mumford believed that cultural rules help people come to grips with the "actual conditions of life" and to "feel at home" by defending "us from the "international style," the "absurdities" of present technology and the "despotism" of "the mechanical order."[27] They are an antidote for our ever-increasing mobility and pursuit of commercial success that causes us, as Luis Ferandez-Gallano states, to "spread ourselves out wider and wider only to become more and more uncomfortable" as we become estranged from our regional cultural roots.[28] Ferandez-Gallano describes our "fragmented lives" as individuals who "long for links, even if feigned."[29] The feigned links that create facile and commercially focused regionalism were one of the main reasons that critical regionalism originally developed as a theoretical concept.

The Australian professor of architecture and urban critic Kim Dovey writes of a quest for authenticity and a feeling of "home" engendered by a "serious disconnectedness in the ecology of person-environment relationships that one might call homelessness."[30] Similarly, the landscape architect Robert Thayer believes that through a compartmentalization of existential questions such as Who I am? and Where am I?, "we have all become, in certain fundamental ways, homeless."[31] This is an especially important issue in areas such as North Texas with its dissipated cultural and natural features that are changing rapidly. The cultural rules in the area are changing faster than the ability of many designers to coalesce them into a meaningful form that will help the population "anchor into" and feel good about the region. Having lived in the area since 1980, this disconnectedness has repeatedly become apparent in conversations and research about the area. Disconnectedness leads to a lack of care and concern for the long-term health and quality of the built environment, which then engenders further estrangement due to poor aesthetic experiences provided by rapid development focused solely on economic forces.

The study of anthropology has determined that our physical and mental worlds are "totally fused" and that the physical has to be a projection of the mental and vice-versa.[32] One important task of design and reason for critical regionalism is to create an existence with deeper significance and purpose in order to "facilitate Man's homecoming," as Aldo van Eyck proclaims.[33] This "homecoming" was not the same imperative through the long evolution of cultural history, where people tended to lead their lives in small and established geographic areas, in contrast to rapidly developing areas today with shifting populations.

If preserved cultural rules are positive influences for population groups, how do they benefit the development of a creative regionalist design methodology or critical regionalism? The answer lies in the approach to cultural environments within a critical regionalism ideology. By creative analysis and creative interpretation of the cultural environment and the cultural regional context, we learn who we are as designers. Both our perceptions and our reactions to regions can become the substance of our developing personalities as designers. The regional elements are absorbed into the imaginative and playful side of our personalities and become the syntax for creativity. This is a crucial step in the development of a design personality, since creative ideas will ultimately find expression back in the physical elements of a landscape. For experienced designers, the cultural context is an opportunity to imbue new creative life into a well-resolved personal design style. By being receptive to new cultural modifiers, we allow our tested and well-resolved design ideas to be given new vitality as they are used to address a new cultural context.

Cultural rules will be most important in landscape architecture projects where rooted culture is a high priority such as in historic districts and in countries and regions with long histories of cultural development. They are a defining regional element for certain cities and regions of the United States and elsewhere. In other areas with less developed cultural rules, the designer will be important as a contributor to their creation as well as their continued evolution. Cultural rules are region- and district-defining elements that are fundamental to critical regionalism and are discussed in greater depth in the coming chapters.

Personal Strategies

The excerpt below on habits and creativity is a good transition to the third area that Bourassa refers to as "personal strategies," one of the strengths of a critical regionalism methodology. They represent the development of an individual's experience, thinking, and taste, which evolves into a personal design aesthetic that will inform and may, if sufficiently powerful and appropriate, transform the cultural rules previously coalesced into regional design styles. As Arthur Koestler notes:

> Habits . . . reduce man to the status of a conditioned automaton. The creative act, by connecting previously unrelated dimensions of experience, enables him to attain a higher level of mental evolution. It is an act of liberation—the defeat of habit by originality.[34]

Personal strategies can be divided into two general types, both of which are highly relevant to designers. The first type is perceptual strategies, or creative ways of seeing and experiencing a region, and the second type is design strategies that modify the landscape. Both strategies can facilitate creative designs. Arthur Koestler (1905–1977), the Hungarian-born novelist, essayist, and journalist, makes a strong case in *The Act of Creation* (1964) that the three major areas of creativity—humor, discovery, and art—involve what he calls "bisociation" or a combining of preexisting things in novel ways to create something new.[35] The perceiving of regional design elements in non-traditional ways and the recombination of those elements into something new is a theme that defines critical regionalism.

Personal design strategies are often categorized as "isms." For example, a designer's preferred personal style can be described using terms such as minimalism, environmental determinism, modernism, process design/functionalism, deconstructivism, art-derived design, new classicism, historicism, industrial picturesque, ranch or farm vernacular, and neo-traditionalism. Personal styles are developed through personal idiosyncrasies, education, travel, formative years spent working for a

Fig. 3.4. The cultural rules of the historic Georgetown neighborhood in Washington, D.C., such as the building massing, sidewalk and street proportions, materials, and the mix of uses, were strong enough to help inspire the "New Urbanism" town planning movement at a time when single-use zoning and automobile-driven development were the accepted wisdom (2009).

Fig. 3.5 (top). Seattle's labyrinthine Freeway Park fountains, designed by Lawrence Halprin and Angela Danadjieva, were highly influential creative interpretations of regional waterfalls using the Brutalist architectural language that was popular at the time (2011). Their echoes can still be seen in fountains throughout the United States.

Fig. 3.6 (bottom). The fountain designed by Boyd & Heiderich, landscape architects for the Myrick Courtyard at the University of Texas at Arlington's College of Architecture, Planning, and Public Affairs (CAPPA) (2019). Constructed in 1984, it was inspired by the Halprin office fountains.

designer with a strong design personality, or through practice experience in general. They may also be the result of the "imprinting" of landscape preferences before the designer becomes self-reflective enough to understand how these influences shaped one's development as a designer. Just as many people are locked into the musical preferences they developed as teenagers, it is also difficult for some designers to transcend the imprinting, either early in life or early in a career, of what they perceive as the "ideal landscape."

The "isms" are a valuable linguistic tool as shorthand for the understanding and communication of a design style. An understanding of these elements helps the designer both to "read" a landscape or a district or a region and to communicate regional character and regionalist ideals to other players in the design process (Figs 3.3 and 3.4).[36] As an educational tool, the "isms" show the novice designer a range of possibilities in a regionally appropriate design. An understanding of a variety of possible design styles can help designers develop the perspective required in order to not accept the personal design aesthetic of a current mentor as the only possible solution. Other solutions will reveal themselves, if the designer is open to them, over time as one changes jobs or is exposed in other ways to a variety of designers with successful personal design aesthetics.

A problem with "isms" is that overweighting the importance of these concepts in the past has led some architectural theorists to reject academic theory outright, without consideration of its usefulness or appropriateness to the work of landscape architecture. Michael Speaks, Professor and Dean of the School of Architecture at Syracuse, has written that "The architecture community is now left to face the future without guidance from the all-knowing theory vanguards that have dominated schools since the 1970s."[37] He is referencing the increasing irrelevance of academic theories that reject popular culture, such as Marxism and Deconstructivism. By embracing the four-part aesthetic and critical regionalism, the study of theory is no longer an either/or proposition. Relevance is achieved through the mitigating factors of regional culture, environmental psychology, and the aesthetics, integrity, and resilience inherent in local ecology.

If a creative designer is informed about the culture and ecology of a given area and the issues involved in a design problem, one may be able to create a design that will be absorbed by a local population and become a cultural rule. The relationship of the individual to a region's culture has been described by Juhani Pallasmaa as the fusing of "conscious intentions, unconscious conditioning, memories and experiences in a dialogue between the individual and the collective."[38] This natural fit of a creative designer and a culture that is ripe for appropriation of their ideas was described decades ago by Dewey and is a key issue in critical regionalism:

> Esthetic experience is a manifestation, a record and celebration of the life of a civilization. For while it is produced and is enjoyed by individuals, those individuals are what they are in the content of their experience because of the cultures in which they participate.[39]

The aesthetics of a design, driven by the passion and excitement engendered by either regional elements or by a personal design inspiration are enhanced by a design process that addresses the four-part aesthetic. This helps keep the resulting design within the range of aesthetic sensibilities of at least a significant portion of the population of users. The goal here is not to lose the emotional fire that inspires the design or the creative vision that absorbs the regional context. To do so would devolve the creative act back to the scientific reasoning of a purely rational or scientific design process, which is often referred to as functionalism. Functionalism addresses the activities and functions for a physical site or for a building without the qualitative overlay that creates inspired designs and moves culture forward. In Chapter 2, I showed how the excesses of functionalism were a key element in the genesis of critical regionalism and how the creative designer will instead combine rational thinking with instinctively derived design ideas that "feel" right, in a subjective way, within both the regional context and the four aesthetic areas described in this chapter. Both intuitive judgment and a well-reasoned design process, developed and tested through experience, are crucial if the designer is to avoid moving too far in either the direction of idiosyncratic responses or, at the opposite extreme, pure, rational, and all-too-often single-purpose problem-solving strategies.

Personal strategies play a role in every type of designed landscape and are one of the strengths of a critical regionalism ideology. They are a higher priority within the four-part aesthetic for landscapes where creativity is more highly valued or for areas where personal idiosyncrasies are more often expressed as a regional design parameter. Thus, bohemian or "artsy" cities such as Barcelona and districts such as Miami's South Beach will be more appreciative of highly idiosyncratic personal expressions than cities and districts that are more historically or environmentally constituted such as the city of Stockholm that celebrates both future viable strategies as an "eco city", and it's very well preserved historical districts.[40] Designers need to expand or rein in their creativity and find the balance that is most appropriate for the cultural rules of a place, district, or region at a particular stage of its development. Critical regionalism is impossible to achieve without singular creative expressions by the designer.

The aesthetic criteria outlined above cover a three-part aesthetic construct as outlined by Bourassa and others. The question then arises: Where do the natural systems and regional ecology that are such an important element of landscape architecture fit into this discussion? Are they a cultural value or simply another personal strategy? Or are they landscape elements that we respond to subliminally and thus become part of environmental psychology?

Environmental Imperatives

Aldo Leopold, a seminal figure in the evolution of environmental and ecological thinking and a land ethic in the United States, is famous for many statements, among them:

Figs. 3.7 and 3.8. Aldo Leopold (top) oversees a prescribed burn of the prairie at the Shack, his family retreat along the Wisconsin River near Baraboo, 1940s; and Dr. Thomas C. Hunt (bottom), reclamation ecologist, observes the same prairie in 2010. Photographs by Carl Leopold (top) and Emily Hunt (bottom). From *Aldo Leopold's Shack: Nina's Story, a New Edition* (Staunton, VA: George F. Thompson Publishing, 2025), 66.

> An innumerable host of actions and attitudes, comprising perhaps the bulk of all land relations, is determined by the land users' tastes and predilections, rather than by his purse. The bulk of all land relations hinges on investments of time, forethought, skill, and faith . . . As a land user thinketh, so is he.[41]

Leopold was very well known as a professor at the University of Wisconsin-Madison during his lifetime, but he is best known today for his work and writing on a land ethic, natural aesthetics, environmental ethics, wildlife management, wilderness preservation, conservation economics, regional ecology, and sustainable agriculture.

He started his career in forestry management after completing a master's degree in forestry management at Yale University in 1909. His career as a thoughtful professional gradually evolved as he looked more and more deeply into the root causes of the environmental and ecological dysfunction that he saw in the U.S. and around the world during the early twentieth century. His seminal and widely read work, *A Sand County Almanac and Sketches Here and There* (published posthumously by Oxford in 1949), shows us that most of the issues, aesthetics, and ethics of land use that are still considered environmentally and ecologically forward thinking have been with us at least since the Great Depression era. It also makes clear that these imperatives need constant nurturing and renewal by thoughtful design professionals and educators today (Figs. 3.7 and 3.8).

Environmental imperatives must be considered separately as an aesthetic category by designers of landscapes. As a matter of personal aesthetic preference, an individual may respond more favorably to cultural environments and may express a lack of interest or even a strong dislike for natural environments. This can be, and indeed is, the personal design aesthetic of some individuals. As designers, however, we no longer have the option of ignoring natural systems. If natural systems are a key to the survival or, at the very least, the quality of life of our species and the myriad species that coexist to create resilient ecosystems on which we depend, then the aesthetics of the natural environment must be part of our design aesthetics and our design vocabulary. Becoming "grounded" in the bioregion is an indispensable component of our appropriation of the environment that anchors us psychologically into a region, our design personality as professionals, and the practical exigency of addressing actual environmental and ecological conditions that sustain life.

The best regionalist architects address environmental issues related to thermal loading, shade, solar orientation, natural versus artificial light, stormwater management and low-carbon footprint materials, among others. This response to climate will have an impact on both the pictorial and tactile experience of dwelling in the buildings. Landscape architects have the opportunity to go much deeper in studying and designing landscapes that can mitigate the environmental footprint and even enhance the ecology of the dense cultural environments in metropolitan areas. These types of landscapes can be referred to as *performative* landscapes in the sense that they are performing both ecological and environmental services in addition to the many other demands of landscape performance. Performative landscapes enhance aesthetics to the degree that the environmental performance is designed to enhance a user's experiences. The innate human response to nature, the cultural value of nature, and the personal appreciation of nature are used to enhance and intensify the experience of these landscapes.

We all have personal preferences for what we intuitively feel is the most beautiful natural condition. Some people are entranced by shady forest environments and others are captivated by the stark sculptural qualities of deserts. These predilections are innate responses to nature, culturally ascribed preferences, or personal idiosyncrasies. Any ecological area, however, can become part of a personal design aesthetic through aesthetic appropriation by a designer. It is important for designers who work in diverse ecological areas to transcend their biases and learn to assimilate the ecological aesthetics of the various environments where their designs are located. They can then creatively design human-made landscape corollaries that perform culturally while also providing meaningful ecological and environmental services in a regionally appropriate way (Fig. 3.9).

Fig. 3.9. Many new developments in the rapidly growing city of Stockholm, Sweden, have embraced the natural systems that provide both regional character and environmental performance to littoral zones (2010).

There must be a type of aesthetic surrender or communion, almost in a spiritual sense, with the experience of the natural features of a given area in order to absorb them into a personal design aesthetic that is adapted to and harmonious with the region. Once this type of communion is attained in a given location, it becomes progressively easier to find the emotional connection to a wide variety of ecosystems and natural features. The literature is replete with poetic writers who have found this type of experience in diverse regions of the world. One of the most prominent of these writers is biologist Edward O. Wilson (1929–2021), winner of two Pulitzer Prizes, who coined the term *biophilia*, which translates as the "love of living things."[42] Biophilia helps a designer become more flexible in the appreciation of natural environments as the natural environment of a given area becomes a symbol of the moral (in the tradition of Plato, Socrates, Stolnitz, and Burke) and as such is seen as a positive aesthetic opportunity. Timothy Beatly, a long-time professor of planning at the University of Virginia, has taken Wilson's vision out of nature into urban areas with his research on what he terms *biophilic cities.* His work focuses on the effects of natural artifacts on human populations and their power to "restore and heal as well as to impart happiness and meaning to life."[43] Beatley recognizes and addresses many of the technical, financial, and political challenges to integrating nature into city planning and design. An additional challenge and opportunity is *regional* ecology, which addresses both human and nonhuman resilience and sustainability. The local ecology is considered, along with cultural rules, as fruitful design material that is engaged in the design process, producing new creative solutions for designs that embrace all four of the aesthetic areas.

The importance of environmental imperatives relative to the other three aesthetic areas is most readily apparent in suburban landscapes and in rural and exurban areas, which I cover more thoroughly in the chapters on creative seeing and plants and natural systems. We will see how environmental imperatives are being used to enhance both the aesthetics and the ecology of the dense cultural environments in cities and metropolitan landscapes as well.

A critical regionalism methodology for landscape architects that endeavors to embrace contemporary thinking and systems must address the aesthetics of the *local* or regional environment, what renowned art critic and writer Lucy R. Lippard calls "the lure of the local" in her pathbreaking book.[44] To ignore this important area negates the unique contribution that landscape architecture brings to the discourse and moves critical regionalism theory back to its roots in architecture, planning, and history.

Conclusion

Natural laws, cultural rules, personal strategies, and environmental imperatives are four areas of aesthetic concern that are fully compatible with the proposed theory of critical regionalism. Environmental psychology is an important part of a rigorous, user friendly, and evidence-based design solution, particularly for special populations. Cultural rules evolve from personal strategies over time, are reflections by a culture of environmental psychology, and are inspirations for personal creativity.[45] Personal strategies are informed by cultural rules and environmental imperatives, and are provided guardrails in the design process by a knowledge of human behavior. Environmental imperatives inform personal strategies, reflect cultural values, contribute to our long-term viability as a species, and respond to an innate human need for contact with nature. The four aesthetic criteria help the profession of landscape architecture move further in the direction of designs that make a more positive aesthetic impact and are more appropriate for users of landscapes.

These four aesthetic areas also take advantage of the individual interests and experience of the various members of a design team. A designer interested in environmental psychology can specialize in designs for special populations and, importantly, keep up with the ever-expanding research in this area in order to disseminate it to other designers working on a wide variety of projects. A designer with an inclination towards culture and history can help the design team "read" the cultural landscape and provide new regional fodder for creative expressions. A designer who is more adept at shape and form can assist others who may be more focused on the other three areas and benefit from their reinvigorating supply of aesthetically qualified material to absorb and use. Finally, the person with a special kinship to nature can focus on the landscapes where this skill is most important and also be an invaluable resource for environmentally and ecologically performative solutions for all designed landscapes. It is no longer realistic to expect one designer to embrace the four areas with the rigor required of our increasingly complex and fragile environments. The four-part aesthetic approach takes advantage of the taste, thinking, and experience of various individuals on a design team and uses them to best advantage.

The profession of landscape architecture has become so diverse that some question what binds us as a profession. Four-part aesthetics help to give landscape architects a group identity and a common philosophical position. This identity is distinct from the other professions—especially planning, architecture, and civil engineering—that overlap with the role of the landscape architect. In a critique of critical regionalism, the architect Steven Moore describes its limitation as being "a purely aesthetic discourse . . . outside of the social and biological conditions that describe normative practice."[46] It is proposed here that if this is true, it is because the theory has been developed by architects with a focus on personal strategies. A narrow focus on *my* thinking, *my* taste, and *my* experience is broadened here to embrace critical regionalism in the context of the four-part aesthetic construct that reflects the values of the best landscape architects and architects. One of the most attractive features of critical regionalism is that, unlike many other personal aesthetic constructs adopted by designers, it is fully compatible with a regionalism that embraces all four aesthetic areas. These four areas can help a design rise above the vast production of "normative practice" to become a more permanent addition to the aesthetic wealth and evolution of a region.[47]

Chapter 4:
Evaluating Critical Regionalism Designs

Design exemplars are something landscape designers frequently look for as a shortcut to understanding a concept, parameter, or technical issue. They offer the additional benefit of direct experience that can transform an understanding of and appreciation for various landscape designs, styles, and "isms." In this chapter, I begin the search for successful examples of critical regionalism that can be used to help understand and utilize the concept. The parameters of evaluation discussed in this chapter help explain why certain exemplars have been selected for this research. These parameters will also help trigger associations with other successful projects that expand a thoughtful examination of the tenets of critical regionalism.

Ideas and Technical Skill

In romantic regionalism or any other well-resolved style, the ideas referenced by a design are well known and easy to gather for design inspiration. Accordingly, the design can be evaluated on the quality and appropriateness of designed and constructed details and the application of the four aesthetic areas discussed in Chapter 3: environmental psychology, cultural rules, personal strategies, and environmental imperatives. In critical regionalism, the details may not be as carefully resolved, and the landscape is often best assessed by the quality of the original *ideas* that engendered its creation.

There is a finite amount of energy and creativity that can be apportioned to any given project in the time allotted for its design. If the time and energy are spent on creating an original concept, then working out all the subsequent details may not be accomplished to the same degree in the allotted time. This is another good argument for a team approach to design, as discussed in Chapter 3, where an original concept of the design may be brought to fruition by another individual more temperamentally suited to design development and construction details. Similarly, a designer may apply creative energy to a well-developed style or theme and develop it to a whole new level. The composer Johann Sebastian Bach (1685–1750) is a good example from a different discipline. The genius evident in his musical works is universally regarded as the pinnacle of baroque musical composition, though we often forget he was writing in a style that was fully mature in its day and often perceived as well-worn and old-fashioned.

Rigor

Rigor is a very salient concept for evaluating designs that express critical regionalism as it involves the application of demanding standards. All tenets of critical regionalism that are present in a design ultimately need to be appraised based on the rigor a designer applies to the design through the process that created it.

The constant reinvention inherent in critical regionalism is an element of rigor that requires the designer to exhibit the courage, effort, and perseverance required to abandon a relatively fail-safe design style for a fresh reconceptualized one. There are many professional pressures pushing a designer to imitate and replicate a successful pictorial design, which often becomes a commercial solution to a design problem and not the creative act that defines the best critical regionalism. As Paul Ricoeur observes: "The problem is not simply to repeat the past, but rather to take root in it in order to ceaselessly invent. Otherwise . . . fidelity to the past will be nothing more than simple folkloric ornamentation."[1]

An assessment of rigor can certainly be applied to the perceptions by a designer of a landscape or building that begins the uncovering of regional inspirations for the subsequent design process. One way to increase the understanding and rigorous perception of a regional landscape or building is to understand the design influences and frames of mind of the original designers. This element of assessment will facilitate the recreation by the observer of the aesthetic experiences and priorities that led to the design in the first place. Combining it with a rigorous personal design aesthetic used by the designer will produce a landscape or building that has a much better chance of transcending the romantic regional and of being perceived both by the local inhabitants and by the visitors to an area as an original aesthetic experience.

Albert Borgmann, a postmodern philosopher of technology, refers to an element of rigor he calls "patient vigor." He defines this as coming to terms with the realities of postmodern design and taking the time to "develop the skills and knowledge that enable us to engage the concrete world."[2] He applies this theory primarily to the relentlessly homogenized suburban developments in the United States, but it is certainly applicable to other areas of rigorous resistance, as outlined in Chapter 1.

The rigorous selection and organization of regional materials is a true test of the integrity and cohesiveness of the design and will directly impact the emotional and intellectual connection to the users. Regional materials are most suitable to the forms that are best adapted to their properties. For example, wood, brick, stone, and gravel paving surfaces all have significant implications as delineators of form. The designer may accept the form implications or play against them to defamiliarize the regional material, as Figs. 4.1 and 4.2 illustrate.

Fig. 4.1 (top). Ubiquitous porphyry paving is used in an unusual way as flowing organic forms at the Hundertwasser House in Vienna, Austria (1997). Concept by J. Krawina (Tu Berlin) and Friedensreich Hundertwasser.

Fig. 4.2 (bottom). Tanner Springs Park in Portland, Oregon, designed by Atelier Dreiseitl, includes an art fence vertically placed and constructed with defamiliarized and repurposed steel rails (2008).

Regional Authenticity and Appropriateness

As Juhani Pallasmaa surmised: "Perhaps the most meaningful form of cultural survival that remains is a regionalism of the mind, the strategy of resistance, the subculture that believes in and searches for authenticity. Not authenticity on ethnographic grounds but of human experience and interaction."[3] In this way, appropriateness within the context of a new design is another element of rigor that applies both to materials and to all aspects of a creative regionalist design. But Lewis Mumford warned that "like a child with a new toy," invention can become an obsession and that "critical discernment" is required to keep it in perspective.[4] Invention based on formalist theory is particularly vulnerable to misdirection whereas, as Lawrence Speck writes, "invention based on tangible realities [the local context] is more likely to provide true service."[5]

In academic form-driven architecture, perceived authenticity is often derived from a sophisticated playing with shapes.[6] Designers using this methodology go through impressive intellectual hoops to create and explain their complex designs. The question then arises as to whether they have an honest emotional, visual, and spatial connection to their design that is transferable to a significant portion of the users. Will the project be one that is appropriated by users as part of their personal identity, or will the result be an academically correct or even brilliant design that is cold and emotionally remote? And for that matter, are all styles equally valid? Are they all manifestations of a personal design language "game" with an equal claim to authenticity? The answers can be found in the appropriateness of each style to a given location and program and in the design's sensitivity to the four-part aesthetic described in Chapter 3. While designs deriving from any personal style may be judged on their own terms as personal design statements, they should also be evaluated based on the appropriate use, in a given place, of environmental psychology, cultural rules, and environmental imperatives. A critical regionalism design is no different and should be studied for how it addresses the four-part aesthetic as an element of contemporary thinking for designs in a specific location with specific programmatic goals.

Ironically, the understanding and use of regional elements and prototypes actually broadens the range of acceptable aesthetics for a region or district. The familiar landscape elements create an instant bond or "knowing" with the population that uses the design, even if the expression of the elements is highly abstract or extremely personal, as in Fig. 4.1.

Another example of using abstract forms with resonance to the local population is Crescent Park in Philadelphia by Stuart Appel, then President of Wells-Appel Land Strategies (Fig. 4.3). The park, at the entrance to the Philadelphia Navy Yard, features a large steel pergola evocative of naval architecture. The pergola can be experienced and appreciated as an original creative landscape element, even though few locals from the Philadelphia area would fail to recognize its connection to naval architecture and its celebration of the Philadelphia naval yard district.

FIG. 4.3. Philadelphia (Pennsylvania): Crescent Park adjacent to the Philadelphia Navy Yard by Wells-Appel, Inc. Image courtesy of Sikora Wells Appel (2007).

The urgent quest for authenticity in our consumer culture can cause designers and end users to embrace design elements of perceived "authenticity" that could otherwise be seen as inappropriate or even ugly. A few years ago, I visited a converted grain mill in a then derelict part of Dallas, Texas, now called The American Beauty Mill Apartments (Fig. 4.4). The mill has been converted into rather expensive rental units embraced by a cadre of young urban professionals. The walls are old and the concrete is crumbling and some of the apartments have very limited outside views or even no views at all. On the surface, the project appears to have all the charm of an abandoned prison or a post-apocalyptic stage set, but what appeals to the people I spoke to about living there is the un-designed nature of the buildings: They were not themed but grew out of the honest cultural environment of their time.[7] Lefaivre reinforces this idea by describing an incident where Charlie Chaplin was walking with Somerset Maugham through "sordid tenement houses and . . . gaudy shops in which are sold that which the poor buy day to day. Chaplin exclaimed: 'This is real life, isn't it? All the rest is sham.'"[8]

While Chaplin was entranced by the picturesque aesthetics of real-life working-class areas, John Dewey focused on the negative attributes of working life. When Dewey writes about factories, he describes them as unabashedly unaesthetic because of his knowledge of the terrible conditions of life that the factory workers had to endure at the beginning of the twentieth century.[9] Today, those same factories and industrial landscapes are celebrated as increasingly meaningful cultural artifacts with an expressive beauty partially appreciated by their remoteness from everyday experience. In Fig. 4.5, one sees one of the earliest and most celebrated examples of adaptive reuse of industrial infrastructure that takes full advantage of the expressive potential of the site. Granville Island in Vancouver, Canada has evolved since the 1970s into a powerful, authentic regional expression of a complex choreography of adaptive reuse, art, and ongoing industrial activities.[10]

FIG. 4.4 (TOP). At the American Beauty Mill Apartments in Dallas, Texas, the region's industrial history and perceived authenticity are pitched to a young and receptive population of urban professionals in the fastest-growing area of the United States (2021). Image courtesy of Brandon Martin.

FIG. 4.5 (BOTTOM). The Granville Island Public Market Courtyard and Market building in Vancouver, British Columbia (2011). Randy Sharp, FCSLA is credited with developing many of the public spaces.

Consider, by contrast, the aesthetic picturesque value of a working contemporary coal-fired power plant or chemical plant. It is harder to see the aesthetic value of the machinery with the contemporary knowledge of the environmental degradation that results. Still, many people who work in the factory will form the same kinds of bonds with it that are formed with any landscape or building. They may even experience the chemical smells as nostalgia triggers, as I did after working as a steelworker in a wire mill in Bridgeport, Connecticut, as a young man. Future generations of people who did not work at the factory, separated by time from the pollution of a working plant, may form their own personal bond and appreciate it as a pure, authentic aesthetic object without the negative environmental connotations.

Studying how a designer negotiates the appropriate line between creativity and eccentricity or overly mannered design is another useful parameter for evaluation. In an appropriate design, the hand of the designer will tend to disappear in direct proportion to the fit of the form to the context. The technique of the designer, if it is mannered and overly obvious, will detract from the *experience* of the landscape. If a design exhibits a sufficient level of appropriateness, it will be experienced, observed, and judged on its own terms. For example, is it an interesting *park* or just an unusual landscape? Figs. 4.6 and 4.7 show the view of the sunken garden overlook at Butchart Gardens on Victoria Island, BC. The pedestrian path leading up to the view through a short, very dark and shady enclosed wooded area is so obviously contrived in setting up the "surprise" of the unfolding panorama that it can actually detract from the *experience* of the world-famous sunken display garden.

Another instructive example of "defamiliarization" occurs in Seattle where the highly idiosyncratic and personal expression created for the entrance to the King County Jailhouse Garden by Martha Schwartz appears jarring and out of place, even within the relatively decorative and artistic aesthetic of downtown Seattle (Fig. 4.8). It exhibits many of the problems associated with Harlequin Plaza (Fig. 2.9) and, in Schwartz's own words, evokes "the feeling of being in a bad dream."[11] Beyond the regional dissonance, it is worth considering if the psycho-social stresses imposed by the legal system are in any way being ameliorated by the stated design intent.

Less than a block away is another more positive artistic landscape expression with a strong connection to Seattle regionalism designed by Gustafson, Guthrie, Nichol (Fig. 4.9). The Seattle City Hall landscape is experienced as an original "defamiliarized" expression with visual ties to both downtown Seattle and to the regional forms and light of the Pacific Northwest.

Adaptation of Personal Design Styles

In addition to looking at context, it is necessary to have studied a designer's previous work in order to evaluate a design as a good or bad example of critical regionalism. By studying previous work, especially in diverse areas, it is possible to see how the personal strategies of a designer have been adapted to each site, region, and program. A single example of the work may give the wrong impression, particularly

FIGS. 4.6 AND 4.7. The sunken garden at Butchart Gardens in Victoria, British Columbia, where the approach (above) sets up the "surprise" of the view of the sunken garden (right) in the spirit of "ha ha" elements in English landscape designs of the eighteenth and nineteenth centuries (2008).

if the observer does not know if the design is simply being repeated over and over. By studying the influences on the designer and not just the product of creativity, it is more likely that an original creative expression will be uncovered. The observation of these successful creative designs is a good intermediary "book" to aid in the appropriation of both new and resolved regional design precedents for later use in the design process. Creative perception and experience of the regional aesthetically qualified material from the "book" facilitates the absorption of ideas into a continually evolving original and creative regionalist design aesthetic.

The creative regionalist designer must be able to grasp the success of a landscape to a local population on its own terms and as a totality, without overemphasis on particular personal stylistic details that may not be as important. For example, in Dallas, Texas, there is an urban development called West Village in an uptown area just north of downtown Dallas (Fig. 4.10). The personal design decisions of the architects are very easy to find fault with from a variety of standpoints:

1. The buildings are constructed of EIFS (such as Drivet) in an overtly historicist and romantic regional style;
2. The landscape details are mostly raw concrete that stains, generally does not age well, and is very underscaled by current "New Urbanist" standards with narrow sidewalks; and,

FIG. 4.8. Stressing novelty over tradition in the King County Jailhouse Garden by Martha Schwartz (2011).

3. There is little attempt at an environmentally future viable landscape with elements such as LID structures or native plants.

The three factors above could cancel any perceptions of positive regard and lead a design critic to deem a project a failure from an aesthetic standpoint. West Village, however, is a very popular mixed-use development with the local population. It is one of the few places in the Dallas area where there are regular crowds of people on the streets and sidewalks, even during the very hot summer months. It would be useful, therefore, to understand what the designers did right and how they made the project so successful despite its obvious drawbacks. For example, William H. Whyte in *The Social Life of Small Urban Spaces* (1980) showed that the way people actually use space, as opposed to the way they describe their preferences for using space, indicates that they prefer crowding in with other people. This could explain the appeal of the under-scaled elements such as the relatively narrow sidewalks. Additionally, the mix of apartments, restaurants, shops, an independent movie house, and other commercial ventures has created a place where people want to go.[12]

This regionally appropriate mix of uses at West Village helps the project transcend the flaws in the decorative details of the design that are both dissonant to the sensibilities of trained urban designers

FIG. 4.9. Seattle City Hall Phase 2 landscape, showing the visual connection of paving in the foreground to the color of Puget Sound in the background at the top of the photo (2008).

Fig. 4.10. Busy street life in West Village in Dallas, Texas, by David M. Schwartz Architects, Inc. (2008).

and at odds with many of the tenets of critical regionalism. Still, the opposite case happens much more frequently. A landscape with a highly resolved design aesthetic (particularly one that photographs well) that is in concert with the sensibilities of contemporary tastemakers will be praised out of proportion to the actual success of the use of the landscape, as was the case with Harlequin Plaza (Fig. 2.9) and the King County Jailhouse Garden (Fig. 4.8). As we have seen, in the opposition between the experiential and the abstractly scenographic, designs that focus on the scenographic are usually deprived of important components for the elicitation of a positive aesthetic response.

A work of critical regionalism can also be usefully evaluated on the insight and integrity of the regional inspiration that has been used to adapt a personal style to a given area. This critique would have to reference other works of greater or lesser value in order to prevent the accusation that it is simply a personal reaction to the work. One way to evaluate how a region and a new landscape work together and are suited to each other is to imagine how well the new landscape would work in other regions. If it appears that it would lose practical and aesthetic value by being separated from its intended region, then it is probably well integrated into the region. Many of the projects used as examples in this book would lose a significant amount of their aesthetic value without the regional context for which they were designed. And this includes the native plant materials used to reflect a region.

Bing Thom (1940–2016), one of the architects most responsible for the evolving "Vancouver style" of architecture, believed that, ultimately, each project can only be evaluated long after it's completed: "Does the building have depth? Poetry? Does it capture spiritual values and satisfy more utilitarian needs? Can the building withstand the test of time? Have we made a difference? Did the building deserve to be built?"[13] These types of questions cannot be answered without understanding if and how a designer has addressed the core principles of four-part aesthetics and critical regionalism to creatively adapt their personal design style to a region's culture and environment. The example of critical regionalism that follows is tested against these principles by using a list of elements of critical regionalism as a starting point for the evaluation of regionalist projects.

Bringing Critical Regionalism to the Industrial Picturesque

Studying elements of critical regionalism in built works involves looking for meaningful regional elements used in creative ways, rigorous imaginative transformation of those elements, the utilization of contemporary thinking and technology, unique design features that provoke critical thinking, and the creation of "bounded domains and tactile presences" that address the experiential aesthetic concerns of landscape architects outlined in the four-part aesthetic.[14] The discussion below illustrates ways that the elements of critical regionalism have found expression in two parks: Gas Works Park in Seattle, Washington, and Northside Park in Denver, Colorado. Gas Works celebrates the industrial picturesque without critical regionalism, whereas Northside Park shows the flexibility of a critical regionalism methodology by exhibiting characteristics of both critical regionalism and the industrial picturesque.

The Industrial Picturesque

The rationale and history of the picturesque and aesthetics have been explored by many writers such as Allen Carlson, Elizabeth Meyer, Steven Bourassa, and by Susan Herrington in an excellent article in *Landscape Journal* entitled "Framed Again: The Picturesque Aesthetics of Contemporary Landscapes."[15] The picturesque is an element of detached aesthetics, focused on the visual, as opposed to the engaged or fully experiential model that involves more of the senses and leads to a richer experience.[16] Picturesque means literally "picture like" and indicates a mode of appreciation by which nature and culture are imagined as artistic scenes. The picturesque differs from my narrower use of the term "pictorial" as is explained below.

At the height of the picturesque movement during the eighteenth and nineteenth centuries in Europe, gentlemanly contemplative observation would be undertaken both with the unaided eye and with a Claude glass. This small, blackened pocket mirror, named after the French artist Claude Lorraine (1600–1682), reduced the tonal values of whatever landscapes it was pointed to as its convex shape simultaneously diminished the vibrancy of the natural landscape that was being viewed and brought more of the scene into focus like a wide angle lens.[17] The observer saw only picturesque scenery and ignored other aesthetic concerns such as, for example, the inconvenient squalor of the rural poor.[18]

The subjective and romantic scenes of the picturesque traditionally referred back to literary and artistic works for their meanings. The concept can be traced to Claude Lorraine who influenced the work of the artist William Gilpin (1724–1804), the writer and landscape designer Uvedale Price (1747–1829), the scholar Richard Payne Knight (1750–1824), and the landscape designer Humphry Repton (1752–1818). Since that time, the concepts have been tied to romantic garden design and the values of tourism with the kinds of images seen in travel brochures, calendar photos, and postcards. This romantic pictorial tradition, halfway between the beautiful and the sublime, is applied here to two former industrial sites that have been transformed into Gas Works and Northside Parks.

The term "industrial picturesque" is defined by what Rick Darke has called "the contemplative power of controlled dereliction" as opposed to the pictorial implications of industry portrayed by, for example, the Italian futurists, the Russian constructivists, or the artistic industrial photography of the photojournalist Margaret Bourke White.[19] These illustrations celebrated the expressive forms of the then *contemporary* industry in the early to mid-twentieth century. Part of the power of the industrial picturesque, however, comes from the same sublime awe at the scale and complexity of industrial constructions.

Just as most people think of places in terms of their physical reality, technology is often understood as physical hardware. This view can discount both the social forces required to create the industrial artifacts of technology and the appropriation by society of the artifact as an element of regional identity. The sociologists Donald MacKenzie and Judith Wajcman explain that technology includes three principal qualities: "human knowledge, patterns of human activities, and sets of physical objects."[20] Knowledge is required to build the object, to operate it, and to determine its relation to natural resources. Patterns of human activities refer to regional practices for solving complex problems through, for example, professions and trades. The sets of objects that are the focus of the industrial picturesque are the things themselves and are useless without the local knowledge base of the local people who use them. This integration of object, site, and culture often binds artifacts of industry to a local population in a way that goes beyond the purely visual picturesque to create a *work-place*. As has been stated, over time, the objects tend to become more purely aesthetic as the memories of their original use, both positive and negative, fade.

The questions moving forward are more about how the aesthetics of the reused sites are designed and the creative performative ecological solutions that mitigate their pollution, and less about the concept or validity of using the sites in the first place. There is a consensus among many landscape architects that the aesthetics, cultural value, and perceived authenticity of derelict industrial infrastructure make it suitable and desirable as a basis for adaptive reuse in new designed landscapes. The balance between preserving cultural features for their *expressive* potential, as exemplified by Gas Works Park, and using them in new ways for their *creative* potential, illustrated by Denver's Northside Park, illustrates the value of critical regionalism for addressing the reuse of industrial artifacts and other regional precedents.

FIG. 4.11. Gas Works Park in Seattle, Washington, showing covered picnic areas and interpretive pavilions, open space, and the former gas-generating towers (2006). Designed by Richard Haag.

Gas Works Park (Seattle, Washington)

Gas Works Park (Fig. 4.11) is the first and still one of the best-known examples of the industrial picturesque in the United States. The highly influential and celebrated park is on the 20-acre site of a former power-generating plant in Seattle, Washington. The Gas Works Park project, designed by Richard Haag, began in 1971 and was completed to its present form in 1988. It marks the beginning of the widespread understanding and acceptance of the industrial picturesque in the United States, and its construction and popular success was an important indicator of the increasing importance of cultural rules and local history in the United States.

Haag chose to preserve many of the original components of the factory site, calling them "a memorial to Rube Goldberg engineering."[21] The industrial components celebrated in the park slow down the transformation of the Seattle landscape to a pace more easily appropriated by the local population as opposed to the clean slate approach to the park design that was originally expected at the site and is most often still employed on degraded former industrial sites.[22]As possible uses for the most iconic elements of the park, the six large gas-generating towers, Haag envisioned "a walk-in cloud chamber, a camera obscura, planetarium, vertical museum, tactile chamber, exploratorium, vertical gymnasium, super-scale fountains, tree-mendous planting urns, games un-invented, and metaphysical demonstrations of hidden dimensions."[23] Any of these visions could have led to a critical regionalism design as the site was creatively transformed. Unfortunately, the promise for new creative designs using Haag's ideas never came to pass, and today the rusting forms shown in Fig. 4.11 are surrounded by security fences and can only be appreciated as picturesque relics at a distance.

Elizabeth Meyer has written that "the monumental structures at Gas Works Park, once the source of technological sublime rapture, now seem less consequential, more of a part of a cast of characters than sole performers within the park."[24] My experiences of the park are similar. With a few exceptions, the park reads as a well-designed space with carefully framed views and a good sequence of movement in a sculptural setting of historic mechanical structures. The rusting artifacts have aesthetic power but feel distant and inaccessible. Because the park never achieved the balance of new and historic uses that Haag envisioned, it is most iconic for its picturesque qualities and does not fulfill the promise of critical regionalism.

Northside Park (Denver, Colorado)

Northside Park is an example of a project that embraces both the aesthetics of the industrial picturesque and elements of critical regionalism. Completed in 1999, Northside Park was designed by Bill Wenk, FASLA, and developed as part of the city of Denver's initiative to build a series of parks along the South Platte River Greenway (Figs. 4.12 and 4.13). The park is an adaptive reuse of an abandoned sanitary sewer plant. Through the employment of a "design by subtraction" method, elements of the derelict sewer plant structure were removed or modified to function within the park's program.[25] Grading and drainage were manipulated to alternately conceal and to reveal the massive treatment-plant structure and to further define park spaces.

In Fig. 4.12, one sees the treatment plant prior to construction. It is easy to imagine how the strong picturesque forms of the existing structure could have been the driving design determinants. In Fig. 4.13, one sees how the design has transformed the treatment plant into an entirely new landscape with passive and active programmatic elements, environmentally viable features, and expressive forms that echo its industrial past.

Visiting this park for the first time was an intense aesthetic experience for me that cannot be duplicated photographically. The site is impossibly flat with a huge 360-degree horizon that encompasses both the Rocky Mountains and the Denver skyline. The infrastructure remnants read as carefully constructed large-scale sculptural objects brought into sharp focus by the intense sunlight present at Denver's 5,200-foot elevation (Fig. 4.14). Wenk purposely removed any cultural artifacts that could have provided a sense of scale to these concrete structures such as fences, furniture, or lighting, thus provoking both the defamiliarization and subsequent critical thinking that are elements of critical regionalism. Notice in Fig. 4.15 that the scale of the sculptural forms is only revealed when a figure is seen directly adjacent to them. And, in Fig. 4.16, one sees how the edges of two new soccer fields on

Figs. 4.12 and 4.13. The landscape of a decommissioned sewage treatment plant in Denver, Colorado, before reinterpretation (1997, top) and soon after its opening in 1999 (bottom). Courtesy of Bill Wenk and Associates.

FIG. 4.14. An endless High Plains horizon at Northside Park with defamiliarized creative elements designed by subtracting material from the original industrial forms of the decommissioned plant (2006).

the site have been defined by making the rim of the old settling basins into curved bench seating. This entirely new use is not immediately apparent to park visitors and will be experienced as a deeper level of understanding over time when they sit on the benches and after they read the interpretive signs that explain the history of the park.

A more preservationist and less creative solution for the reuse of settling basins is shown in Fig. 4.17. This internationally famous and very compelling example of the industrial picturesque in Germany keeps the settling basins intact as preserved expressive picturesque landscape elements. The contrast between the uses of the settling tanks at Northside Park and Landscape Park Duisburg Nord clarifies the contrast between the ethos of looking backward and the ethos of looking forward with expressive echoes of the past.

Another important feature of the design of Northside Park is the adaptation of a regional drainage way to give form to the park and to address water quality and wildlife habitat considerations. The park is located at the out-fall of a regional urban drainage basin. The existing drainage infrastructure included a large concrete channel and a detention pond whose functions had to be maintained. The design reroutes the storm flows through a new large phytoremediation bioswale within the park. This increases the quantity of developable land adjacent to the park and supports wetlands on site, providing significant water-quality benefits to the regional water system and connecting the park to important habitat areas.

FIGS. 4.15 AND 4.16. Local teenage boys at Northside Park provide scale for the structures (top) and curved benches at the edge of new soccer fields at Northside Park were created from the edges of former settling basins (2006). Also, see Fig. 4.12.

FIG. 4.17. Preserved settling basins at Landscape Park Duisburg Nord in southwest Germany, created in response to a 1989 redevelopment plan for the heavily polluted Ruhr industrial district (2010). Designed by Peter Latz and Partners.

The final form of Northside Park is the result of a design process that focused on adding typical park program items, such as the soccer fields, to the treatment plant site while retaining a specific volume of structure. The layout of the soccer fields, site drainage, and internal circulation were designed to reinforce the axis and cross axis that organize the overall site form shown in Fig. 4.13. The design mediates between the demands and expectations that go with conventional park development, the design potential of adaptive reuse of structure, natural areas and wildlife habitat development, water quality, environmental reclamation, and storm-drainage design. The result is a unique park experience that builds on the cultural and picturesque precedents of Gas Works Park by creating a personal creative interpretation of the park's industrial past that is in concert with the ideology of critical regionalism.[26]

In the list below, I summarize elements of critical regionalism exhibited by the new landscape at Northside Park.

1. Elements of Four-Part Aesthetics
    a. Natural Laws
        i. The landscape is purposely defamiliarized (environmental psychology)

b. Cultural Rules
   i. The park preserves enough of the derelict industrial infrastructure to make it a meaningful part of the history of the area; interpretive signs reinforce the learning opportunities; the program is tailored to the regional population.
c. Personal Strategies
   i. The landscape is a rigorous, unique, and site specific creative expression.
d. Environmental Imperatives
   i. The large bioswale and new wetlands express the aesthetics of the local ecology for these conditions and are used as spatially defining elements.

2. Elements of Critical Regionalism;
   a. A critique of the perceived excesses of modernism, functionalism, and enlightenment rationality: Northside Park is designed to evoke an aesthetic experience much more powerful than the programmatic or functional elements, such as soccer fields, would otherwise evoke.
   b. A critique of the romantic, picturesque approach to regionalism: The Denver skyline and the Rocky Mountains are addressed as distant views, but no attempt is made to transfer experience by *reproducing* familiar icons of the region.
   c. An embrace of the postmodern emphasis on place, rather than space: Both place and space are addressed, but the experience of the place is actually enhanced by the open-ended and ambiguous control of space that reinforces the open planar landscape in this part of Denver.
   d. A desire to create landscapes that balance a celebration of regional diversity with the benefits of universality: The regional elements are enhanced with contemporary park development methods, safety issues (both ADA and CPTED), and the contemporary infrastructure that goes into a park design in the United States.[27]
   e. An embrace of regionally defining physical, environmental, social, and cultural elements: The expressive industrial forms are creatively reused, the flat topography of the site is celebrated, and the regional context of the Rocky Mountains, other industrial users in the area, and the city of Denver are a strong part of the experience of the place.
   f. A desire to make the landscape an object for intellectual contemplation as well as sensual pleasure: The sculptural forms are deliberately defamiliarized; the large scale and unique design of the forms strongly provoke contemplation.
   g. A distrust of grand design solutions and an embrace of incrementalism: The park is a unique project that stands on its own and is not a lesser part of a much larger development.
   h. A desire to create a bounded space where the excesses of endless megalopolitan development and a consumer driven culture are resisted: The unique creative expression of Northside Park makes it a highly imageable space with a strongly distinct presence.

3. Elements of problematic design aspects that critical regionalism is intended to address that were not found.
   a. Academicism
      i. The project is not a pure form-driven endeavor that would be just as, or even more effective, if it were placed in another context.
   b. Eclecticism
      i. It is a unique response to the site and program as well as the creativity of the designer and not a facile expression that "anything goes."
   c. Kitsch
      i. It is not a kitschy, overly derivative, or facile regional expression designed for purely commercial reasons.
   d. Historicism
      i. Northside Park is not a historical recreation without reference to modern technology and programming; the creative hand of the designer has the potential to move culture forward.

Conclusion

The industrial picturesque is an aesthetic that looks backward with expressions of nostalgia, history, memory, decay, melancholy, the passing of time, and the sublime. Bill Wenk addresses industrial infrastructure more as an echo and less as the literal preservation, recreation, or interpretation of history, in harmony with the ideology of critical regionalism. The landscape architect, author, and educator James Corner has described an approach to landscape design that is a dialogue between a designer, the landscape, and those encountering it, with the explicit notion that all three are undergoing continuous change.[28] This idea is in accord with the reconceptualization that is a hallmark of critical regionalism, combined here with the industrial picturesque.

In the upcoming chapters, I cover in more detail some of the many issues that need to be addressed in order to move the design process in a creative direction that can produce landscapes with the regional aesthetic power of Northside Park. These issues will be clarified with a focused and rigorous evaluation of selected evolving designed regional precedents.

Chapter 5:
Critical Regionalism and Place

Regional Boundaries

An understanding and appreciation of regionalism is a resistant force that works in the background of all design activity as a responsibility toward the greater good. The region becomes a de facto client that is modified and will suffer or benefit from design decisions. The benefits of a design approach that addresses the imperatives of regionalism will accrue to the local population in such areas as cultural integration, ecological and environmental performance, psychological attachment to a place, and many others. A regionalist approach will help a design firm's commercial development by showing clients that not only are their region and district (by "district" I mean a smaller, imageable enclave around the project that offers site specific inspiration for creative regional design) taken seriously and celebrated in the design process, but also that a keen understanding of the quirks of a region's development and infrastructure are a part of the firm's design thinking. Finally, regionalism will help the individual designer by keeping the design process fresh with continually renewing regional design influences to play off and to combine with contemporary and historic world culture. This will encourage the creation of imageable enclaves with an expressive and compelling enough character to become attractants within the fabric of a region and thereby contribute to the development of an overall regional character.[1]

Patrick Geddes is considered a seminal figure in the evolution of the *idea* of a region. For him, the region was the most logical repository for connecting all human activities that unite the opposite poles of rural and city life. His interest in typologies led him in 1909 to develop the idea of the "valley section" that follows a river course from its inception in the mountains to the sea. The section connected the various topographic regions and demonstrated the interconnected occupations that benefit from regional relationships, such as miners and woodsmen in the mountains, hunters and shepherds in the grassy lower hillsides, and farmers and fishermen in the valleys closer to the sea. The occupations join together to form a cooperative society of people in the same way that communities of plants form mutually beneficial relationships. Geddes's regional ideas were originally inspired by regional plant associations, which he studied during his academic tenure as a biologist.[2] He developed his philosophy shortly after Charles Darwin's theory of evolution was published. A period when the study and classification of both natural and cultural typologies was a strong component of the ethos of the era. This conceptual connection of biological and cultural organization has found continuing resonance with regionalist thinking. It has elevated the influence of Geddes in contemporary discourse beyond his peers, and his influence historically with such regionalist luminaries as Lewis Mumford and Ian McHarg.

The first step in the understanding of local character is to define the boundaries of the region or district that are most appropriate for an understanding of the influences for a particular design. The idea of boundaries is very problematic as the multivalent and overlapping criteria described below will show. Nevertheless, practitioners do not have the luxury of endless analysis and must make concrete decisions about regional boundaries and how to address them in each of their designs. Therefore, all of the regional criteria below should be seen as points of departure that may or may not come into focus as the most relevant parameters when a designer becomes increasingly familiar with, as Forster Ndubisi writes, the "interacting physical, biological, and cultural phenomena that establish [a region's] natural and cultural character over time."[3]

Sometimes a regional context will be obvious, particularly in well-established urban enclaves. Many landscape architects began thinking about regions and districts after reading Kevin Lynch's terrific book, *The Image of the City.* First published in 1960, this book is still indispensable for landscape architects as a starting point for an understanding of the district character of highly evolved cities and the metaphysical or psychological community that is formed with a personal mental map of a district. Lynch's breakdown of cities into districts with paths, nodes, edges, and landmarks, however, may not be as useful for many of the rapidly developing areas that have been a principal focus of the evolving theories of critical regionalism, since the areas have had insufficient time to coalesce into these mature city typologies. The definition of a regional context in these types of areas is another opportunity for personal creativity and careful interpretation. There is a lot of confusion and disagreement in the literature as to the definitions of regionally defining parameters for these evolving areas. The focus of my research is on elements that contribute to experiential landscape aesthetics and to critical regionalism as outlined in the previous chapters.

The boundary of the region is not where something stops but rather where an enclave begins—what the German philosopher Martin Heidegger (1889–1976) calls its "presencing." This more indefinite boundary encourages designers to consider not only the enclave that is the object of a design, but also its relationship to other areas within a reasonable sphere of influence by car or mass transit. The boundary is where the collision of styles and forms is most likely to create innovative ideas that can be developed later in the centers of the established enclaves.

Regional influences can be visualized as a series of nested circles or a more typical bubble diagram. These circles will change depending on the place and the type of design undertaken. A theoretical example for an urban enclave would place the immediate context at the level of direct experience in the center. The next circle is the "imageable enclave" or mental map of the district as outlined by Kevin Lynch and others. The larger circles of influence could be the city, the metropolitan area, the native biome, and, finally, the region of local materials. The material region has been defined recently by the LEED and SITES certification programs as a 500-mile radius from the site, but the circle could be much smaller if cultural factors are prioritized over the energy savings that determined the 500-mile radius. A still larger circle can be a large culturally derived regional construct such as New England or even an entire country. The final circle that surrounds all the nested circles is universal civilization that continually aids in the creative evolution of a place.

Doug Kelbaugh advocates a view of critical regionalism for which the agenda of the program is secondary to the agenda of the overall site or district. The visual environmental context and the historic context then become the prime influence on the outer appearance of form "at the expense of structure, technics, materials, and function."[4] This is another example of a tenet of critical regionalism that needs to be translated to apply to a landscape design. In landscape design, there is no "inner" and "outer" form; there are only "inner" and "outer" areas of the landscape. In this view, the part of the landscape that is visible to users would be more influenced by both visual and non-visual neighborhood and district design elements, discussed in detail in Chapters 6 and 7, than the portion hidden from view by plants or structures such as an interior courtyard or a residential back yard. The integrity of the district is reinforced by the outer form while allowing ample room for personal expression in more private areas.

In Figs. 5.1 and 5.2, one sees the Shops at Legacy in Plano, Texas, considered by many designers to be the most successful example of an early "New Urbanist" town center in the Dallas/Fort Worth area of North Texas. The landscape design for the project was led by Paul Shaw (1959–2015), first at Huitt-Zollars, Inc. and then with RTKL, Inc. Phase One of the project was completed in 2001, and the mixed-use project was still under construction and growing as of 2025. This terrific example of a live/shop/work/play district was created in an area that featured huge office parks with large tracks of vacant former farm and ranch lands between them. The expression of the surrounding area was quintessentially suburban. The Legacy design team purposely made the perimeter of the development that faces the main arterial street (Legacy Drive) look like a more typical suburban automobile-oriented shopping district with low-rise retail and plenty of parking (Fig. 5.1). As one ventures into the district, block by block, the expression becomes progressively more urban with increasing density and a more pedestrian-oriented scale (Fig. 5.2). The suburban periphery helped the project fit into the character of Plano and encouraged suburbanites to filter in and explore the district without the psychological impediments that can be engendered by the sudden appearance in a suburban district of a truly urban expression.

FIGS. 5.1 AND 5.2. The Shops at Legacy in Plano, Texas, showing suburban expression (TOP) at the northern perimeter and urban expression (BOTTOM) several blocks inside the project (2019).

Place

Critical regionalism's most prominent cultural precept is the creative creation of "place" that acknowledges local culture, social institutions, political issues, ecology, construction techniques, climate, topography, and many other elements of the regional context.[5] Albert Mayer defines the "place" or enclave as a "tapestry of many figures, each distinct with its own color and character but [interpenetrated] into a total interrelated excellence."[6] And as Jeffrey Cook writes:

> Architecture becomes regional when designed to respond to local, natural, and man-made place . . . place is an expression of integrated ecologies of climate, resources, and culture . . . local materials have color, texture, and fiber. All have particulars of quality . . . the various zones of a region overlap each other in patterns that require the articulation of human judgment . . . neither culture nor nature are hardlined provinces.[7]

Cultural geographer Edward Relph wrote at length about the sensitivity necessary for an authentic understanding of "place." He refers to his model of the philosophy of *being* as *environmental humility*, derived from Martin Heidegger's writings.[8] Environmental humility is defined by Relph as both a deep respect for and a continual striving towards a profound understanding of both the built and natural or un-designed landscape. Relph advocates the appropriation of places in order to add meaning to our lives through our care and concern. He defines appropriation as the moment of insight when we see [landscapes] for what they are through the concealment caused by "familiarity, forgetfulness, the narrowness of science, and the comforts and seductions of materialistic life."[9] Appropriation does not mean an uncritical reverence for either natural systems or celebrated built works. Instead, as Relph continues, "It simply means caring for, protecting and appropriating places."[10]

The designer should, therefore, never threaten local values with a detached expertise which can lead to "'self estrangement' as landscapes are increasingly designed by invisible, abstract, social forces unrelated (or alien) to . . . inward impulses."[11] Alienation is essentially experiencing the world and oneself passively, receptively, as the subject separated from the object.[12] By contrast, appropriated spaces add meaning to our lives and become a type of anchor for our self-identity. The regional context then facilitates the transformation of the sensual pleasure derived from a successful landscape design into a deeper level of interaction and communication, what George Santayana calls the "hushed reverberations" of region that lead to a richness of living experiences.[13] As Aldo Leopold has commented:

> The shallow minded modern who has lost his rootage in the land assumes that he has already discovered what is important . . . History consists of successive excursions from a single starting point, to which man returns again and again to organize yet another search for a durable scale of values.[14]

Landscape architects have many opportunities to experience the rich interactions tied to their identity because of landscapes that are their creation. When they enter into a constructed landscape they have designed, it can appear to them as one of the most beautiful landscapes they can imagine. The landscape is beautiful precisely because every design element refers to some part of the designer's personal design aesthetic. Although the forms and textures may have an inherently pleasing quality to many people, it is the personal associations that create the most powerful connections to the experience of the place. By using design elements that are referent to a local population, designers are trying to recreate a small portion of that feeling for the people that use a space, a portion that goes far beyond what would be experienced by a general population not emotionally tied to the regional elements. The "transferred value" of the emotional triggers that the designer extracts from the regional context are consciously or subconsciously conveyed to the user.[15] The user perceives and experiences a creative transformation of a common regional past and participates in a shared regional memory. The following passage, written in 1863 by the poet Charles Pierre Baudelaire (1821–1867), demonstrates the long history of this important concept and reinforces its value as a timeless verity of creative regional design:

> Beauty is made up of an eternal, invariable element, whose quantity it is excessively difficult to determine, and of a relative circumstantial element . . . Without the second element, which might be described as the amusing, enticing, appetizing icing on the divine cake, the first element would be beyond our powers of digestion or appreciation, neither adapted nor suitable to human nature.[16]

Referential creativity has also been compared to the evolution of language where the meaning *embodied* in words, related here to the intrinsic meaning of regional elements, is inextricable from the new creative meaning of a written work.[17] Both words and regional design elements will have personal associations that people will experience in a work in complex, sometimes surprising, and divergent ways.

In order to elevate the priority of regionalism in the very complex development process in the United States, it is imperative to develop and articulate a focused ideology of regionalism. The subject-object relation is dynamic and subject to who has the advantage in power relations.[18] This reality is readily exemplified by the development process in the United States in which the various stakeholders, such as developers, banks, design consultants, regulators, public constituency groups, and marketing consultants, are in a continual competition for influence. Each of these constituencies must be convinced that a regionalist approach will, ultimately, be beneficial to their particular concerns as landscape architects and architects use a region to enhance the experience of place.

Regional Parameters

Regionally defining parameters will vary according to the qualities of the region itself and the scale of the region that is the focus of study. For some large regions, a natural systems approach is the most appropriate organizing principle, for which watersheds are often the prime regional determinant. River watershed entities such as the Tennessee Valley Authority (TVA) tie whole clusters of cities and rural communities together with a common set of goals and priorities. Regionalism differs here from traditional city planning in that it accounts for both groups of cities and the increasingly important open spaces between them. The cities are seen as contributors to regional issues that are not thought of as isolated problems to be solved by individual cities, counties, or even states. Another example of large-scale regional planning that transcends individual cities is the landscape architect Phil H. Lewis (1925–2017) who showed, as early as the 1960s, how water corridors and drainage basins in Wisconsin are closely correlated with regional settlement patterns. The two examples of the TVA and Wisconsin reflect a historical regional logic that developed over time from conditions on the ground. These types of regional organizations should never be utilized as typologies that can be imposed on an area without a thorough analysis of the development and natural conditions of a region.

While some regional development patterns are organized around water, others are tied together regionally by an effort to resolve negative influences such as air pollution and traffic congestion. Cities can join together to solve regional problems and to respond to shared opportunities. The North Central Texas Council of Governments (NCTCOG) is such an entity that helps define the region of north-central Texas. The mission of NCTCOG is to "assist local governments in planning for common needs, cooperating for mutual benefit, and coordinating for sound regional development."[19] NCTCOG serves a 16-county region of north-central Texas anchored by the two largest urban centers of Dallas and Fort Worth. NCTCOG has more than 230 member governments, including all 16 counties served, numerous cities, school districts, and special districts that have banded together to create a type of political regionalism.

Still other regions are more influenced by cultural ties to history, migration patterns, and stylistic traits. For example, regional cultural rules derived from European immigrants can unite the disparate geographic features and political entities of New England. Additionally, the diverse cities in the American Southwest have a common tie to immigrant groups from Hispanic cultures. While regional influences spread much more slowly in the past with slower migration patterns, in recent years there have been more examples of the rapid spread of regional cultures in the United States as communities of recent immigrants have coalesced far from the historical entry ports of cities such as New York and San Francisco.

Regional patterns, aspirations, and histories are important factors in understanding regional contexts. Just as a person must develop their own personality in order to have healthy relationships with other individuals, so a regional personality is required to have successful relations between regions in the design process of critical regionalism.[20] The widely influential architect and design theorist Christopher Alexander (1936–2022) describes this regional personality as "the natural receptacles for language, culture, customs, and laws." He believes that if the power of nation-states is not ameliorated by being decentralized into regions, the states can be culturally destructive influences that impede both the quality of life and the environmental and ecological health of the planet.[21]

Bioregionalism

Bioregionalism is a large-scale cultural and social construct that draws from both the natural sciences and the humanities. A bioregion is defined by the unique patterns of natural characteristics that are found in a specific area. People are also counted as key components of a place's identity, as exemplified both by the adaptive cultures of early inhabitants and by the activities of present-day "reinhabitants" who strive to harmonize in viable ways with the place where they live. Anthropological studies, historical accounts, social developments, customs, traditions, and the arts can all play a part.

Bioregionalism, at its core, according to bioregional activist Peter Berg, has three main goals:

1. Restore and maintain local natural systems;
2. Practice sustainable ways to satisfy basic human needs such as food, water, energy, housing, and materials; and,
3. Support the work of reinhabitation.[22]

Bioregionalism in the United States is partially a reaction to the political boundaries drawn up as the nation expanded westward, "partly by sheer haste, partly by ignorance of actual resources, and partly by political theories which sought to override the facts" on the ground, as Lewis Mumford proclaimed.[23] Bioregionalism advocates recognize that there are strong cultural determinants to perceptions of region but feel (*very* strongly) that the bioregion is a less subjective and more productive way to categorize regions.

Elevation can serve as a bioregional determinant whereby areas of similar elevation, even if separated by great distances, have similar bioregional issues.[24] A corollary is a similarity of ecosystems where mountain areas in southern climates have a close ecological relationship to areas of lower elevation further north. For example, this phenomenon has led plant hunters to find and introduce species from the mountains of northern Mexico into similar climates at lower elevations in north-central Texas. Bioregionalism is distinguished from other types of regionalism by an emphasis on natural systems, both for the ecological health of a region and for their use as metaphors for design inspiration. In bioregionalism, natural systems are one of the keys to our psychological and our physical health as well. Jim Dodge, an early writer who helped catalyze the definitions of bioregionalism, described the understanding, design, and implementation of bioregional landscapes as "our first environmental art."[25]

Bioregions can be defined by biological criteria; for example, there is a regional biotic shift when 15 to 25 percent of the plant species are different from one region to another. This shift can be caused by either climate or soils. Bioregions frequently overlap and commingle, making their use in informing design a cultural and personal activity—a reflection of human "perceptions, goals, and purposes," as Gary Coates writes.[26] The denser the cultural environment, as Coates continues, the more complex the interactions are between the bioregion and constructed landscapes that appropriately address the "psychological, aesthetic, emotional, social, and economic needs of the human inhabitants of the area."[27] By mediating between the purely exploitative and the desire for pure ecologically driven preservation or restoration without regard for cultural determinants, new options for creative and ecologically performative landscape designs continually emerge. These creative solutions can be used both to develop new areas and to enhance existing cultural landscapes with the ecological and aesthetic opportunities presented by the bioregion. The Roxhill Bog in Seattle described in Chapter 8 is an example of a project that has carefully integrated both human and biological determinants.

Peter Berg describes two important concepts of bioregionalism as "living in place" and "reinhabitation." Living in place means keeping a balance among "human lives, other living things, and the processes of the planet."[28] Reinhabitation means combining the working with and restoration of the ecological relationships of a place with both social and environmental priorities. This Berg excerpt on reinhabitation amplifies the discussion above of Relph and his ideas on environmental humility:

> Reinhabitation means learning to live in place in an area that has been disrupted and injured through past exploitation. It involves becoming native to a place by becoming aware of the particular ecological relationships that operate within and around it . . . It involves applying for membership in a biotic community and ceasing to be its exploiter.[29]

Bioregionalists consider this biological appropriation to be a minimum requirement for a long-term strategy of human survival. As Aldo Leopold so powerfully and famously warned in his famous 1949 essay "The Land Ethic," "We are remodeling the Alhambra with a steam shovel, and we are proud of our yardage."[30]

Exposure by the public to representative samples of regional natural character can lead to a much greater understanding of and a sense of belonging to a region, and to the issues involved in ecological management and restoration.[31] Bioregionalists lament that people in the United States know much more about property and political boundaries than the life forms and ecological processes that pass around and through them. They ask questions such as:

1. What is the carrying capacity of a bioregion?
2. What kinds of activities are most beneficial and most detrimental to it?
3. What is the best way for people to become informed and to get involved in bioregional issues?
4. How can watershed restoration be used to restore bioregions and bioregional thinking among inhabitants?

A map of the bioregions of Texas (Fig. 5.3) and similar regional maps are reproduced in many books on plants and ecology. The map illustrates how the bioregions transcend city and county divisions and also demonstrates that such maps often do not cross state boundaries to show how bioregions connect to adjacent states. The maps produced by the United States Environmental Protection Agency show the overlap of 120 defined ecosystems across states, though not across countries.[32] Bioregional thinking across countries is more important than ever as the impact of fencing of all types, including on the U.S. border, becomes a feature that can impede the free movement of many species that is required for their survival.[33]

Robert Thayer, a landscape architect with the sensibilities of a planner, has written a very thorough treatment of the topic of bioregionalism in his book, *LifePlace: Bioregional Thought and Practice* (2003). He focuses on three essential questions that are useful for developing a regionalist design ideology: Who am I? Where am I? What am I supposed to do? His answers, which define his ideas of bioregionalism, are strongly influenced by rural California, where he works and lives.

This brings up one of the essential challenges with bioregionalist thought in landscape architecture theory. Many landscape architecture academic programs are located in small towns and cities, so it is natural for professors who study design theory to focus on the preservation of natural areas or the integration of farmland into developments that surround small cities and towns as Thayer does. Most landscape architecture practice, however, is in larger cities where the issues of highly complex interactions of nature and culture in human-made and ecologically performative environments are more immediately relevant. Additionally, in the current practice of landscape architecture, there is much more of a need for focused and flexible regional understanding as opposed to the breadth and depth engendered by studying a single region over many years, made possible by academic practice. Landscape architects create landscapes in diverse areas and professional practice demands do not generally allow the time required to analyze and reflect on the important ramifications of a specific place or even a specific theory. In Chapter 8, I present an example of the depth required to reconceptualize urban nature and how it may call into question the way that the profession of landscape architecture is presently constituted.

Thayer's approach is, however, invaluable both as a resource for landscape architects who are looking for practical methods of regional engagement and as a window into established thinking about regions. He lists a wide range of disciplines with a regional focus and interest groups that are useful to an understanding of a bioregional approach:

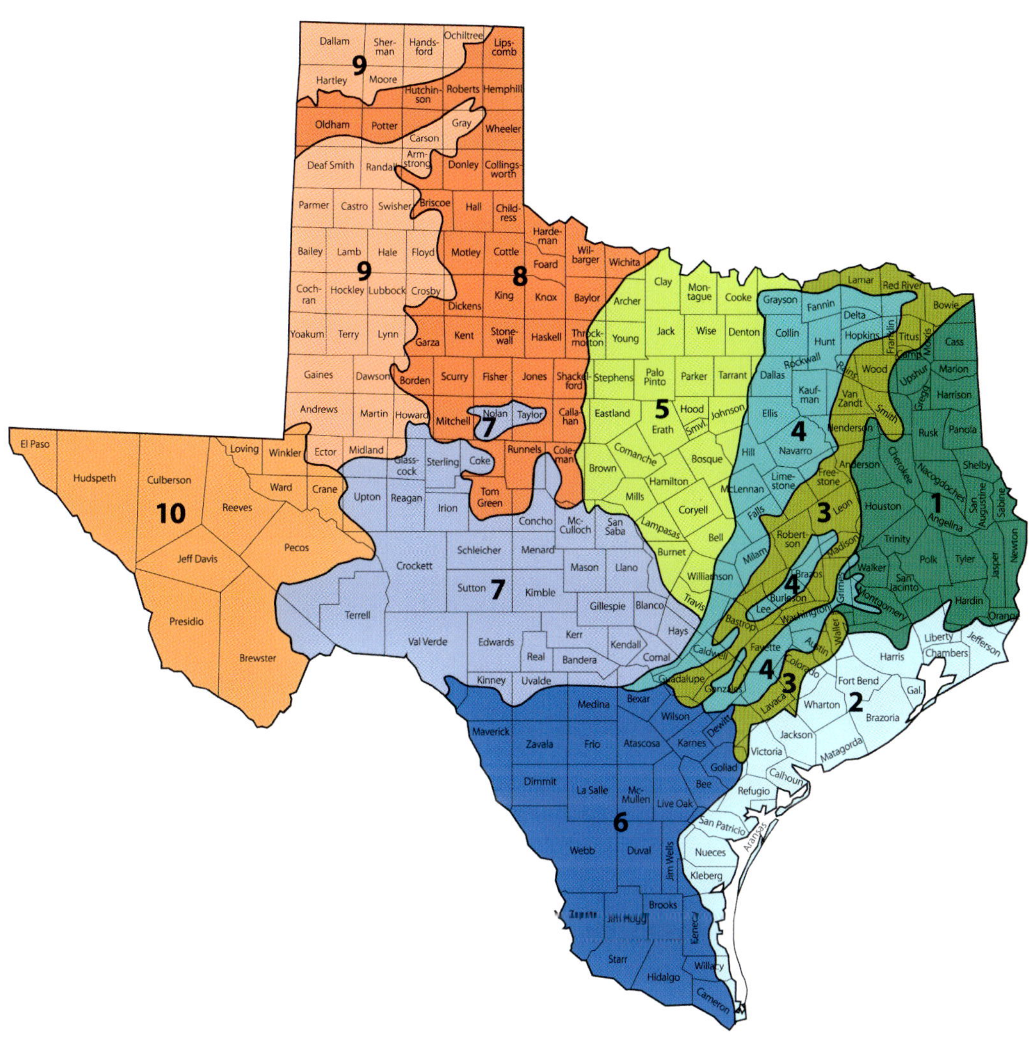

1. Pineywoods
2. Gulf Prairies and Marshes
3. Post Oak Savannah
4. Blackland Prairies
5. Cross Timbers and Prairies
6. South Texas Plains
7. Edwards Plateau
8. Rolling Plains
9. High Plains
10. Trans-Pecos Mountains and Basins

Fig. 5.3. Map of bioregions within Texas. Courtesy of the Botanical Research Institute of Texas, Fort Worth.

> From ecosystem geography comes a fuzzy natural way . . . to partition the earth . . . , from ecology comes an understanding of . . . natural assemblages or associations, . . . from ecosystem management comes a pressing need to holistically manage land . . . in scientifically defensible chunks, from regional theory, planning and landscape architecture comes a battery of methods and techniques for analyzing, planning, and managing land on the regional scale, from architecture . . . comes the ability of tuning the built environment to the conditions of the natural region, from alternative economics comes the means of strengthening . . . regional economies, from sustainable agriculture comes means to link food producers and consumers, from social and political theory comes participatory democracy . . . capable of solving regional problems, and from artists, poets, painters, and writers emerge a sense of the true nature of culture.[34]

Reading *LifePlace* reinforces the notion that regional issues are not limiting, secondary, or less significant than other design concerns. Thayer also shows that although regional issues are endlessly complex, individuals or small groups have the ability to make an impact at the regional level without becoming professional politicians.

Other Regional Theories

Timothy J. Cassidy, an architect, landscape architect, planner, and historic preservationist, offers a similar approach to Thayer's, although he identifies his theoretical approach as *reflexive regionalism.* Like Thayer, Cassidy has utopian aspirations and reflects the values of a career spent studying regional influences of a rural area in minute detail. His belief that a building with regional expressive qualities cannot be designed but rather must *become* regional over time through use and its associated meaning, is not very helpful to practicing professionals who must make design decisions every day. This is especially true in critically resistant areas such as north-central Texas where a rapidly shifting population and a dissipated natural and cultural context make this becoming much more difficult. The role of the designer is elevated in these types of areas to facilitator of a "virtuous cycle" where meaning is ascribed by landscape architects and architects and subsequently amplified and appropriated by users. Cassidy's embrace of farm and industrial vernacular is very important for a relatively undeveloped area such as southeastern Pennsylvania but not as directly resonant with landscape architects who practice in metropolitan areas with much more complex and evolved cultural modifiers that are often more difficult to interpret.[35]

Barbara L. Allen, then the director of the graduate program of Science and Technology Studies at Virginia Tech University, wrote about a similar sentiment with a description of *performative regionalism.* She also describes a reflexive process whereby "identity is a performative construct [which] . . .

could be understood as a 'film set' . . . that derives its meanings from the activities that have taken place there."[36] Her writing illustrates the difficulty of approaching architectural theory from outside the discipline. The results, though very carefully considered, can seem obvious, superficial, or not resonant to a practicing designer. For example, she asks, "Does regionalism have to apply to broad geographical parts of a nation or state, or can we have micro-regions within cities?"[37] The idea of the enclave (the micro-region) is one of the prime tenets of postmodernism, critical regionalism, and many of the examples of built works cited in this book. Additionally, her statement that regionalism is 10 percent built form and 90 percent "defined by what people do" is unreasonably simplistic, particularly when related to landscape architecture. It negates the strong regional modifiers of built works, ecology, topography, and climate in favor of the criteria of her primary area of concern: sociology. There is not sufficient agency given to the past and to the psychological value of regional influences as nostalgia triggers and anchors for identity. She also diminishes the resistant capacity of designers in favor of mitigating design issues with an overweighting of the important public involvement process. This reflects a fundamental distrust of the capacity of design professions to address regional issues in a comprehensive way. Allen's statement that, "once the spatial dimensions of human activities are satisfied, the visual appearance of the built environment is open" is a return to "form follows function," a regressive approach that can easily lead to either the populism of romantic regionalism or a pervasive eclecticism with all its attendant problems for cultural integration and regional identity.[38]

The study of bioregionalism, reflexive regionalism, performative regionalism, and many other regional typologies offer useful lessons for a designer considering a critical regionalism approach. The ideas they contain can become an important constituent of an educated sensibility that combines regional elements and universal expressions to elevate regionalist design thinking gained through education, professional experience and the evolution of their profession.

Vernacular Influences on Critical Regionalism

As Jeffrey Cook writes: "too often . . . [vernacular] . . . examples of uncanny brilliance are appreciated only as picturesque relics, as romantic projections, or as refined products of some limited technology rather than as pivotal human solutions that embody cultural persistence across time."[39] The term "vernacular architecture" applies to various practices and the flurry of writing on the theoretical stands on those practices. These encompass, as Gabriel Arboleda articulates, "primitive or aboriginal architecture; indigenous architecture; ancestral or traditional architecture; folk, popular, or rural architecture; ethnic or ethno-architecture; informal architecture; the so-called 'anonymous architecture' or 'architecture without architects,' and even 'non-pedigree' architecture."[40] Critical regionalists study examples of vernacular architecture for its place-centered or region-centered spatial arrangements and material details, in contrast to popular and academic architectures that are often more recognizable by time or style periods. They understand the vernacular is a result of cultural factors; physical forces are considered secondary and modifying conditions. As evidence for this position, they note that similar conditions of climate, materials, and site have produced a great, formal diversity of architectures throughout the world. Ian McHarg, in keeping with his focus on the planning level, expressed the opposite view during the 1960s by placing the physical forces of science at the forefront in creating a "workman's creed" for designers. Even McHarg, however, was a strong advocate for the instructive value of vernacular design at the level of human experience, especially as it relates to natural processes, materials, and forms.[41]

Professor of architecture Amos Rapaport promoted the study of cultural influences on vernacular built form over the then prevailing priority of functionalist explanations in his influential book *House, Form, and Culture* (1969).[42] He proposed that . . . "given a certain climate, the availability of certain materials, and the constraints and capabilities of a given level of technology, what finally decides the form of a dwelling, and molds the spaces and their relationships, is the vision that people have of the ideal life."[43] The prioritization of cultural determinants was later reinforced by William Bechhoefer in an essay about teaching regionalism by pointing to researchers, including the psychologist Edward T. Hall, who studied cultural differences in spatial perception and interpersonal behavior; J. B. Jackson, with his vivid descriptions of vernacular built works; and Christopher Alexander, whose pattern-language approach can be utilized to study the way people actually use both landscape and architecture.[44] This focus on understanding a population's vision for the ideal life is especially important in reemergent cities as they fill with new residents who are, as Kristina Hill declares, "increasingly more educated, younger, disproportionately single, and relatively wealthy."[45]

Labelle Prussin is another researcher who sought to understand the cultural factors that lead to vernacular design. In her book, *Architecture in Northern Ghana* (1969), she combined architectural and anthropological methodologies to arrive at an understanding of architectural forms and details as well as ethnographic information about the social context in which the architecture functions. She observed that "materials, technology, range of economic activity, social organization, religious and secular ideology, as well as historical factors, all had an influence on architectural form."[46] The understanding of "cultural rules" that inform design decisions for critical regionalism is amplified by addressing these kinds of issues in such a systematic way.

Critical regionalists try to understand the "richness of information" inherent in vernacular architecture by striving to understand the inhabitant's point of view, rather than taking a purely visual approach to place analysis. Professor Eleftherios Pavlides, like Prussin, believes that the form systems generated by folk or vernacular architecture are the most basic physical manifestations of cultural determinants, factors that influence growth and development factors, and the values that a given people impose on their architecture: "In its nature and value, folk architecture is viewed as timeless, uniform, severely utilitarian, and as representative of a people's 'soul . . . [It is] . . . architecture of necessity by contrast to architecture of pride.'"[47] The architect, planner, and educator Balkrishna Doshi amplifies these sentiments with a description of vernacular design as being most in concert with social conditions and with conservation of natural resources. He believes that ignoring these time-tested design solutions will lead to increasing misuse of resources and accelerating degradation of the environment.[48]

Well known vernacular architecture not historically designed by design professionals also includes, among its many styles, adobe structures found throughout the world, including the western and southwestern United States.[49] Mumford believed that, with reference to buildings designed without the benefit of architects in the colonial period of the U.S., the limitations of vernacular design are what provide early American buildings with their charm. Such limitations as "lack of labor, lack of materials, or [even] lack of taste" can become potentially positive and useful regional parameters.[50] Old frontier houses are seen as "functional [and] free from improper use of material, unnecessary ornament, imitated details, illogical imported ideas of plan or style, or inherited bad habit."[51] They have thus served successfully as a starting point for the development of regional styles of "modern" houses in the same regions.

Suburban residential homes in the United States can be considered a contemporary manifestation of the vernacular as described by Mumford. According to the architect and historian Anthony Alofsin, about 98 percent of these homes are designed without the benefit of an architect. Alofsin describes suburban homes in relation to the professional culture of architects and critics as a "another foreigner in our midst" that is "more responsive to public taste . . . than the architecture profession."[52] This thinking elevates these ubiquitous homes to at least a data point for designers, in the quest for a better understanding of regional popular taste.

A discussion of the vernacular in relation to landscape and garden design reveals the difference between highly evolved regional garden styles and critical regionalism. The evolution of vernacular landscape typologies can lead to tremendous expressive qualities such as those embodied in Japanese Zen gardens. These gardens could be understood as a type of critical regionalism in that their forms and materials abstract and defamiliarize the natural landscape of Japan. The form is so stylized and so often repeated, however, that the multiple iterations put the work firmly back into the vernacular vein, albeit a very carefully crafted and artistic vernacular. The original impetus that created the style has been developed by perfecting it and not by reconceptualization as it would be in a critical regionalism design process.

Each society and each mode of production can lead to its own particular types of places.[53] Moore expands on this idea by proposing that the differing qualities of designed spaces are more a matter of technology than the result of aesthetic choices. This might certainly be true in less prosperous and less developed regions. In technologically advanced and wealthy countries, however, we have seen a huge

FIGS. 5.4. AND 5.5. The Museum of Pop Culture in Seattle, Washington: (TOP) a building designed as an art object without vernacular or tectonic limitations (2006) and (OPPOSITE) looking up at the titanium "Purple Haze" wall at the EMP (now MoPop) in Seattle (2006).

variety of aesthetic choices available given enough resources. Recent development of computer-aided design, as seen in Figs. 5.4 and 5.5, have shown both the promise and the peril of highly idiosyncratic architectural statements made possible by new technology privately funded by massive concentrations of wealth. A return to the historic influences of a regional vernacular that can slow the pace of cultural transformation must, therefore, be a very conscious decision by a regionalist designer who has the full modern technological building technology arsenal at their disposal.

The building shown in Fig. 5.4 is influenced by a deconstructed electric guitar, used by the architect Frank Gehry as inspiration for the model of the building, and by rock music used as inspiration for the "Purple Haze" wall (Fig. 5.5), both influenced by the Seattle-born musician Jimmy Hendrix. Additional technological regional influences of the electronic Music Project (now Museum of Pop Culture—MoPop) come from the software and advanced manufacturing techniques used for construction of the MoPop that are similar to those used by the aircraft industry to build metal planes. The enormous Boeing Aircraft plant just south of Seattle is a big part of the regional industrial development of the city. In Fig. 5.6, one sees another example of a parametric building in Hong Kong that is tied to the waterfront landscape by more perceptible regional influences.

FIG. 5.6. The iconic Hong Kong Convention and Exhibition Centre was designed by a team led by Larry Oltmanns of Skidmore, Owings & Merrill LLP, in association with Wong & Ouyang (HK) Ltd. (2016). The parametric roof evokes the regional forms of gull wings, the ubiquitous watercraft in Hong Kong Harbor, and the many hills that surround the harbor.

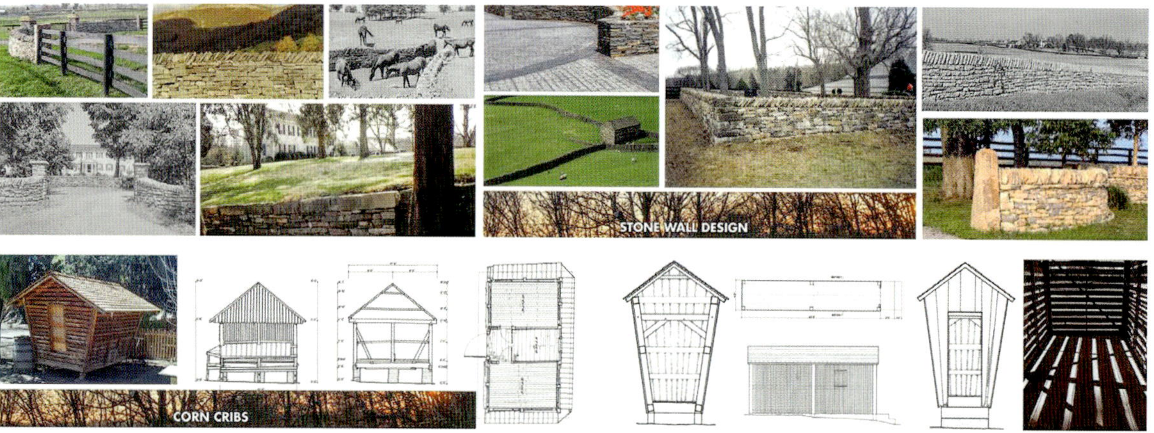

FIG. 5.7. Vernacular influences for landscape design in a new subdivision called "Light Farms" in Celina, Texas. The reference images above, assembled by Mesa Design Group, Inc., show natural wall materials and historic agriculture constructions, used as inspiration for the "Agrarian theme of the amenities and architecture, celebrating family life and the history of this site." Courtesy of Mesa Design Group. Quote from Light Farms: http://mesadesigngroup.com/portfolio_page/light-farms/; accessed in September 2021.

Fig. 5.8 (top). Arched loggias at Mission Francisco de la Espada, completed in 1731, in San Antonio, Texas (2007).

Vernacular designs, whether approached as artistic or as purely functional, are unlikely to be perceived as critical regionalism in the sense that they are not designed in a self-reflective way and usually do not provoke critical thinking. The influences of vernacular design can, however, inform and "refresh" the cultivated design aesthetics of landscape architects using a critical regionalism ideology. In Fig. 5.7, one sees vernacular design influences for the design of a new subdivision north of Dallas, Texas. The image board was for a new large subdivision North of Dallas called "Harvest."

In Chapter 6, I explain how the vernacular form of the *acequia* (irrigation ditch) has become part of the design vocabulary of San Antonio, Texas. San Antonio designers have embraced other elements of historical design that can better be described as traditional architecture into the San Antonio regional style. In Figs. 5.8 and 5.9, one sees the arched colonnades at Mission San Francisco de la Espada, established in 1731, and Mission San Jose, established in 1720. Arches have been a feature of many styles of Spanish architecture since Roman times. They would certainly be unremarkable in many contexts throughout the world. In Texas, however, they are an emblem of the regional Spanish heritage of the city that separates its historic regional influences from other large population centers such as Dallas/Fort Worth and Houston. This historical Spanish form appears

Fig. 5.9 (opposite). Arches at Mission San Jose (1720) in San Antonio, Texas (2007).

Fig. 5.10. (top) Arched aquifer at the Lady Bird Johnson Wildflower Center in Austin, Texas (2007).

in many guises throughout the city of San Antonio, Texas, both on buildings and as freestanding elements in the landscape.

The landscape architect James E. Keeter used the arched form in the regionalist Texas landscape at The Westin La Cantera resort and hotel in San Antonio. The form has also spread into other areas of Texas. In Fig. 5.10, one sees the colonnade adjacent to the entrance walk of the Lady Bird Johnson Wildflower Center in Austin, designed by J. Robert Anderson, FASLA (principal), Eleanor McKinney (now with EMLA), and Darrel Morrison, FASLA. In Chapter 6, I also discuss how displaced regional modifiers, such as transferring the Spanish arch motif from San Antonio to Austin, can sometimes work against an authentic approach to cultural integration and should sometimes be seen as universalizing influences rather than as local signifiers (Fig. 5.11).

The arched forms extracted from the Missions in San Antonio and used throughout the city are not critical regionalism. They are, however, a culturally integrative influence that inhabits the design space somewhere between historicism and creative romantic regionalism. They are now firmly entrenched in the public imagination of San Antonio and ripe for a reconceptualization as a critical regionalism statement that uses them in a new creative way.

FIG. 5.11. An arched colonnade at the River Walk in San Antonio, Texas. Designed by the Houston office of SWA (2007).

Contemporary vernacular influences can range from the mundane to the artistic. Lily Yeh in Philadelphia is an example of an artist and social activist who has tapped into the artistic sensibilities of one of the most socially and economically disadvantaged populations in the United States. Her Philadelphia-based Village of Arts and Humanities (1986–2004) stands out as a spectacular regional vernacular exemplar (Fig. 5.12) in the urban enclave of North Philadelphia.[54] The pristine condition of the various works in a very high crime and economically disadvantaged area testifies to the appropriation of the art by the local African-American population. Yeh wrote that she is sensitive to the needs of the community to be participants in her art rather than mere observers. "I've come to conceive of the Village as a living piece of sculpture . . . in which sculpture is a communal event. The walls are shaped and touched by people's hands, including as many people from the community as possible."[55] The work of Yeh, in cooperation with the local population, has created new contemporary vernacular influences that can become important positive elements of district character into the future.

A very small scale and simple example that illustrates both the promise and the peril of finding contemporary vernacular influences became evident to me a few years ago in a funky "SoHo" area of downtown Dallas called Deep Ellum (Ellum being African-American slang for Elm Street). This district was at that time full of clubs, restaurants, bars, original hand-painted murals on walls, art galleries, as well as offices and an increasingly upscale residential population. I was walking to a restaurant for lunch

Fig. 5.12. The Village of Arts and Humanities (1992–1994) mural at Guardian Angel Park in Philadelphia, Pennsylvania (2006).

when a landscape element stopped me in my tracks. It was a "garden" of 300-to-500 pound limestone boulders placed in a linear strip about three feet wide in a planting area next to an iron fence that enclosed a restaurant courtyard. I had never seen anything quite like it (Fig. 5.13). Was this a garden of rocks or a work-in-progress? It was definitely regional in that local limestone was used yet not designed in any way I had ever seen before in the area.

As I was taking pictures of the rocks, the owner of the restaurant came out looking very agitated and concerned. He was afraid I was someone who was going to complain about the landscape feature and, perhaps, report him to the city for a code violation.[56] He explained that the reason the rocks were selected and placed in front of his fence was because they were too big to pick up and discard but too small to sit or lie down on. The owner was actually using the rocks that I found so aesthetically compelling as a device to keep homeless people away from his fence! To me, however, the bed was a defamiliarized statement of "stone" that was very much in keeping with the arty nature of the district and a new, albeit very simple, vernacular regional expression that could be worth appropriating.

The rocks illustrate that, while there are elements that are clearly regional and elements that are clearly not regional, many elements will fall into the broad unclassified area between the two, as

FIG. 5.13. Limestone "Garden" in the Deep Ellum district of Dallas, Texas, removed in 2017 (2016). Courtesy of Google Maps.

elements that have not as *yet* become recognized as regional by either insiders, like the restaurant owner, or outsiders such as designers like myself. Being open minded to empirical observation and not constrained by pre-conceived notions can lead to design revelations that are meaningful and can enrich the region, despite the sometimes questionable intentions implicit in their inception. The examples of industrial forms featured in this research certainly reinforce the point.

Lessons from Solana, a Large Modern Office Park in North Texas

A discussion of the Solana Office Park development in North Texas is instructive for an understanding of regional boundaries and design issues. Solana is a good example of an attempt at large-scale regional integration imposed on an enclave by outside forces. In this case, the outside forces were IBM, the landscape architects Peter Walker and Martha Schwarz, the other design consultants, and the developer. The project opened in 1988 and remained true to the original design intent until a major renovation was begun in 2015.[57]

Fig. 5.14. Solana's town center in the Mexican modernist style by the architect Ricardo Legorreta and the landscape architects Peter Walker and Martha Schwartz (1997). Completed in 1988.

Background

The Solana (which means "place in the sun") Office Park lies approximately 15 miles northwest of the Dallas-Fort Worth International Airport and straddles the cities of Westlake and Southlake. The project, built as the IBM Southwest Regional Headquarters, consists of a village and recreation center, a marketing center, and an office complex that encompasses more than seven million square feet of office space for 10,000 to 20,000 employees (Fig. 5.14). The developers outlined two principal thematic elements of the project. The first was the desire by Maguire-Thomas (the original developer) to connect the project with Mexico and Latin America, as he stated, "The historical Mexican influence in the region was something that seemed to tie it together."[58] The second was, as Peter Walker writes:

> The desire to feature the landscape as a major influence on the overall design of the project. History, a sense of place, regionalism, landscape restoration and conservation; all of these concerns addressed at Solana can be associated with two movements of the last twenty years, environmentalism and postmodernism . . . The dominant concept, the traditional walled hacienda, with its compound of buildings, so familiar in Texas and the Southwest, reveals the

> design team's concern for history, regional character, and the native landscape. . . . The native landscape is dominant, when viewed from a distance. . . . . The buildings and roads were laid out so as to preserve the uplands and hills dotted with ancient post oaks, some three hundred acres of pasture, and the verdant flood plain.[59]

The statement that follows by Peter Walker, FASLA, and Murotani Bunji indicates some of the goals of the design of Solana:

> The buildings, gardens and parking plazas are laid out in tight compounds which are urban in density yet rural in expression, resembling haciendas of Texas and the Southwest. The parking plazas resemble orchards; canals recall irrigation ditches. As on a farm, these features respond to existing environmental conditions, and they are also composed so that the entire man-made environment can be experienced as a work of art.[60]

The regional features described and subsequently used as design inspiration, such as walled haciendas and irrigation ditches, are as foreign to the landscape that existed in North Texas at the time as the Gothic style of Europe was to Rice University in Houston and the University of Oklahoma in Norman, when they were built in the "Prairie Gothic" style. The Hispanic culture that produced both the walled hacienda and the drainage channels (see the discussion on acequias in Chapter 6 and Figure 6.4) never came much further north than San Antonio (more than 300 miles to the south) until well after World War II when these typologies were no longer being constructed. This is not a critique of the forms of the project; rather, it shows that the design team was neither aesthetically tuned in to the region nor to the district where they were *actually* producing the new landscape.

As Peter Walker observes: "It's interesting that our age, which is in a way so vast, with the airplane travel and so forth, is trying to achieve intimacy. I know that every time I try to achieve grandeur, clients instinctively tighten up. They don't want it. And I have had to fight to do things big."[61] This statement is a fair representation of a pictorial and formalistic approach, often a feature of landscapes designed by Peter Walker, as opposed to the experiential aesthetic approach advocated in the discussion of four-part aesthetics in Chapter 3. The combination of a developer based in Los Angeles and a design team from San Francisco, New York City, Los Angeles, and Mexico City led to a vision of a North Texas style that is foreign enough to the area to be considered a strong expression of their individual styles and not a reflection of the region's culture or environment. The design team utilized only the most immediately obvious components of the North Texas landscape, the relative horizontality of the region and the savanna ecosystem, which is preserved only in entirely undesigned areas. It should be noted that these preserved areas ultimately became placeholders and have since been developed into typical suburban typologies. The team stopped exploring the North Texas region (as opposed to a vague notion of Texas or the "The Southwest") at that very superficial level and reverted to the familiar and highly resolved

FIG. 5.15. Solana's evocation of an irrigation ditch (2005). Photograph courtesy of Wade Miller.

vocabulary of their individual design styles. While claiming to embrace the region, Walker has made the statement that there "is no tradition here [in North Texas]."[62]

The water feature immediately west of the IBM Westlake complex (Fig. 5.15) is an instructive example of intentionality versus perception. The linear water feature is designed to be evocative of Hispanic irrigation ditches (see Fig. 6.14). An informal survey of nine people sitting outside of a building next to the pond indicated that none of them had any idea what it was intended to represent, and all referred to it as "the canal." The huge scale of the feature has abstracted it to the point that it is very difficult for an observer to ascertain the conceptual meaning. Additionally, there is little likelihood that further reflection would reveal a regional connection, as there is no regional precedent for the scale or geometry of the feature. There are no historical irrigation canals in North Texas, and even the concept of an irrigation ditch or an agricultural drainage channel is very alien to an office worker in a metropolitan area that, as of this writing, has a population of more than eight million people.[63]

A jarring transposition of displaced styles is certainly not limited to architecture or landscape architecture. A parallel can be found in the art world. Many fine-art objects transported from their original context by the modern art markets have lost their original meaning within the context of the cultures that produced them. They then become pure specific art objects and lose a portion of their expressive value and potential to assist in the evolution and integration of local culture. Similarly, landscapes that are manifestations of the aesthetics of a designer and do not embrace regional influences may be successful aesthetic objects but lose one of the key elements that create a strong emotional connection to a user group. If the designer strays too far from regional normative practice or uses too many elements that are not referent to the region, the design may be experienced as another culturally disintegrative eclectic landscape.

Solana is an interesting and successful project in an abstract and conceptual sense, but it falls short in the criteria of cultural integration, experiential richness beyond the purely visual, and environmental and ecological responsiveness to the region in the developed areas. By embracing a more rigorous reading of the character of North Texas, the depth of the expressiveness of the project could have been increased. This includes experiential depth, historical depth, depth of stylistic variety, and a depth of learning opportunity that is difficult to accomplish with an all-encompassing design solution created by detached professional expertise.[64]

Just as the true test of regional adaptability of plant materials is the ability of the plants to reproduce and propagate successfully in a given environment, the true test of rightness of fit for a regional design is its adoption in some form by other designers in subsequent works. There have only been two other major public buildings in the Mexican modernist style built in the area as of 2023—more than 30 years since the construction of Solana. They are the Latino Cultural Center in Dallas and the Fort Worth Museum of Science and History, both designed by one of the architects of Solana, the Mexican architect Ricardo Legorreta. Solana shows that it is rarely possible to get too far out in front of clients with enough building to have an impact on the development of a regional style.[65] This certainly was the case with Solana. The unusual geometry, heroic scale, Mexican colors, and lack of regional modifiers also create a barrier to the "appropriation" of the project by the people who live and work in the area. By 2017, the project was stripped of much of the original Mexican character intended by the designers and was renovated back to a more typical expression for office parks in North Texas.

Conclusion

This chapter is a small window into the endlessly complex modifiers that create both the physical and mental manifestations of a region. Regionalism is most often approached in writing by referencing the history of an area or with references to literature, film, and other creative works not tied directly to the physical, cultural, and natural artifacts of region that apply to critical regionalism and four-part aesthetics.[66] Essays and books on regionalism, featured throughout this research, are very valuable as they help sensitize the designer to both the wide range of possible conceptions of a region and the societal implications of a regionalist approach. They are endlessly interesting and informative and help to develop a personal ideology that can lead to critical regionalism and a powerful connection to places. Jim Dodge expands on this idea with an emphasis on regionalist practice over formalist theory for the creation of a connection with the user: "Call it whatever seems appropriate—enlightenment, fulfillment, spiritual maturity, happiness, self-realization—it has to be earned, and to be earned it has to be lived, and that means bringing it into our daily lives, and working on it."[67]

After an appropriate region and district have been determined for a given project, the next step is to uncover the local physical, biological, and cultural determinants that are most useful for a new creative regionalist design. In the next two chapters, I begin a detailed discussion of some of these determinants.

Chapter 6:

CRITICAL REGIONALISM AND CREATIVE SEEING

Critical regionalism has been described as an ideology that sets the direction for a personal design aesthetic or design process. The tools of critical regionalism that help consummate the design process, such as defamiliarization, resistance, understanding of regions, and now undertaking a creative and flexible search for regional and district defining parameters, are personal formulations that require philosophical exploration and reflection. This chapter on creative seeing, therefore, begins with a more general discussion in order to facilitate a wide-ranging inquiry into the important and sometimes idiosyncratic arena of creative perception of a region. Examples then follow that are more concrete, that tie the theory to successful projects, and that clarify the concepts. A few of the many methods that can be used with regional elements in the design process are then discussed. These design practices are used to help illuminate various design approaches that inform an understanding of critical regionalism. As Juhani Pallasmaa writes:

> The human task of architecture is not to beautify or to humanize the world of everyday facts, but to open up the view into the second dimension of our consciousness, the reality of images, memories, and dreams.[1]

This quote echoes a much earlier philosophical thread that Patrick Geddes wrote about in his 1905 essay, "The World Without and the World Within: Sunday Talks with my Children," in which he divides the world into the "out-world" of an objective, fact-based reality and the "in-world" made of memories of that reality. He proposed an "Act-Deed" formula that resonates with the theories of critical regionalism. The formula outlines a deeper world of design that flows from facts to memories, to plans, and finally to acts or implementation.[2] Geddes later amended this to encompass the continual changes that cultural environments experience whereby acts lead to facts on the ground, are reinterpreted through memory as dreams, and then find expression in further actions he called "Deeds."

Designers draw on common environmental experiences created from an understanding of the deep well of interactions with shared surroundings. Without this understanding, the landscape is a mere aggregation of natural and cultural artifacts with no particular metaphysical meaning. Through the sensibilities of an individual, the landscape accrues both objective and subjective meanings that cannot be easily separated. Understanding the potentiality of these meanings through the ability to "read" an environmental context is important for both design professionals and for professionals in academic practice who are interested in training designers with an elevated regionalist sensitivity.[3] The continuing technical advances in the creation, manipulation, and dissemination of images for the study and communication of regional exemplars facilitates this process of discovery for both designers and clients. As William James proclaims:

> Now however fixed these elements of reality may be, we still have a certain freedom in our dealings with them. Take our sensations. *That* they are is undoubtedly beyond our control; but *which* we attend to, note, and make emphatic in our conclusions depends on our own interests; and, according as we lay the emphasis here or there, quite different formulations of truth result. We read the same facts differently. "Waterloo," with the same fixed details, spells a "victory" for an Englishman; for a Frenchman it spells a defeat.[4]

What defines a critical regionalism design may not be any specific, nor even recognizable, manipulation or embellishment of the forms uncovered; rather, it is the creative "seeing" of regional elements and their subsequent reinterpretation into new creative landscape designs, that moves a project towards critical regionalism. The psychological stage is set for the process by an excitement in observing the character and details of a site, a district, and a region. The excitement can be thought of as an intrinsic part of human nature—the natural laws discussed in Chapter 2. It taps into our embedded hunting instinct and the astonishing capacity of humans to observe and process the environment for that purpose. The more experienced the vision, the more design elements that provoke design responses will reveal themselves.

Revelations need not be, and indeed cannot be, entirely describable in words or even images. The intuitive grasp of a site is an emotional feeling that helps to guide the design process to a convincingly resolved conclusion. An emotional engagement with both the region and the response from our inner selves is crucial to consummate the most successful regionalist design of which the designer is capable. This emotional intelligence will guide subsequent study and reflection into the nature of the experience of the place. We may analyze the site in a cognitive way, but our affective sense of the place cannot be entirely explained in a rational way. We can be rationally systematic in making sure we direct our attention to as many relevant natural and cultural artifacts as possible, but it is our poetic imagination, triggered by an emotional connection, that will create new responses and forms.[5] Perhaps these emotional responses are one element that can create, or contribute to, what we call the "spirit of the place."

There is an ever-increasing temptation to understand a site by using analytical tools that are available on the computer due to their low cost and easy accessibility. Additionally, as was discussed in Chapter 4, a familiar, well-resolved design style is almost always the path of least resistance as professional opportunities far from familiar areas present themselves. Both issues raise the importance of taking the time to create an emotional connection with a new area, through *direct* experience, before attempting a critical regionalism design in that particular place.

Interest in regionalism is an interest in the physical environment that extends and informs the purely personal proclivities of a designer. This regional interest grounds the designs. It gives them an expressive background, a "back-story," without which proposed design solutions can be perceived as merely capricious, overly personal, and lacking in substance. It gives us a greater opportunity for intuitive insight without the arduous process that can arise from a lack of renewing material for a design's inspiration. The insight is then refined through analysis and critical thinking to give the design body, weight, and perspective.

The examples of regional elements presented in this chapter are not intended to suggest a comprehensive checklist of elements to look for when determining regional or local character. Every area will need to be viewed on its own terms, but my examples demonstrate a broad range of perceivable regional delineators. Regional elements used for creative design cannot be studied scientifically or as systematically as one can the local ecology or historic elements. The ability to see new regional parameters with the rigor to make them meaningful requires a process that starts with a sincere desire to find them based on an understanding of their importance to the design process. Perceptual sensitivity gained through effort and experience is then given validity through analysis and synthesis. This analysis is the opposite of traditional scientific inquiry (reductionism) in that it seeks to relate the observed details to the whole rather than breaking the whole down into its constituent minutiae.[6]

The artistic eye of the designer, developed through experience, will guide the many decisions that lead to a critical regionalism design and to what Dewey referred to as "aesthetically qualified material."[7] Just as art imposes a pattern on the void, so creative regionalists sift through the vast quantity of eclectic, and often confusing, regional irrelevancies and the superficialities of many cultural artifacts to make choices about which elements to amplify and celebrate. Historical precedents, manifested in the landscape and buildings, are also keys to understanding the intrinsic value of contemporary artifacts based on the evolutionary trajectory of a place. These elements can become a treasure trove of key drivers for design decisions that address the character of a contemporary regional aesthetic. The resulting regionalist design helps a population make more sense of the environment they dwell in.[8] Elizabeth Meyer describes this as finding " . . . the particular in the productive as well as the toxic, the transposed as well as the transgressive, the found and the made . . . [creating] site-specific design, emerging out of its context but differentiated from it."[9]

The designer slowly develops a regionalist sensibility to the point that there is confidence in a personal ability to assess the validity of the elements extracted and not a concern about always seeking confirmation or the successful precedents that will make the design into something "fail-safe." The fail-safe attitude can devolve a critical regionalist design back into a commercial or romantic regional design that places a lower priority on artistic perception, personal creativity and moving culture forward.

The essences of region, extracted and qualified for new landscapes by the designer, gradually disseminate into the popular perception of region. There is no limiting cultural or regional *a priori* except in the most academic or superficial reading of regional design influences.[10] Over time, the entire regional context (the cultural rules) can be transformed by a rigorous examination of successful regional elements and prototypes and their subsequent creative reuse in new landscape designs. Just as an enhanced understanding of adaptation of a biological species to a particular environment should inform ecological design decisions, the more knowledge a designer has about all aspects of a place, the more likely it is that the designer's ideas will be received positively and propagated into a region.

Developing Creative Regional Perception

One of the most exciting, challenging, and treasured sensibilities for the creative regionalist to develop is a personal regionalist aesthetic. Every perceptive regionalist designer will manifest a unique personal response to the cultural and natural conditions of regions. The designer is not just creatively transforming a given or even obvious set of regional elements; rather, one of the most imaginative areas of the entire design process happens when the designer perceives, experiences, and thinks about a region.

It is very important for this regional experience, and experience of a particular place, to be *in situ*, in person. A designer will gain more about the region through direct observation and experience than by simply relying on the words and illustrations of a previous observer. Some of the most powerful aesthetic experiences of landscape will be triggered by seeing projects in person that seemed only mildly interesting in photographs. Robert Thayer echoes this sentiment by stressing the importance of avoiding virtual reality experiences of place and getting out into the landscape to achieve a true sense of the region and place. This is especially important when visiting unfamiliar landscapes far from home that have the potential for use as design inspiration on the universal civilization side of the critical regionalism equation. John Dewey relates this to the art world:

> Escape from the familiar environment to a foreign one is often a means of enlarging subsequent experience, because the excursions of art create new sensitivities that in time absorb what was alien and naturalize it within direct experience.[11]

In Figs. 6.1 and 6.2, I show two very well-known projects that made a tremendous impact on me in person in a way that they never did when previously encountering them in the many photographs that accompanied articles written about them. The experience of the masterful manipulation of spaces as one moves through Seattle Freeway Park and the aesthetic power of the engineering of the bridge over Granville Island in Vancouver left impressions that have had a strong impact on my subsequent design thinking.[12]

The Granville Island Bridge is a particularly instructive example due to the integration of the bridge with the district's character and the careful control of the experience beneath the bridge by the designers. Spaces under bridges are often considered "lost space" in urban areas suitable only for

Fig. 6.1. The promenade at Seattle Freeway Park by the office of Lawrence Halprin with Angela Danadjieva (2006).

parking or, perhaps, for an artistic statement or as a transitional space to be traversed as quickly as possible. On Granville Island, the historic industrial character that is an integral part of the adaptive reuse of the island is reflected and reinforced by celebrating the forms of the complex bracing that connects the concrete bridge's supports to the elevated eight-lane road above. This connection can easily be seen and understood from photographs. What is harder to illustrate photographically is the way the bridge, built during the 1950s, reads on site: as a large-scale urban canopy or porch that is carefully integrated into the experience of the development as well as a welcome place to shelter from the frequent rain events on the island. The visitor center for the mixed-use development is placed squarely under the bridge, reinforcing the adoption of the area as an integral part of the landscape and as an important amenity. The vines on the concrete supports and ornamental plants around their bases provide texture and human scale. The overhead plane shrinks and defines the outdoor spaces.

A steel canopy of similar height, shown in Fig. 6.3, was created at great expense at the Phoenix Convention Center in Arizona. The Phoenix canopy acknowledges the perceived aesthetic viability of this type of structure for shelter, enclosure, and aesthetic power. A comparable effect was created at Granville Island by appropriating into the design process the commanding aesthetic potential of the existing engineering of the bridge and using it to create a new defamiliarized and very imageable

FIG. 6.2. Bridge over Granville Island in Vancouver, Canada. This third iteration of the bridge was designed by a team led by Vancouver city engineer John Oliver and completed in 1954 (2008). For an 18-minute 1954 movie showing the construction of the bridge, see https://viewpointvancouver.ca/2021/09/01/vancouver-1954-opening-of-the-granville-street-bridge/; accessed in Decemeber 2021.

FIG. 6.3. The Center Steel canopy of the Phoenix Convention Center, designed by the firm Populous and completed in 2009, with stone colors inspired by nearby desert canyons (2014).

landscape that is now an important component of the district character of Granville Island. The bridge is at a height high enough to keep traffic sounds and smells at bay but low enough to provide a sense of enclosure and awe at the sublime scale of the engineering. The soundscape is another element that does not translate from the site to the photo. Even as there are eight lanes of traffic traveling on the Granville Street Bridge, the traffic sounds are barely perceptible due to the thick asphalt paving that mutes the sounds of the tires. Bridges are frequently paved with concrete, and often with grooved concrete, for improved water runoff. This ruins any possibility of using the spaces below them due to the intolerable roar of traffic's intrusion into the landscape experience below.

By visiting Granville Island in person, landscape architects will experience the success of the design and gain renewed appreciation for the potentialities of urban infrastructure as an important element of regional character. By experiencing regional prototypes on site and combining them with personal design sensitivities, the designer can more easily move away from a rote copying of the elements without a personal, emotional connection to them. Learning to see the regional context with clear, knowledgeable, and creative vision creates a *passion* for a design, in that *particular* place, that facilitates the creative act needed to bring forth a superior design.

The contemporary difficulty is certainly not the *breadth* of information available to designers. With the Internet, printed literature, and videos available today on almost every conceivable region, as well as the ease of travel to project sites, designers have more than enough potential regional information. The problem is developing the ability to understand the information with much greater *depth* and rigor. Lawrence Speck describes a process to develop this ability whereby the designer "tinkers, crafts, accepts, rejects, adjusts, and reacts."[13] When applying this to landscape design, natural and cultural systems can be given more equal weight than with building architecture. As Aldo Leopold famously wrote about the effects on ecology by development, "To keep every cog and wheel is the first precaution of intelligent tinkering."[14] The greater the depth and breadth of regional understanding, the greater the potential for design creativity that has a lasting influence on the place and the region.

Critical regionalists not only want to understand and use the surface qualities of regional form systems, but also to question and reinterpret the thinking that led to those systems. An understanding of the underlying history, principles, and forms that make the local landscape aesthetics positive or negative for the end users, is thus used by the designer to qualify regional material for subsequent use as part of their personal design ideology and process. Lewis Mumford warned that "it is much easier to copy ornament than to find out all that needs to be found out about the geology, the soil, the climate, the working conditions, and the sacred customs of the neighborhood for which a building is designed."[15] His statement elevates the importance of adding a rigorous research component to on-site, primarily visual observations, which may be missing important design information due to the flawed perceptual filters of the observer. More and deeper ideas from both research and observation lead to expanded creative design opportunities in both the cultural and the ecological/environmental realms.

Studying the current conditions of a given area will also give the designer a better chance of choosing appropriate universal archetypes that are in concert with the project's goals and district's character. Designers who seek to understand any style or period of "universal" environmental design must understand, as Rexford Newcomb notes, not only "the history, the genius, and the social and religious customs of its builders, but also the geographic, geologic, and climatic conditions of the land of its inception."[16] This becomes increasingly important as the influences of universal civilization become more and more ubiquitous in a rapidly developing world.

For example, the heroic scale of a baroque French landscape may be more appropriate for a large institutional space where a projection of power and control is intended, as in the original instance, and not as appropriate where spaces scaled for comfortable human activities are desired. Therefore, even if a baroque-inspired and heroically scaled landscape such as Solana (discussed in Chapter 5) is part of the regional fabric, it may still be an inappropriate regional archetype for use in critical regionalism because the ideology of its baroque inception could be inappropriate in many district and project contexts.

A frequent problem faced by landscape architects is being overly influenced by the climate where the designer is actually working as opposed to the climate where a design project is located. For example, European parks often have large treeless and unprogrammed open spaces that are very popular with big-city populations in cooler climates with frequent cloud cover and few open space opportunities. When these types of spaces are created in the hot climate of North Texas by European designers or designers from the United States from cooler areas, the spaces tend to be neglected and unused. The need for almost complete shade cover, enclosure, and differentiation of "endless megalopolitan space" and for the imperative for heavy programming are two critical research or observational components that sometimes do not make their way into the design process of landscape designers from Europe. In Figs. 6.4 and 6.5, one can see the contrast in the heavily programmed and shaded Klyde Warren Park in Dallas, Texas, with the Tilla-Durieux-Park in Berlin with its large minimalist tilted plane of open lawn (both parks are about five acres).[17] Understanding how Germans and Americans use and appreciate outdoor spaces would be crucial to the success of emulating the visual qualities of either project as an example of universal civilization across continents.

The combining of the local and the universal makes the critical regionalism designer very aware that every local artifact and spatial arrangement is part of an infinite whole. Attention will bounce back and forth between the immediate experiential aspects of the site and design and the infinite boundaries of past experiences and imagination. In Fig. 6.6, one sees the paving pattern of the World Trade Center Plaza in Denver, Colorado, designed by the Denver office of Design Workshop. The careful detailing that is a hallmark of the firm was used to design a pattern that is both creative and unique enough to provide a strong identity for the project as a regional expression at the site level and also evocative of Colorado's High Plains as they are seen from the air. The Plaza patron's attention is directed both to the present and immediate experience of the place and to the experience of air travel and the connection of

FIG. 6.4 (TOP). The heavily programmed and shaded children's garden at Klyde Warren Park in Dallas, Texas, designed by the Office of James Burnett, soon after its opening (2012)

FIG. 6.5 (BOTTOM). Large treeless open space at Tilla-Durieux-Park in Berlin, Germany (2010). Designed by DS Landschapsarchitecten.

FIG. 6.6. The World Trade Center Plaza in Denver, Colorado, by Design Workshop, is evocative of a grid-like agricultural patterning as seen from the air (2006).

the site to the vast Colorado High Plains region. The regional connection is a secondary level of understanding that may take time to notice and comprehend. The multiple levels of meaning will help keep the project as a subject for regional reflection long after the more obvious and easily understood design elements have drifted back into the natural attitude, as described in Chapter 1.

Seeing and the Evolution of Regions

It is important to consider the level of sophistication and cultural development in an area or district when looking for regional modifiers. Just as "New Urbanism" can be considered early successional urbanism, or incipient urbanism, with resulting conventions of scale and form, so, too, can certain areas be considered "pioneer communities [that] have never been noteworthy for developed artistic expression."[18] This is not to denigrate the regional potential of these areas but rather to calibrate regional seeing to the ecological, folkloric/artistic, and functional regional design influences that are most likely to be useful as elements for appropriate design at a particular stage of their evolution. To always keep in mind that it is often very difficult to notice on first encounter the everyday elements that are most loved by the local population. It is important that these early influences, both natural and cultural, be preserved in some form for each region in order for designers and other people to understand the essential regional elements that coalesced into a later mature regional style. The creative regionalist designer will then search for the "catalysts" that will point the way towards an emerging regional vocabulary as the area develops. This process is akin to the development of ecological communities that must go through stages of succession in order to arrive at a more stable and unique climax condition. The pioneer species may decrease over time but are crucial to the success of later successional species. Similarly, the early influences of cultural landscape design will, in time, give way to regional influences that are more appropriate for a later stage of development.[19] The adaptive cycle and capacity of each region is different and contextual. How each cultural framework behaves from one phase of development to the next depends on the scale, context, internal connections, flexibility, and cultural carrying capacity (resilience) of the system.[20]

Pallasmaa has written that an authentic regional tradition cannot be invented; one must rather "rediscover and revitalize" both elements of style and hidden dimensions of culture.[21] The designer will need to determine, after a rigorous search for regional traditions, how implicit to be in the creation of new conventions. Every tradition evolved, at some point in time, from a personal creative act that was in concert with a receptive culture. The balancing of tradition with creativity is difficult, sometimes ambiguous, and a true test of the rigor required for a critical regionalism methodology. This is especially true in areas that are coalescing into more dense and mature cultural environments.

Some designers consider regionalism to be a less evolved and less sophisticated design determinant. Mumford warned that although the regional is often associated with "the rough, the primitive, the purely local," it is actually the culmination of a long, complicated process and emerges very late in cultural development.[22] It takes time to advance, as Kristine Woolsey writes, "a shared vision, recognizable by the inhabitants as representing the history and culture of a place. A vision . . . with overtones of nostalgia."[23] This emergent regionalism can then become an architectural "school" that is important as both a pedagogical and a cultural institution that forms and mirrors the emerging regional tradition.[24] Patrick Geddes described this as a *school of thought* that:

> . . . may express itself sooner or later in schools of education. The types of people, their kinds and styles of work, their whole environment . . . represented in the mind of the community, and these react upon the individuals, their activities, their place itself.[25]

Early cultural development, such as the Vietnamese brick ovens pictured in Fig. 6.7, will usually involve agriculture and industry which, when combined with the creative seeing of natural features, will begin the slow process of giving form to regional expressions. The United States has many fewer pre-industrial cultural development exemplars to draw from compared to other areas of the world such as Asia. Konjian Yu has written eloquently about the value of learning from what he calls the "deep form . . .

peasant's approach . . . , the structure underlined by processes and patterns" that evolved from pre-industrial cultural development as a response to survival.[26] His company, Turenscape, has used these principles to design award-winning parks in places as diverse as China, Chicago, and Austin (see Fig. 8.3). The *methods* used to extract "deep form" can be applied to each region where the concept is applied as a universalizing component of the design process. If, however, the Chinese forms are treated as a transferable typology, as a literal transference of lessons learned from the long history of China, much of their value will be minimized because each region always has a unique set of physical conditions and pattern of cultural evolution. Ethnobotany is another discipline where landscape architects can learn empirically derived best practices and their compelling forms from the long evolution of pre-industrial societies, especially as they apply to extreme climates such as dry areas.

A beautiful and simple example of critical regionalism that combines the influences of industry, nature, and creative expression is the Salmon Bone Bridge designed by Seattle artist Lorna Jordan and installed as part of the Longfellow Creek Legacy Trail in Seattle, Washington. The bridge (Fig. 6.8) offers an observation point for fall salmon runs, the restored creek channel, and native vegetation. The design of the bridge is both a powerful and evocative creative form that abstracts the shape of a salmon and an expression, using simple industrial pipe material, of the salmon industry, which was such an important part of the early development of the city of Seattle. The highly original form of the bridge is

Fig. 6.7. Ben Tre, Vietnam, near the Mekong River, where the compelling forms of ovens for traditional hand-made brick were still fired with agricultural byproducts such as rice hulls (2016).

Fig. 6.8 (top). The Salmon Bone Bridge in Seattle, Washington, designed by Seattle-based environmental artist Lorna Jordan, as seen in 2008.

Fig. 6.9 (bottom). The Canoe Bridge at False Creek in Vancouver, Canada, designed by PWL Partnership Landscape Architects (2011).

also a clear example of defamiliarization, especially when comparing the bridge to the vast majority of prosaic pedestrian bridges that are not objects worthy of notice or objects capable of provoking critical thinking. In Fig. 6.9, one sees a more recent bridge designed by PWL Partnership and built for the 2010 Winter Olympics Village on False Creek in Vancouver, Canada. The "Canoe Bridge" is also a creative regional expression and is defamiliarized by its computer-generated parametric form. It is designed to evoke the ribs of the canoes and kayaks that are frequently seen in the boating area to its north. The steel grating on the walkway allows views of the water below and creates fewer shadows on the water to maximize habitat value.[27] Even as the sleek, high-tech form of the canoe bridge is in concert with the overall character of the new district, it is not as culturally integrative as is the Salmon Bone Bridge, for it largely leaves out the historical natural and cultural forms of Vancouver. The Canoe Bridge and the entire new development on False Creek in Vancouver offer very faint echoes of the long history of the area before the Olympic Village was built. The development is, however, a reflection of the Asian-influenced modernism and contemporary high technology building systems that are becoming a signature of the "Vancouver style" (Figs. 6.8 and 6.9).[28]

The two bridges illustrate the complexity involved in the decisions made by designers about their role in the extraction, creation, and evolution of culturally integrative stylistic elements. A number of years ago, a major national landscape architecture firm based in Colorado held a retreat to determine if there is such a thing as a discernible "Colorado Style" of landscape architecture. Through a telephone interview with a landscape architect who was a participant, I learned that the conclusion was that there is not a "Colorado Style." If a regional style for a rapidly developing areas such as Colorado or Texas is not discernible to a design team, then landscape designers who wish to embrace a critical regionalism methodology must focus on the process of *developing* a regional style based on a heightened sensitivity to the regionally defining elements that are most appropriate to a place at its current stage of cultural evolution—the intellectual succession (cultural evolution) that shapes and is formed by design decisions.

Seeing Topography and Natural Features

In landscape architecture, a fundamental feature of design methodology for a regionalist designer is the degree to which historic and cultural precedents are balanced with an understanding of and appreciation for local natural features and topography. For example, when designers talk about the inherent horizontality of Midwest design, they refer to both the views surrounding us and to the movements of the eye. In "Big Sky" grasslands of the Great Plains, the eye also tends to sweep horizontally as one scans the vast horizon. Strong vertical elements are few and far between except in city centers. This creates a certain rightness of fit for horizontal elements, which tend to feel more like a part of the linear fabric

FIG. 6.10. Texas State Cemetery in Austin, Texas, by Lake/Flato, Architects, showing the main entrance building filling the valley between two small hills (2009). Courtesy of Hester and Hardaway.

of the landscape. Photographer David Robertson describes these regions as containing "a flat horizon that just 'won't go away,'" as shown in Fig. 4.13.[29] A horizon, writes Rob Thayer, that is defined by "the immensity of the sky, with its cloudless summer blue blaze . . . and the lack of a feature foreground."[30]

The San Antonio architecture firm Lake/Flato has taken advantage of both the horizontality of the general landscape and the rolling hills of the Texas Hill Country in its design of the Texas State Cemetery in Austin (Fig. 6.10). The valley between two low-lying hills is spanned with a building that starts and ends as a wall and "reads" as part of the wall. The spectacular limestone construction of the building, evocative of both traditional/historic limestone construction and abstracted natural limestone rock formations, is a ceremonial entrance and a visitor center.

Another example that takes advantage of subtle site topography is in North Texas and was designed by Stan Cowen, the managing director of Mesa Design Group, Inc. in Dallas. Landscape elements are used to reveal the gradual rise and fall of the relatively flat landscape. At the Valley View Municipal Complex in Irving, Mesa designed a series of concrete and metal pedestals that represent the railroad track along which the city of Irving was founded (Fig. 6.11). The pedestals run from the

Fig. 6.11. The Valley View Municipal Complex in Irving, Texas (2008). The pedestals accentuate the site's subtle topography and express the path of a historic railroad line.

entry sign at the front of the property, through the building, and out to the back of the property. The terminus of the pedestals is a huge model of a railroad spike that is part of a large sundial. The tops of the pedestals are perfectly level, thus accentuating the slowly changing topography and making noticeable (defamiliarizing) the otherwise almost imperceptible changes in grade. The strong axis created by the pedestals is also a formal organizing device for the circular geometry of the campus. The design response to the site topography and the abstraction of the history of the site moves the project towards the realm of critical regionalism.

Other landscapes evoke a wide variety of topographic shapes. In the Blackland prairie area of North Texas, for example, there are subtle natural features called gilgai. Gilgai are two- to four-foot-tall mounds caused by highly expansive clay soils that appear throughout undeveloped virgin prairies (Fig. 6.12). I was part of a design team that used this idea as a point of departure for a small park in the city of The Colony, Texas, when I was working at Huitt-Zollars, Inc. The mounds at Scholars Park, in the Austin Ranch development, are expressive of the local topography and can also be used as a type of furniture for lounging at gatherings (Fig. 6.13).

FIG. 6.12 (TOP). Natural gilgai at the 1,443-acre Clymer Meadow Preserve in North Texas a few weeks after a prescribed burn in spring (2013). The burn was managed by The Nature Conservancy, which owns the land for the preserve in conjunction with other landowners.

FIG. 6.13 (BOTTOM). Abstracted "gilgai" landforms at Scholars Park in The Colony, Texas, designed by Huitt-Zollars, Inc. (2008). Courtesy of Chia Yin Wu.

Fig. 6.14 (top). Gas Works Park in Seattle, Washington, by Richard Haag, showing a constructed landform evocative of the surrounding Seattle landscape (2019).

Fig. 6.15 (bottom). Seattle Harbor Steps leading down to the waterfront designed by Arthur Erickson and Hewitt, Architects (2008). Courtesy of Heath House.

At Gas Works Park in Seattle, Washington (Figs. 6.14 and 4.11), the hill that was created from polluted soil from the former gas-fracturing plant has a certain rightness of fit with the surrounding topography. The scale and gradient of the hill would be out of place, however, in an area such as North Texas that does not have the steep streets leading down to the water's edge that are such a ubiquitous feature of the Seattle landscape, as illustrated by the harbor steps in Fig. 6.15.

The topography and natural landforms of a region can be the starting point of form with social objectives and financial realities receiving equal and simultaneous consideration.[31] Topography is, by definition, site specific, and it can help mitigate typology or generic design with a unique response to both the site and to the building or landscape with a new creative design that Frampton refers to as "*place-form.*" He is especially wary of designers who obliterate the character of existing landforms or who conceive of their design as "a freestanding aesthetic object."[32]

Topography is one of the special insights that landscape architects bring to the development process. They are the most qualified professionals on a design team for the understanding and advocacy of how to best combine the poetics of landform with the technical details of site engineering. Topography will increase in importance as designers move towards less expensive and more resilient hydrologic and grading practices in landscape development. The advocacy of regional character is another tool to sell the practical and aesthetic values of existing topographical conditions to prospective clients.

Abstracting Other Natural Features

One of the most iconic images in the history of landscape architecture in the United States is Ira's Fountain (Fig. 6.16), also called the Portland Auditorium Forecourt Fountain, built in 1971 and designed by Lawrence Halprin's office with important contributions by Angela Danadjieva. The fountain is a good example of how critical regionalism has been in the mainstream of practice for many years, though few people explain their work using the term. This work abstracts the many waterfalls coming down from the Cascade Mountains watersheds (Fig. 6.17) into an original expression that reflects the sensibilities of both the designers and the *zeitgeist* of the modernist period in which they were immersed. Some people have referred to this historic style of modernism—popular from the 1940s to the 1960s—as *Brutalism*. Brutalism was a style where exposed rough-concrete finishes and chunky blocky forms coexisted, especially in works influenced by Le Corbusier.[33] The fountain incorporates the ethos of brutalism in a way that meets the criteria for a work of critical regionalism. The design uses the then contemporary technology, addresses the International style of the time, has a regional natural form as its inspiration, and is a defamiliarized expression of the personal design aesthetics of Halprin and the Halprin office.

Fig. 6.16 (top). An abstraction of the Northwest's waterfalls in Ira's Fountain in Portland, Oregon, by the office of Lawrence Halprin (2008). Halprin often produced work that, according to Laurie Olin, "reveled in aspects of nature: water, stone, and plants; used abstractions of natural processes and form that dramatically exploited a number of its attributes, such as generosity of scale, redundancy, amplitude, color, patterns, texture, movement, sound, modulation of topography, and light . . . engendering sheer joy for many, and in a manner we associate with "being in nature." As quoted in Laurie Olin, "Water, Urban Nature, and the Art of Landscape Design," in Frederick R. Steiner, George F. Thompson, and Armando Carbonell, eds., *Nature and Cities: The Ecological Imperative in Urban Design and Planning* (Cambridge, MA: Lincoln Institute of Land Policy, 2016), 395.

Fig. 6.17 (bottom). Upper Multnomah Falls near Portland, Oregon, served as an inspiration for Lawrence Halprin's Ira's Fountain and Lovejoy Fountain, both in Portland, Oregon (2008).

Fig. 6.18 (top). The Richmond City Hall forecourt, by Chris Phillips, FCSLA of Phillips, Fervaag, Smallenberg, was completed in 2000 (2008).

Fig. 6.19 (bottom). The two arms of the Frasier River that border the city of Richmond, British Columbia (2018). Courtesy of Google Earth.

The abstraction of natural features is a design thread that continues to provide a rich source of inspiration to contemporary designers. In British Columbia, the Richmond City Hall landscape (Fig. 6.18) was designed by Chris Phillips of Phillips, Fervaag, Smallenberg (PFS Studio), a landscape architecture firm in Vancouver. For this design, the pure experiential qualities of the watershed of Richmond were not evoked as was done in the Halprin Ira's Fountain; rather, a microcosm of the topography and hydrology of the city was abstracted in miniature. Richmond is a low-lying city surrounded by water that functions hydrologically much the same way as areas of New Orleans. An aerial photo (Fig. 6.19) illustrates the city of Richmond's containment within the floodplain between the North and South arms of the majestic Frasier River. The entire city is at or below sea level and is protected by large dikes and a series of drainage channels whose water is forced out to the rivers by large pumping stations. The south plaza at City Hall is a particularly evocative abstracted expression of both the flat island of the city within the two branches of the river and the shifting network of intertidal islands and sandbars that ring the city.[34] Additionally, the Richmond City Hall landscape, completed in 2000, addresses more contemporary issues in landscape design that were not as central to the focus of the design process at the Halprin office during the 1960s. These issues include a reference to a *particular* place (Richmond) and not a *universal* archetype (waterfall), a palette of plant materials of Asian origins (such as *Rhododendron japonicum* 'Hino Crimson') that acknowledges the approximately 50 percent of the population with Asian ancestry in the surrounding area, native plants, and art pieces that trace the evolution of the city from estuary to farmland, to bedroom suburb, to its latest aspirations as a cosmopolitan city. The close ties to the region are creatively expressed through a contemporary style of modernism that carefully integrates landscape with architecture.

Both Ira's Fountain and Richmond City Hall are firmly within the stylistic periods of their time. They are examples of how an understanding of the subtle regional formal complexities of modernism is required to successfully extract regional elements from an area that has developed largely since World War II. The style of Ira's Fountain was repeated in areas ranging from Seattle Freeway Park to the large fountains of Halprin's FDR memorial in Washington, D.C., completed in 1997. Similarly, Chris Phillips's modernist style has been expressed in another city hall project in Bellevue, Washington (Fig. 6.20). As was the case in Richmond, Bellevue City Hall responds in a subtle way to the geography of the city, located between Lake Washington and Lake Sammamish. The Halprin and Phillips projects show how critical regionalism methods can lead to new styles reflective of the place, the time, and the designers of spaces. They also point out the importance of reconceptualization, as the similarity of the approach used by both offices for multiple projects began to devolve into a "fail-safe method" of repeating the elements and strategies used to design a very successful and creative project.

The two works by Phillips are relatively subtle in their use of regional modifiers. Most people will probably not immediately grasp their connection to the region, except with signage, as the references are at the planning scale. This relatively subtle expression of the region would then be another secondary level of comprehension that takes more time to register, as is the case with the Denver World Trade

FIG. 6.20. Seattle's area lakes are abstracted at Belleview (Washington) City Hall, designed by Chris Phillips (2008).

Center Plaza (Fig. 6.6). In the meantime, the restrained beauty created by the geometry and the materials draw the visitor's attention to the landscapes and tie immediate experience to the evolving modernist contemporary style of the recently constructed districts in Richmond and Bellevue.

The designed landscapes that represent critical regionalism and use natural features as their point of departure can also reference regional natural features in a way that is accessible to a wider population. A successful example is Founders Green at the redeveloped Stapleton Airport in Denver, Colorado (Fig. 6.21). Founders Green is itself a regional variation (conceptually) of Isamu Noguchi's famous and influential *California Scenario* sculpture garden in Costa Mesa, California (1980–1982).[35]

Founders Green was designed as a community focal point that tells the story of water in Colorado, with mountains rising out of the Great Plains as the beginning of the story. According to Mark Kopatz, the project's lead designer for the firm Nuszer-Kopatz, the project combines both natural and cultural history (Fig. 6.22). Design influences include mountain water sources, serpentine river valleys, canyon walls etched by water, and a pavement grid evocative of agricultural patterning. The designers strove to make the project expressive of the regional elements without making them into overly obvious or literal copies of those elements, as was done at the Gaylord Texan, discussed in Chapter 2. They found

Fig. 6.21 (top). A poetic evocation of the Denver watershed at Founder's Green, designed by Mark Kopatz of Nuszer-Kopatz (2006).

Fig. 6.22 (bottom). Landscape architect Mark Kopatz (left), at Founders Green with a "slot canyon" wall and abstracted "mountain" water source of his design (2006).

FIG. 6.23. The Mental Health and Retardation Center in Laredo, Texas, where a simple steel trellis with hog-wire mesh is familiar and expressive to local ranch workers (2009). Courtesy of Hester and Hardaway.

that a regional project narrative is a successful way both to present the project design to the client and to aid the client with marketing efforts. The result is an urban art park, purposefully contextual, with layers of design intent that encourage the user to go back multiple times to notice and fully appreciate.

Seeing Regional Decorative Elements

The most easily recognizable understanding of a region by both designers and users of landscapes involves the constituent parts of a design or what are sometimes referred to as the decorative details. One area to look for to determine the appropriateness of the detail is the relative cost of the materials typically used in the regional landscapes of the area. In 1995, I worked on the landscape design of a new Mental Health and Retardation Center in Laredo, Texas, with Rosa Finsley, the lead designer and owner of Kings Creek Landscaping, a landscape design/build firm. The center was a replacement for an old World War II-era building that exhibited an impersonal, institutional character. The new center was broken down to a more human scale in a "hacienda" style that is easier for the local Hispanic population

FIGS. 6.24 AND 6.25. Overscaled light fixtures dominate the Surrey Central City Plaza and Forecourt in Surrey, British Columbia, and reinforce the regional visual language of the similarly overscaled wood-and-concrete columns in the main atrium lobby of adjacent Simon Frazier University (2008).

to relate to and to feel comfortable in. The various small buildings of the new center were surrounded by courtyards featuring familiar native and adapted plants, rustic water features made from local stone and prefabricated concrete watering troughs, and fencing and arbor structures made with simple industrial materials (Fig. 6.23). The buildings, designed by Lake/Flato, were similarly designed with familiar stucco, stone, and industrial materials. The result was an award-winning design that avoided the disconcerting impersonal and institutional aesthetic of the older building and contributed to a sense of ease for a regional ethnic population in times of very difficult personal circumstances.

Other decorative details, such as light fixtures, benches, paving patterns, and the complexity of planting designs, can be integral to the cohesive design of an area based on their regional or district appropriateness or seem jarring and forced if designed inappropriately. In Figs. 6.24 and 6.25, one sees the heroically scaled light fixtures that are a successful and integral part of the landscape design for Central City Plaza in Surrey, British Columbia, by PFS Studio. The scale and form of the fixtures make sense within the context of the spectacular space frame in the adjacent building, constructed from wood, a material that is historically associated with the heavy timber construction of British Columbia. The frame and building, designed by Bing Thom Architects, support the main atrium of Simon Frazier University—grafted to the top of an existing shopping mall. The scale of a local, decorative feature, the exterior lights, has helped a creative new exterior design reinforce the visual context created by the regionally influenced architecture. It is easy to imagine how these heroically scaled light fixtures and building details could appear wildly inappropriate in other contexts.

Degree and Type of Regional Ornamentation

The prevailing extent and character of ornamentation is also a regionally defining parameter, distinct from the types of artifacts. Instructive examples of this occur in Seattle, Washington, and San Antonio, Texas. Both cities require that one percent of the budget for public landscape projects be devoted to art, and both cities have a highly decorative tradition in both their public and private developments. This decoration tends to be widely diffused in both places, with many small elements geared towards a pedestrian scale as opposed to other cities, such as Dallas, that tend to have larger and much more elaborate decorative design statements that are more widely scattered throughout the urban fabric. As a result, a highly ornamental aesthetic is appropriate as a regional normative practice for both areas.

The *type* of decoration in the two cities, however, is very different. San Antonio's is a reflection of strong craft traditions passed down for generations, largely from the Hispanic population (Fig. 6.26). During the nineteenth century, San Antonio had the largest community of artists of any city in Texas.[36] An important component of regionalism in San Antonio evolved out of the ability by those artists, as Steven Fox observes, to "transform the old, the derelict, and the 'other' into icons of regional identity."[37] In Fig. 6.27, one sees a well-designed recent creative interpretation of this tradition at The Shops at

Fig. 6.26 (top). A pagoda in the Japanese Tea Garden at San Antonio's Brackenridge Park, showing regional artisan traditions (2007). The garden was developed by Park Commissioner Jack Lambert and completed in 1918.

Fig. 6.27 (bottom). San Antonio craft traditions were used to provide expressive content to a new development at The Shops at La Cantera in San Antonio (2007). Phase One, designed by J. Robert Anderson, FASLA, Landscape Architects of Austin, Texas, was completed in 2005.

FIG. 6.28. Growing Vine Street from the "Trillium Project" in Seattle, designed by Charles Anderson with "Beckoning Cistern" by artist Buster Simpson and completed in 2003 (2008).

La Cantera development in San Antonio, with ongoing contemporary craft traditions of metal, stone, decorative paving, and tile.

Seattle's decorativeness, by contrast, is reflective of the vibrant *contemporary* art scene that has been a big part of the aesthetic of the area for many years and the more recent focus on ecological future viability. A good example is the Vine Street Cistern steps designed by Charles Anderson, FASLA, to help mitigate stormwater pollution before it spills into Puget Sound (Fig. 6.28). As is typical in Seattle, the cistern steps became an opportunity for a public art piece with the addition of a work created by Buster Simpson that includes a metal hand reaching out of the cistern to accept the rainwater from the adjacent building.

The two approaches taken by Seattle and San Antonio inform every detail element of design, including paving, walls, water features, furniture, lighting, and plant materials. Their regionalism can

Fig. 6.29. The Epicenter Apartments in Seattle's Fremont district, by Bumgardner Design, fit comfortably into the region and the artistic sensibility of this creative urban enclave (2019). For more information and pictures, see: https://bumgardner.biz/projects/portfolio-posts/epicenter/.

be seen as a state of mind and "not a matter of materials or a way of building."[38] Seattle is an example of an area that has a regionalist bent for encouraging and nurturing a contemporary creative state of mind versus other areas, such as San Antonio, that focus more on celebrating the past and more traditional craft practices. This contrast is illustrated in Figures 6.27–6.29.

Seeing Spatial Sequences

Not every city's visual character will be as immediately accessible for creative regionalist design as those of Seattle and San Antonio. The original impetus for this research was the quest for regional expression in the rapidly growing Dallas/Fort Worth area of North Texas. As in many relatively new and rapidly developing population centers of the United States, the problem with creative seeing of this region is the *dissipated* meaning found in ordinary regional landscapes. Here, the job of the regional designer is to coalesce and amplify these meanings until they become obvious enough to register an emotional and/or intellectual reaction with both the design team and the users to cultivate what architect Alvar Aalto calls "the gift of seeing the beautiful in everything."[39] Obviously, not every cultural and natural artifact

Fig. 6.30. A hierarchical spatial arrangement of the lively harbor is dominated by the Fairmont Empress Hotel in Victoria, British Columbia (2008). The hotel defines the spatial domain with its 45-degree influence and its visual dominance.

will register as aesthetically qualified material, but there is usually much more to work with if a sincere effort is undertaken to find regional and district expressions of culture and nature to use as points of departure for a critical regionalism design.

An example of a sometimes overlooked regional element to study and utilize in areas with subtle regional signifiers is the degree to which sequential spatial ordering is prevalent in the landscape. For example, is the regional spatial exemplar a hierarchical centered arrangement dominated by an emergent building or are the spaces more de-centered with a continually unfolding geometry that may be best appreciated by moving through the spaces?[40] Seeing cities as a progression of storyboard-like sequences of framed stills that illustrate sequential seeing was famously proposed by Gordon Cullen in the book *Townscape*.[41] A range from hierarchical to serial spatial organization can often be found in older versus new urban development. In "New Urbanist" projects, the outdoor spaces and architecture that defines them tend to be more uniform in terms of style, massing, height, and scale, often due to the financial constraints of incipient urbanism that result in low rise buildings of the same four or five stories. Broad sidewalks are often designed as open spaces and paved linear parks, punctuated with a series of experiences that are best appreciated sequentially (see Fig. 5.2). In older, more established urban areas, such as Victoria, British Columbia (Fig. 6.30), a hotel, government building, or church with associated landscape may dominate a space and impose its presence on the landscape within its sphere of influence. This influence is sometimes explained by the "45-degree influence" principle where a space feels like it is in the spatial domain of a building or other object if it is within a line drawn at a 45 degree angle from the top of the structure to the ground: a 1:1 relationship of height to distance. Visual prominence as a near or distant landmark defines and reinforces the spatial domain as well. These two examples illustrate spatial experience as a determinant of regional form as an addition to the decorative details of a region. The ever-increasing use of aerial imagery, animation, and video technology greatly facilitates the documentation of the sequences that are such an important part of many regional landscape experiences.

Aesthetic Relativism

Understanding, aesthetic appreciation, and appropriation of regional elements will inevitably involve criticism of built form. According to Dewey, criticism is more important as an "explication of the content . . . as to substance and form" than as a basis for placing positive or negative value.[42] The designer who embraces critical regionalism must try to understand and appreciate the regional context in both a subjective personal sense and *also* in as non-judgmental a way as possible. The tentacles of conventional wisdom can block designers from being open to new potentialities, even if revealed by their own observations. This is not to imply that an original regional insight is easy to obtain. It takes effort, but only through this deliberate undertaking can the critical regionalist unloose the constraints of convention and uncover a new creative vision. It is what Dewey calls "a test of native sensitiveness and of experience matured through wide contacts . . . and demands a rich background and disciplined insight."[43] The rich background is developed by knowledge of a variety of regional traditions that facilitate an understanding of the importance of perceived regional elements. How would a designer otherwise know that a particular element is representative of a region and not of a universal expression? Similarly, how would the designer know, after the initial excitement of uncovering it, that an element is worth incorporating into the design process? The designer who understands and appreciates a variety of regional styles will make better use of *unique* regional expressions.

Rather than consciously searching for unique regional expressions, many designers with whom I have discussed regionalism understand the idea of regional elements as those that are generally accepted in an area as regional. Although it is certainly not necessary or even desirable to eliminate the accepted regional icons, forms, and materials, the creation and evolution of creative regionalist styles require a singular imaginative vision that is powerful enough to contribute to conventional wisdom and the cultural rules of the area. This will move the designer beyond a simple re-editing of an existing, recognized regional context.

The creative vision of the designer must remain flexible to new manifestations of the infinite complexity of regional environments, with the perspective necessary to transcend the products and influences of our aesthetic biases. As a designer makes an honest attempt to appreciate the regional cultural and natural context, it is also helpful to understand why something is unappealing. This forces the designer to look into their tendencies and prejudices. The designer can thus "grow" as a person and appreciate and appropriate landscape elements that were formerly unknown or that triggered unpleasant associations. Those associations may not be an intrinsic part of the elements themselves, such as the factories mentioned in Chapter 5 or as seen in the cotton scale in Fig. 6.32.

The ability to appreciate regional elements on their own terms is akin to learning to appreciate art or music from ancient cultures and distant lands. For example, when we see folk art or medieval art, we do not judge the works based on the most rigorous standards of contemporary design. Rather, we attempt to understand and appreciate the work on its own terms within the context of its creation and in relation to similar works we have experienced. The recalibration of our aesthetic sensibility required to appreciate forms separated either geographically or temporally from the familiar greatly expands our perceptual filters and is well worth the effort. Since each project, region, and district will need to be addressed on its own terms, the possibilities are both infinite and endlessly stimulating for the design process. Every style and 'ism' from every epoch has enthusiasts and practitioners with talent and integrity. The ability to connect emotionally with the sensibilities of these designers will lead to a much richer inventory of elements to use for critical regionalism. It will also help prevent the designer from believing there is no usable regional context, as was the case with the designers of the Solana project (Figs. 5.14 and 5.15). The designers of Solana were susceptible to an offhand condemnation of a regional style because it was not in concert with their sophisticated taste or preconceived design ideals.

Aesthetic sensitivities must be carefully calibrated to *both* the cultural and the natural features of an area. Some places are culturally rich, and some have a great deal of easily appreciated natural beauty.

FIG. 6.31. Texas gayfeather (*Liatris punctata var mucronata*) blooming in October at Blackland Prairie Park in Arlington, Texas (2013).

Others are culturally dissipated or have natural features that require effort to uncover and celebrate in landscape design. For example, a flower such as Texas Gayfeather (*Liatris punctata* var. *mucronata*), which could appear as a relatively commonplace specimen if placed in a lush botanic garden, evokes a much more meaningful aesthetic experience when seen growing in its native hot and dry prairie habitat without human intervention (Fig. 6.31).

All local natural contexts serve as important design inspirations, even if they are no longer readily apparent in the location being considered for development. Natural landscapes have *intrinsic* aesthetic value, as was pointed out in the discussion of four-part aesthetics in Chapter 3. They become more important to aesthetics as one begins to understand the infinite complexities and almost unimaginable time frame that was required for their creation.

Coalescing subtle regional meanings requires a mindset that both carefully addresses conditions as they are and eagerly anticipates what they could *become* on their own terms. This is very different from designers who wish to impose a vision for a lamented lost landscape on an area that is seen as culturally or physically "inferior," based on a narrower ability to recalibrate the designer's fixed assumptions about which design parameters should be appropriated into the design process. Bringing *reinvented* lost cultural and natural features back into a dissipated context is one of the prime reasons for creative regionalist designs. A sincere search is conducted, with an open mind, to find regional influences that may have been previously unknown to the designer or even to the inhabitants of an area. The designer develops a complex web of cross-referential and mutually reinforcing design ideas. Paul Ricoeur warns that it is never easy to be tolerant of a wide variety of places and landscape styles while remaining true to our own design identity. Regional communication with people from cultures that are different from one's own is possible "by the means of sympathy and imagination" and can be compared to the way we relate to characters in drama or literature.[44]

There is a profound relativism in a regionalist experience by a mature regionalism designer. We all have what psychologists call a situational personality, referring to how a person reacts under varying circumstances. A flexible situational design personality is also very important to the fostering of creative regionalist design in a wide range of regional conditions.[45] The opposite is also true. Expressions of landscape architecture that exhibit great technical skill may not be appropriated into the design process due to being "out of sync" with contemporary conventional wisdom that no longer values the designs. A wide knowledge of regional and design traditions will allow the observer to see through misplaced stylistic reinterpretations, inappropriately derivative designs, sophisticated academic exercises, or simply hackneyed expressions that have been rendered meaningless by overuse.

We have all seen the phenomenon of adults listening to the music that defined their adolescent years. The abundance of classic rock stations in every corner of the United States proves this point. It seems that just as there is a window in human development that permits language to imprint very easily up to a certain age, so it is with music and many other aspects of our daily lives. Advertisers covet the 18–34-year-old demographic for this very reason: They know that these are the years when taste and buying habits are being formed and that these tastes then travel with us through the rest of our consumer lives. The intense memories that are formed between ages 10 and 25 are referred to in research as the "reminiscence bump." This phenomenon, actively researched since the 1980s, occurs because teen years and early adulthood are when people are most preoccupied with forming the internalized life story that develops into an identity.[46]

It should come as no surprise, therefore, that our taste in landscape is often developed either in our youth or during the early years of practice as a young impressionable designer. I have personally seen many landscape architects whose taste in landscape design is heavily, if not predominantly, influenced by the place or places where they first came to understand and appreciate landscape architecture. This seems to hold even if they have spent the majority of their lives far away from the "imprinted" landscape in a vastly different environment or even on the other side of the world in a completely new country. This powerful fixation on landscapes with deep personal meaning makes it even more imperative that designers learn to "read" the places for which they are designing and learn to appreciate them for what they have to offer as unique places, even if this uniqueness is strange at first impression. Adding resistance to subconscious design, driven by personal design predilections that are acted on without reflection, to the resistance components of critical regionalism discussed in Chapter 1 will keep the designer self-aware and critical of the implications of their personal proclivities. Just as the child growing up learns to develop a more complex palette for the experience of food, so the nascent regionalist designer will slowly, and with considered reflection, develop a broader ability to understand, appreciate, and appropriate into the design process both successful regional prototypes and design influences from diverse areas.

The cultural geographer Edward Relph describes a way of seeing in which the observer attempts to see what is actually there in a place without overly imposing personal values and prejudices. By seeing in this way, the designer, according to Relph:

> . . . acknowledges that individuality is the essential quality of a place, it is what sets place apart, makes it itself, a reflection of ecological diversity and human variety, and an expression of people's accomplishments.[47]

The Insider and Outsider Perspectives

We will never understand and experience the local context in the same way that local inhabitants do. For that matter, every local inhabitant will experience the local landscapes in a slightly different way. We can, however, bring our educated aesthetic sensitivity to bear on a region in a way that celebrates one's personal creative perception and understanding of the area that was formerly unknown to us. Bourassa calls this the "outsider perspective." A very important truism that applies to most design projects is that outsiders tend to perceive landscapes more easily as aesthetic objects, while insiders tend to see things in terms of their practical importance. It is much easier for an outsider, as most members of design teams are, to see a region creatively without all the baggage of precedent and knowledge of obstacles to creative reinterpretations of a region.

The outsider's perspective is well documented in areas ranging from business consulting to such luminaries as Freud, Einstein, Charles Ives, and, famously in the field of landscape architecture, Garrett Eckbo, James Rose, and Daniel Kiley, who developed their breakthrough ideas on modernism while largely alienated from the traditional academic environment of their time. Academic insiders are very adept at the politics of moving their ideas through the obstacles and objections imposed by the gatekeepers in journals, books, and conferences. Yet they can slow the process of innovation through their acceptance of and acculturation into the established mainstream thought and taste of their professional peers. Academic outsiders have a greater affinity to the sensibility required for design, where innovative designers gather as much information as possible and then move forward with the best thinking and the best solution they can muster without being unduly stymied by seeking the endorsement or criticism of colleagues. There is a parallel with ecology here that Aldo Leopold called "an evolutionary mandate for individualism."[48] Creative outsiders provide alternatives and a way forward as design styles and methodologies lose their utility in the cultural, physical, and economic evolution of regions.[49]

Bourassa cites a variety of studies on insider and outsider perspectives, mostly using photo-elicitation, that compare the landscape preferences of various groups of design experts and non-experts, outsiders and insiders. The first finding relevant to creative seeing is that "professional experience reduces the likelihood that landscape architects will be able to estimate the preferences of their clients."[50] This finding underscores the importance of appropriation of the regional context as previously described. The second relevant finding is that landscape architects, architects, and non-experts exhibit strong differences in landscape preferences. In Chapter 3, I introduced the research team of Kaplan and Kaplan. The team conducted a study of 107 college students in 1973 that revealed that architecture students prefer images of buildings, landscape architects prefer designed landscaped settings with buildings, and the general student population preferred unadulterated enclosed natural settings.[51] These findings further reinforce the need to approach the seeing of regional elements with a broad and relative perspective that encourages us to transcend one's personal *and* professional biases.

Place Making and Transformation

The central precept of critical regionalism is a special sensitivity to a region that enhances the identity and intensifies the cultural significance of place making.[52] As the American architect Romaldo Giurgola has written:

> I believe that it is in the making of coherent connections in time, history, and cultural identities . . . that a building becomes true architecture. That making of clear connections with a cultural past and present is very different from the sophisticated playing with shapes, which often passes for architecture today.[53]

The use of connections to place for a critical regionalism design can be described in biological/behavioral (environmental psychology) terms with a discussion of "rhyme." To rhyme, as Doug Kelbaugh suggests, "images must be neither too similar nor too dissimilar to each other. In the former case, the human tends to lose interest too easily and in the latter case to become confused and discouraged too easily."[54] The "happy medium" between these two extremes can produce a pleasurable biological response in humans. This response then becomes an important component of what we refer to as beauty. Without an appropriate level of abstraction and creativity, the designer cannot develop a design to the level that provokes critical thinking while also making the work a personal statement. Critical regionalists, however, transform familiar architectural language with a careful enough process that the result will "rhyme with ... historic precedents" in a perceptible, if sometimes subtle, way.[55]

Transformations are sometimes discussed in terms of a critical response to a region using modernist design principles as a starting point, as in the examples of the Portland Forecourt Fountain (Fig. 6.16) and Richmond City Hall (Fig. 6.18). This approach can help bridge the gap in design philosophy between some modernist and postmodernist designers. It encourages a designer to bring all of one's "baggage of the brain" to a project while still furthering the adaptation to region that enhances the place-making advocated by regionalist designers. The architectural educator Ann Cline expresses this idea as follows:

> While we may begin with the perfect geometry of modernism, we do so fully intending from the start that this perfection become altered in ways that become the more expressive because they are referent to something [regional] . . . we now have a network of deviants . . . and in each deviation we are introduced to the heart of the matter. When we deform this shape in this place, we find we are most satisfied by this deformation which might draw its inspiration from some element defamiliarized, or from some feature typified. The deformation begins the insistence upon the key steps to critically regional design, and at the same time relates them globally: the collection of cousins . . . reunited to family.[56]

The critical regionalist designer is likewise impelled to develop a first impression into something more lasting and meaningful through experience, comparison, and precedent. Considered and experienced judgment separates the designer from the narrower design sensibilities of the layperson or the inexperienced designer. Often the first impression of a landscape, the *gestalt* or impression of the unified whole, is what creates the strong germ of an idea for the design. This seed, once planted in the mind, according to Santayana, "breeds a hundred more, sometimes slowly and subterraneously, sometimes . . . with a sudden burst of fancy."[57] If intuition is the sudden expression of seeds of inspiration planted by the environment that have been growing for some time, then it follows that appreciation and aesthetic absorption of regional elements can also emerge as original intuitive ideas after an incubation period. The regional elements thus feed the fires of intuition and provide a catalyst for creative intuitive expressions. This first impression, however, will fade in time and will need to be followed by a more analytic phase whereby the regional elements are processed intellectually. This phase helps the designer catalog these emotional experiences and develop from them a heightened understanding of their reactions and, most importantly, the intrinsic validity of the elements to the design process.

Some regional elements used in design can be experienced more powerfully when their original context is removed. Elements that are considered pedestrian, commercial, or hackneyed, for example, can be rearranged and transformed into a successful design that can celebrate, criticize, or simply provoke critical thinking about the elements. The designer assimilates the material and reissues it in a fresh and creative way. The regional material is then once again the raw material for the landscape but not necessarily the *substance* of the design in the way it would be in a romantic regional landscape. This realization will allow a designer to accept the use of a broader range of regional elements without feeling hackneyed or provincial. Examples of well-recognized and ubiquitously used regional materials and forms used in new creative ways appear in many guises throughout this research.

Metaphor

Let's begin with a quote by author Donald Schon:

> New concepts do not spring from nothing or from mysterious external sources. They come from old ones . . . new concepts emerge out of the interaction of old concepts and new situations, where the old concept is not simply re-applied unchanged to a new instance but is that in terms of which the new instance is seen.[58]

A landscape metaphor occurs when a landscape feature recalls multiple instances of a feature with something in common. By causing us to see one thing in terms of another, metaphors help us to see things in some manner that is new to us. On this point, S. J. Brown writes, "Essentially, it is the process by which all new ideas come into being."[59]

FIG. 6.32. A large steel cotton scale from Aledo, Texas (2008).

Metaphor can help us understand a given work of landscape architecture. At the very least, an understanding of metaphor will aid in its enjoyment. A metaphor can also be negative and detract from the experience of a new landscape design. I received a personal lesson in this regard when I purchased a cotton scale at an agricultural antique store in the small town of Aledo, Texas, many years ago. The scale had a powerful expressive form, looked rather like a Nike swoosh, was more than ten feet long, and was made of heavy iron (Fig. 6.32).

To me, the form was very arresting and the fact that it was a working cultural artifact more than 100 years old made it even more compelling, but I should have known that cotton scales are regarded as artifacts of slavery by the local African-American population in Texas. This was pointed out to me very forcefully by several Dallas-area residents to whom I showed it. It certainly would have been vitally important to understand this connection in order to use the object or the form in a landscape design.

This charged cultural artifact could never be neutral among African Americans in the cotton growing areas of the southern United States. It is, of course, impossible to predict with perfect accuracy how the metaphoric elements of a project will be received and understood—both in the short and long term—but there is a better chance that the designer can control the perception of metaphors with a conscious and rigorous understanding of regional design influences and the seeds of their creation within the regional context.[60] Understanding the complex range of perspectives within various population groups in a given area could be the purview of a design team member focused on cultural rules, as outlined in Chapter 3.

Japanese gardens are one of the best-known examples of gardens that use metaphors for nature and life. These metaphors are created from a variety of materials. For example, gravel is used in the Zen garden as a metaphor for water surrounding the carefully selected stone "islands."[61] Another water metaphor in Japanese gardens is *Mazzus repens*, a very low creeping groundcover that blooms either white or blue in the spring, used for the "water" surface of pond-shaped features. This type of landscape metaphor can be adapted, using critical regionalism methods, for areas outside of Japan rather than literally copying the Japanese metaphors, as is commonly done in recreations of Japanese gardens in the United States. For example, in North Texas a metaphor that uses the "oxbow," or bend, of a meandering river as the point of departure would have resonance with the local population in the same way that shapely rocks typically used in Zen gardens are evocative to the population of the islands of Japan.

Metaphor is one of the best-known devices that apply to the arena of semiotics. Semiotics, when applied to landscape architecture, can be used to study the tools that carry the message of design language from a designer or a landscape to the users of landscapes. These tools include metaphor, metonymy and many other interesting and productive ways of understanding how symbols communicate design intent.[62]

Metonymy is a transfer-of-meaning process by which an artifact in the landscape is used to refer to another that is related to it. For example, we often hear of the Wall Street versus Main Street divide when it comes to economics. Wall Street is a metonymy for the stock market and the investment class and Main Street a metonymy for small business. In my professional practice as a landscape architect, I have learned that these types of symbolic meanings apply to many plants as well. The association of our native grasses and grasslands in the North Texas area where I live with the ideas of dereliction and lack of care is a serious issue to address for anyone seeking to bring their regional expressive qualities into metropolitan areas. The term "cow pasture," which would be a prairie in North Texas is most often used as a derogatory term, as in "the yard looks like a cow pasture," meaning that it is not being satisfactorily maintained by typical suburban standards. The exotic *Nandina* sp. are similarly viewed as symbols of dereliction in the North Texas language of landscape. Many people in the area have a visceral dislike of this plant that is often found growing around poorly managed older landscapes after being planted when it was more popular in the twentieth century. The study of semiotics as they apply to landscape perception is another helpful tool in critical regionalism that helps us understand and bridge the gap between intentionality by the designer, the expressive potential of regional material as uncovered with creative seeing, and the likelihood of its perception, understanding, and appreciation by the end users.[63]

Preservation, Re-creation, Interpretation, and Transformation

A good way to evaluate the appropriateness of regional forms and materials is to consider the options available for expressing regional design elements in new landscape designs. If preservation, re-creation, and interpretation of an element are part of the cultural history of an area, then the transformation that moves a design in the direction of critical regionalism is more likely to be expressive and meaningful to the local population.

An example of this concept is the regionally appropriate use of the irrigation ditch or canal as a metaphor for projects throughout the San Antonio area. The Spanish term for these structures is *acequia* (pronounced ah-see-kyah). *Acequias* have been in use in the San Antonio area since Spanish colonial times. These small community-operated waterways brought water from rivers and lakes to distant agricultural fields. During the early 1700s, Franciscan monks established six missions with crop fields that were irrigated by *acequias* along the San Antonio River. Using floodgates, the *aguador* (water master) controlled the volume of water sent to each field for irrigation and for such auxiliary uses as

FIG. 6.33. The preserved Espada Aqueduct or Acequia in San Antonio, Texas (2007). Photograph courtesy of the San Antonio Conservation Society.

Fig. 6.34. Recreation of a working *acequia* at the San Antonio Botanic Garden (2007).

bathing, washing, and powering mill wheels. Today, nearby farms still use water from this system.[64] Remnants of an historical *acequia* at Mission San Francisco de la Espada (Fig. 6.33) still exist as a *preserved* historical vernacular regional element. At the mission, water is carried over Piedras Creek by the Espada Aqueduct—one of the oldest preserved arched Spanish aqueducts in the United States.

All six of the missions flourished, and the most famous of them, the Alamo mission, evolved into present-day San Antonio. The Alamo had an *acequia* that remained in use until 1912, when the city filled it in and generally erased the historic water conveyance system from local memory. Recently, renewed archaeological interest has resulted in excavations of small portions of the historical structure and subsequent recreation behind the chapel on the grounds of the Alamo. In Fig. 6.34, one sees another *re-creation* of a working *acequia* in the San Antonio Botanic Garden. This re-creation, in a high-profile and often-visited place, helps move the form of the *acequia* from an obscure historical context to one that is generally recognized by the local population.

The San Antonio-based architecture firm Lake/Flato has used the expressive potential of the *acequia* to good effect in ways that go beyond preservation and re-creation. The Portal San Fernando, in San Antonio, is a transitional space that connects the historic Main Plaza near the Alamo with the popular River Walk. The architects designed scale models of various water features, including an *acequia* with a working wooden floodgate (Fig. 6.35). This *interpretation* of the historic regional forms for moving water is fun for people of all ages and encourages them to absorb the history of the area.

The high profile given to the *acequia* form in San Antonio led to its adoption as a point of departure for a more subtle and transformed expression of one at Trinity University in San Antonio (Fig. 6.36). The combination of preserved, recreated, and interpreted *acequias*, as well as those actually still

Fig. 6.35. Opening day at Portal San Fernando in San Antonio, Texas (2005). Courtesy of Lake/Flato Architects.

Fig. 6.36. An abstracted acequia at Trinity University in San Antonio, Texas, by Robert A. M. Stern, with Rialto Studio Landscape Architects (2007).

in use for irrigation, assures that an abstracted or metaphorical *acequia* has a higher probability of being understood by the local population as a creative use of a local form. Thus, the use of the *acequia* metaphor as a signature water feature at Trinity University is *both* a creative *and* an expressive interpretation of an historic form of water conveyance in the region.

The *acequia* metaphor is a very obvious and celebrated regional archetype in San Antonio. The more obvious the regional element transformed, the more radical the transformation can be without losing its ability to be expressive. Similarly, a more subtle or abstract regional modifier will need to be expressed with increased clarity in order to have a fair chance of being understood and embraced. This is especially true for expressions of natural systems that are often only vaguely understood by local metropolitan populations, such as the plants and plant communities of the Edwards Plateau, Blackland

Fig. 6.37. An acequia at the Dallas Botanic Garden by Warren H. Johnson of Fallcreek Gardens, Inc., with Schrickel Rollins and Associates (2014).

Prairie, and the East and South Texas Plains that surround San Antonio. Understanding these systems is further complicated by shifting climate patterns, which brings opportunities for new creative transformations of shifting natural systems but may also make historically popular naturalistic design expressions impractical and less appropriate.

The *acequia* metaphor has also been used for a water feature 300 miles north of San Antonio at the Dallas Botanic Garden (Fig. 6.37). In Dallas, the metaphor becomes a curiosity that has little cultural resonance with the local population, although it is a very well designed and executed landscape. It is more like a museum artifact or a more carefully executed romantic regional expression than a celebration of a meaningful historical cultural tradition. There is a tendency in North Texas, because of its relatively subtle and dissipated regional character, to look to other areas of Texas for regional inspiration. Designers in the area rarely go through the process that occurred in San Antonio of bringing an actual regional element back to public perception. Texas is a very large state that has developed with influences from many ethnic groups. The Spanish influence of San Antonio has not been a feature of the local history of North Texas until recent years with the influx of immigrants from Central and South America. Therefore, historical Spanish influences, even from San Antonio, should be considered universal civilization influences, as outlined in Chapter 1, to be adapted and creatively transformed to the North Texas region in a critical regionalism process rather than historic elements to be re-created.

Conclusion

We have seen in this chapter some of the regional elements to consider and a small sampling of potential methods that can be used to incorporate regional design parameters into creative and expressive landscape designs. These examples demonstrate how valuable seeking these regional elements is to the pursuit of an ideology that embraces the principles of critical regionalism. The designer who embraces critical regionalism develops an element of passion in discovering and interpreting these regional elements. The understanding of the design potential of regional factors raises the level of appreciation of a region above many of the local inhabitants, the insiders, who may be only dimly conscious of the regional character of the landscapes where they dwell. The passion for regionalism grows as elements from contrasting areas are observed, compared, and absorbed into design methodology by a heightened awareness of regions. This awareness can be likened to the heightened sensibilities of an artist and is stoked by a continual influx of new regional design information. Transformations gleaned from observing regional influences keep the design process fresh and facilitate a spontaneous emotional engagement of the designer's sensibilities with the work at hand. As the designer taps into the aesthetic sensibilities imprinted on a regional population, there is a much better chance that the resulting landscape will not be experienced as "inert geometry"[65] but will instead be "redeemed by conscience and art."[66]

A methodology for designing creative regional expressions with an ideology corresponding to elements of critical regionalism is a time-tested idea that lost currency during the modern period. Lewis Mumford in 1938 wrote about a creative regionalist process that is similar to critical regionalism. His methodology advocated "exploration, scientific observation, imaginative reconstruction, and finally, transformation by art, by technical improvement, and by personal discipline."[67] The search for meaning that led to the theory of critical regionalism was especially active during the 1980s and 90s, when the postmodern reconsideration of design imperatives was most intense. The continuing dearth of creative regional expression in many new designs indicates that the design theory needs persistent advocacy and renewal. The regional context is replete with opportunities for tacit knowing by local populations—elements that both stimulate cultural evolution and preserve cultural memory.[68]

Denis Donoghue (1888–1965), an English professor, author, and literary critic, wrote frequently about form in poetry and music in a way that is resonant with the tenets of critical regionalism. The following quote from Donoghue ties creative seeing back to the practice of creative regionalist design and provides a window into critical regionalism's roots in English criticism:

> If we try to separate form from substance, we turn form into an abstraction that . . . make[s] it an ally of reactionary art. . . . Form transfigures what otherwise merely exists. . . . It is not a creation from nothing, but a further creation from the otherwise created. Form is substance as imagined, not merely received; transfigured, not mined.[69]

Chapter 7:
Critical Regionalism and Non-Visual Regional Elements

The selection and use of regional materials is a true test of the integrity and cohesiveness of a critical regionalist design and will directly impact the aesthetic connection of the new landscape to the users. Non-visual regional influences are sometimes the most important cultural and natural determinants that define a region or district. They enhance every experience of place by addressing in design the full range of senses and not just visual elements gleaned directly from creative observation of an existing designed or undesigned context.

Non-visual elements make regionalism accessible to people with impaired vision such as the celebrated blind architect, Chris Downey.[1] Downey is a good example of how learning to design for special populations can expand the definition of sensory experience for all people, as the senses that may be providing subconscious cues are consciously addressed in the design process. Non-visual elements can also be an important key to understanding appropriate regional responses to "critically resistant" areas (as described on page 11) and places with rapid shifts in demographics that bring new influences to an existing context. Designers can study the predilections and history of populations as design cues, before these cues have been imprinted on the landscape by development. Non-visually derived design influences also arise from regulations such as form-based codes. Regulations are part of the broad panoply of development infrastructure that includes the important elements of construction materials and craft traditions as well as the ethos of the professionals who design, pay for, and implement new construction projects. Elements of this development infrastructure are always evolving and the changes appear after construction as visual elements to appropriate as part of the regional fabric.

Non-Visual Experiences in Critical Regionalism

As discussed in Chapter 3, landscape architects and architects often give pictorial aspects of design the most attention. The compromises needed to bring a project to completion are most often between the visual experience created by form, materials, and placement, and the budget or the functions of a landscape. A regionalist who does not consider the non-visual senses as a priority for aesthetic perception is missing opportunities for a subtle connection to place in areas where regionalism is problematic and dissipated or the evocation and enhancement of a more powerful experiential atmosphere where regionalism is a stronger feature of the landscape.

Aldo Leopold offers an example from 1929 of an intense multi-sensory perception of region that can inform design decisions and elevate regional experiences by users. The excerpt below from a poem written by Leopold is primarily an homage to the sounds of the Pinyon jay, but also evokes the regional non-visual elements of texture ("silky"), temperature ("basking"), and scent (of "cedar").

Ho for piney lanes of sunshine
On the tops of basking mesas!—
Ho for singing groves of piñon
On the foothills in the fall.
Ho for lanes of silky gramma,
Tang of sage and scent of cedar
On the pleasant hills of autumn
Where the Piñoneros call.[2]

Sounds are a usable and transferable component that enhances a powerful regional experiential atmosphere. Consider, for example, the sounds typical to the Colorado mountains: relentlessly moving water from streams and murmuring brooks or the rustling of leaves from trees with loose petioles such as aspen trees. Other evocative regional sounds include the sounds of sea and surf, the characteristic sound of rain on roofing materials or large-leaved plants, the sounds of local birds, animals, and insects, wind whistling through structures, ships and train horns, fountains, music such as the misty diffuse ambient sound of distant bagpipes, calls to prayer and church bells, Japanese "deer catchers" and the bell-like sounds of a suikinkutsu fountain, and many others.[3] A big part of the experience and memory of visiting castles in Europe, for example, is the feeling and sound of the crunch underfoot when walking on the ubiquitous gravel used for pathways.

Other non-visual sensory opportunities include the feeling of humidity near water features, the warmth of sun pockets, and the cooling benefits of shade, all of which are heavily influenced by a region's climate relating to dryness or humidity, precipitation, wind, intensity of sunlight, and temperature. A more esoteric and controversial example is magnetoreception: the perception by humans of magnetic fields. Dr. Connie Wang led a research team that countered the long-held belief that humans have lost the ability of many other vertebrates to sense and use magnetic fields, and she revealed "a strong, specific human brain response to ecologically-relevant rotations of Earth-strength magnetic fields."[4] These new frontiers in sensory interactions with the environment need further study, as an adjunct to the study of environmental psychology, in order to learn their potential in the design professions. The information these internal senses provide to the human brain is continually fading, reviving, and rearranging to help create our personal experience of place.[5]

Complex and often subtle sensory reactions are another reason that it is important for designers to visit and spend as much time as possible in a landscape that is being developed. The designer will glean sensory information that can help inform design decisions, even if it is not fully consciously processed. The problems associated with some European landscape architects designing in non-temperate areas of the United States that were discussed in Chapter 6 can be addressed by designers spending more time experiencing the distant area for which they are designing with a focus on outdoor non-visual sensations, particularly those related to climate.

The scent of popular local plants is another fruitful area often used for regional investigations. Information on heirloom plants, both native and introduced, is widely available as a resource for traditional regional plant aromas coming from leaves, flowers, and fruit. For example, in the Mental Health Mental Retardation project in Laredo, mentioned in Chapter 6, we used Mexican oregano (*Lippia graveolens*) for some of the ornamental flowerbeds.[6] This plant is used for both cooking and medicine by many populations throughout Mexico and in South Texas. The scent of this plant provides an immediate and powerful connection between the new institutional landscape of The Center and the South Texas Hispanic population of the area. Mexican Oregano is native to South Texas and is root hardy only as far north as San Antonio. It requires a commitment to regional plant research for designers from more northern latitudes, even in Texas, to discover and utilize the benefits of this plant for South Texas populations.

Landscape materials are also an opportunity for aromatic cues. Regional mulches have characteristic smells, both new and as they decay. In a similar vein, cut wood and the oils placed on them are evocative of districts and regions as are other hardscape materials such as stucco and loess that have a noticeable scent that can permeate entire neighborhoods. Both loess and stucco are used extensively in Africa and the U.S. Southwest where there are loess soils. The smells inherent in regional ponds, rivers, and other water bodies can evoke strong emotions as they also help to define districts.[7] The scent of food has the most powerfully evocative effect and is accordingly seen as vitally important to regionalist landscape planning and design. Food affects many senses, including smell, bodily sensations of hunger and satiation, visual cues, and even sound and tactile pleasures. Food vendors on streets, farmer's markets, community gardens, and places to eat, gather, and linger are more characteristic of some regions and districts than others. They are examples of how the study of use patterns, including non-visual sensory cues, can lead to the discovery of regional prototypes with, as Panos Koulermos says, "plan and form generated by appropriate and similar organizational conditions."[8] These types of regional typologies must be uncovered and understood in order for their creative transformation in a new design to accomplish the more incremental change that is a hallmark of postmodern design philosophy.

The texture of materials is often used as a regional variant. Some regional concrete formwork is relatively rough, as is the case in Hastings Park (Fig. 7.1). Other concrete, such as that in Beck Park (Fig. 7.5), is perfectly silky smooth. Stone has similar regional variations. Cut, planed, sanded, chopped,

FIG. 7.1 (TOP AND OPPOSITE). Landmarks featuring "traditions, sounds, foods, and aromas" along Jefferson Boulevard in Dallas, Texas, as captured by Petrine Abrahams, an M.L.A. student at UT-Arlington, for a studio project on a district's character (2009).

and natural stone all have regional texture implications. The textures of the stone itself will also work for or against a regional expression and are a good reason, along with the more regularly addressed carbon footprint implications of transporting stone and the regional visual cues, to seriously consider a regional stone. Sedimentary stone, such as limestone or sandstone, will have a very different texture, regardless of how it is finished, than harder materials such as marble or granite. The tactile qualities of the stone used for walls, seats, flooring, water and other features, can tie a project to the region or they can be just another imported artifact that dilutes regional character.

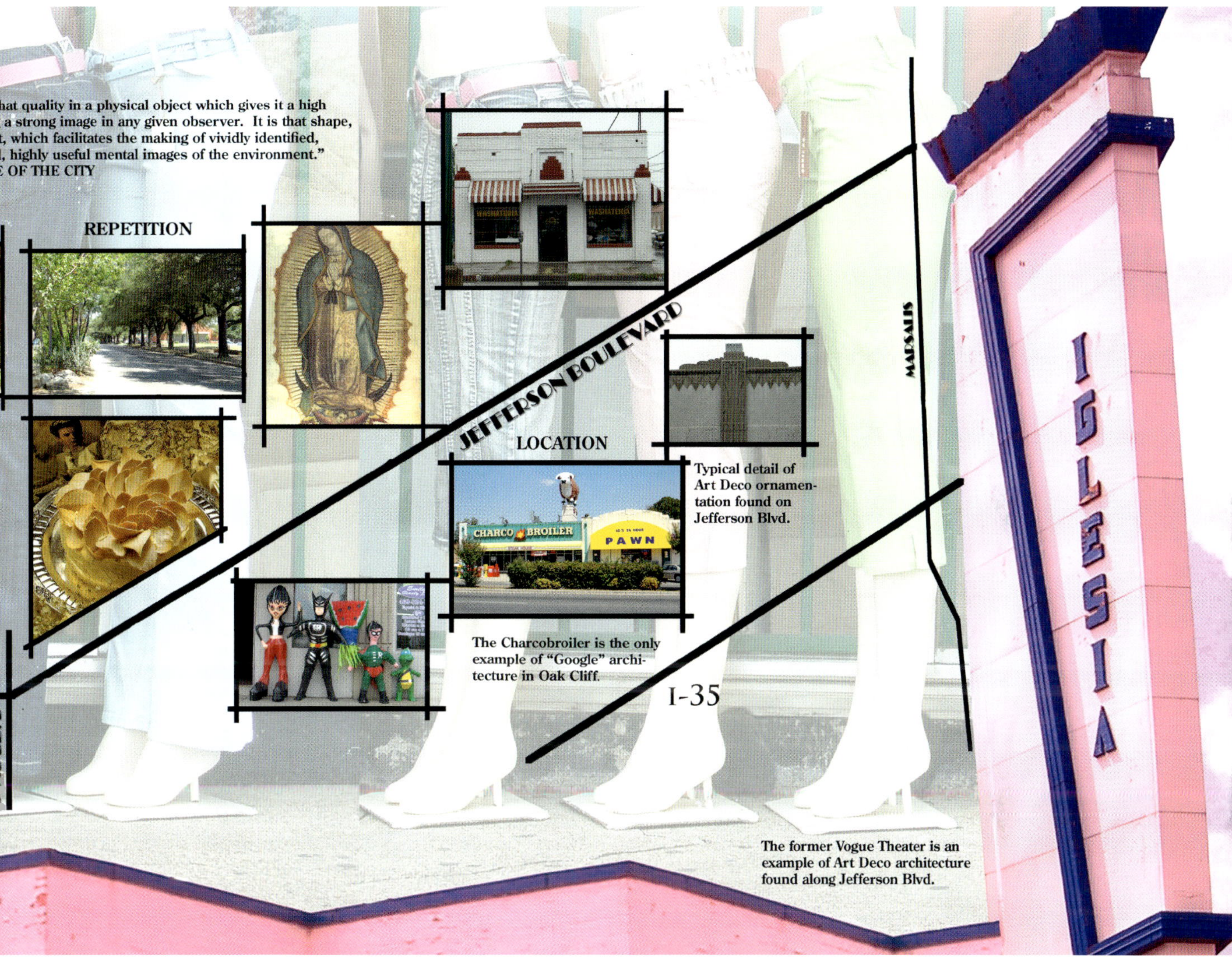

Opportunities for taking advantage of non-visual landscape cues need to be approached with the same flexible and creative spirit that was described for visual cues in Chapter 6. Some of these cues will be obvious, such as the aromas of food and plants, and some will be relatively subtle, such as the musculoskeletal sensations created by moving through a space, the kinesthetic and the haptic senses keyed to the effort required to move through them, which varies with regional topography, distance, and scale.

In Fig. 7.1, Petrine Abrahams, in a project undertaken for the studio I taught at the University of Texas at Arlington, captured her take on the best elements of district character that the Jefferson Boulevard district in south Dallas, Texas, had to offer at the time. The non-visual regional Hispanic influences of music and food have helped her to celebrate and amplify the visual image of the district character as part of the site analysis process.

FIG. 7.2. A computer model by David Hopman, showing the cruciform shape of Henry C. Beck, Jr. Park in Dallas, Texas (2003).

Regional Technological Network

Steven Moore proposes a regionalism based on Bruno Latour's *technological network*: "By technological network, Latour refers not just to sets of [visible regional] artifacts but to the social networks that construct relationships between human knowledge, human practices, and nonhuman resources—the latter being the stuff—steel, wood, water, etc.—from which the objects themselves are made."[9] The design influences of both historical and contemporary local technology are an important addition to those of historic memory and forms, traditional materials, climate, and nature.[10] Local construction techniques and craft traditions can be non-regional, making them part of universal civilization, or they may be regional, in which case they can inform the regional design influences of the landscape architect. In either case, they allow the regional influences that are manifested in the contemporary craft of construction techniques to inform the design process for hardscape elements and plant materials the way they have throughout the history of built form.[11] This idea was especially resonant during the nineteenth century and influenced writers, such as Ruskin, who furthered the evolution of the Arts and Crafts movement that immediately preceded modernism.[12]

Fig. 7.3. Henry C. Beck, Jr. Park in Dallas on opening day (2004).

An example of a regionalist work that was inspired by the technological network of Dallas is the Henry C. Beck, Jr. Park, built in 2004 with principal design by Spindrift Al Swaidi (daughter of Henry C. Beck, Jr.), and Mesa Design Group, Inc., for whom I was a landscape architect working on the project at the time (Figs. 7.2–7.5). The park pays homage to Henry C. Beck, Jr., who took over a thriving construction company in the Dallas area after his father's death in 1948 and built it into the largest construction company in Dallas. He is credited with being most responsible for the construction of the Dallas skyline at a time when both the International style and early postmodernist buildings called for simple use of materials and spare use of ornamentation.[13] The park celebrates these historical modernist attributes with structural materials intended to be expressive on their own terms without ornamentation: finely worked architectural concrete, bush-hammered concrete (a favorite of Beck, Jr.), mill-plate steel, bronze, Pennsylvania bluestone (slabs and crushed), wood, and cascading water.[14] These elements are used as regional elements for the park because they were important elements of the historical technological network of Dallas and the life of Henry C. Beck, Jr., an important regional figure in the physical development of the city, and not necessarily because they are ubiquitous elements in the visible contemporary built environment or resonant with recent design trends. The park also reads as an architectural ruin with a cruciform shape that has meaning to both the life and family of Henry Beck and to the people of Dallas—a significant percentage of whom are actively religious (Fig. 7.2).

Fig. 7.4. Key players in the relationships that created the form and materials of Beck Park: (left to right) Jeff Turner, ASLA; Spindrift Al Swaidi; Tary Arterburn, FASLA; and John Spiars, PE (2004).

Fig. 7.5. This bush-hammered concrete retaining wall (left) and a sharp edged 18-foot-long, finely formed high fly-ash concrete wall at Beck Park (right) celebrate Henry C. Beck, Jr.'s affection for finely crafted concrete (2009).

FIG. 7.6. A palette of monotone gray materials defines the Modern Art Museum of Fort Worth, Texas, with finely honed architectural concrete that heavily influenced the technological network of North Texas (2017).

The architectural concrete used for the walls in Beck Park is a good example of a recent addition to the regional material palette in the Dallas-Fort Worth area. Silky smooth and very finely and carefully formed concrete was used as a principal building material for the celebrated Modern Art Museum of Fort Worth designed by Tadao Ando, completed in 2002. The craft of the material captured the imagination of local design consultants, engineers, clients, and contractors, the "technological network" of North Texas. The DFW area, already known for its extensive use of concrete, was "ripe" for adoption of the material and it immediately became a popular addition to the regional palette.

Beck Park is an honest expression of the economic, social, design, and technological culture of Dallas in 2002 when it was designed, an expression that arose both from a series of relationships and from the spare modernist forms of much of the Dallas arts district to which it is adjacent. John Spiars, PE, shown in Fig. 7.4, was the engineer for the project as well as the engineer responsible for the finely honed concrete at the Modern Art Museum of Fort Worth.

The appreciation of technique, however, is no substitute for genuine *aesthetic* appreciation, grounded in the four-part aesthetic. The Modern Art Museum of Fort Worth is a large edifice with gray concrete walls, grey metal, and even gray stone in the landscape (Fig. 7.6). The pervasive gray color can be viewed as a depressing or monotonous feature when considered through the lens of environmental psychology. When the museum is visited by design consultants, however, there is an almost universally enthusiastic reception of the building, partially caused by the tremendous care and expense that was exercised in crafting the satiny smooth and perfectly straight concrete surfaces with spectacularly crisp and sharp edges and corners. This appreciation, based on the technological network that produced it and not just through visual perception, goes well beyond the attention and appreciation the layperson normally accords raw, grey concrete. Contemporary architectural concrete is an example of how the development community can adopt a regional consensus that celebrates a form, material, design technique, or construction process that may be more problematic for the aesthetics of the typical end user. While the material is a genuine expression of the regional technological network, the resulting aesthetic exhibits some of the same problematic modernist characteristics that led to the postmodern movement. It places visual form and a new regional material derived from a technological network above the actual experience of dwelling in the space, which should be informed by the four-part aesthetic described in Chapter 3. The prioritization of form and material over the broader four-part aesthetic at Beck Park results in it being experienced most often from a distance for its sculptural forms. The park does not invite the public to enter and linger comfortably, even if they choose to. In this respect, the aesthetic experience of the park has similar problems to the experience at Harlequin Plaza as described in Chapter 2.

Technological networks created many cultural elements that we now recognize as regional determinants such as the explosion of cast-iron work during the early nineteenth century that are now associated with New Orleans and other cities that developed during that time period. The ubiquitous cast iron work that helps define regional character was not present to observe when it was constructed. It had to be introduced and then accepted by both the technological network of the time and the owners of the buildings and landscapes who appropriated it. During the International style of the twentieth and twenty-first centuries, however, we have seen the negative side of overbuilding using the technological efficiency of concrete, steel, and glass curtain wall structures such as those in Dallas in Fig. 2.5. This problem will continue to be an issue that will require conscious vigilance and creative and thoughtful solutions as the pace of change accelerates with better and faster computer design and manufacturing systems. Cognitive psychologist Daniel Levitin wrote that, "in 2011, Americans took in five times as much information as they did in 1986," a symptom of what has been called "the quickening" that is accelerating and outstripping our ability to adjust.[15] We will need to address the four part aesthetic and find a balance between using the computer to generate new forms, using modern tools to facilitate design and construction of those forms, and creative regional designs that address cultural precedents. I write this as someone who is very familiar with these tools and who has taught many classes in computer modeling and rendering to graduate landscape architecture and architecture students. The pace of change that facilitates appropriation by the local community will need to be an item for careful study so that it can be a more purposefully determined parameter for designers and decision makers when pursuing large-scale parametric interventions.

An instructive example is the large canopy structure at Pacific Plaza in Dallas by HKS architects and SWA landscape architects shown in Fig. 1.8. The design combines past and future by taking advantage of new and currently pervasive advanced computer aided manufacturing techniques for the punching of 58,290 holes in its 322 unique metal panels. The holes are an old railroad morse code and represent every stop along the Texas and Pacific Railroad between New Orleans and El Paso, albeit in a very abstract way that is difficult to discern even with careful explanation. There has been an explosion of custom made punched metal panels in recent years since the technology to make them has been perfected and has become widely available. SoFi Stadium and entertainment complex in Inglewood, California, is perhaps the most famous recent example. The stadium features a large parametric punched metal roof that was also designed by HKS, the designers of the Pacific Plaza Pavilion. The punched metal material may, in time, be appropriated as a popular regional material in North Texas. Its introduction at Pacific Plaza, however, is the result of the technological network of design and advanced manufacturing at the time of its completion in 2019.

Another good example is the Liège-Guillemins railway station in Belgium. The Liège railway stations have been reflective stylistically of their time periods since the nineteenth century. A new station designed by the renowned Spanish architect Santiago Calatrava was completed in 2009. The TGV station receives high acclaim for its poetic use of light and space.[16] The important question that relates to critical regionalism is the relationship of the station to the existing community of Liège, shown in Fig. 7.7. It is certainly a shocking juxtaposition when experienced in person and appears, almost literally, as the abstract and alien forces that Leo Marx warned about in my discussion in Chapter 6. I had a similar feeling visiting the station that I had when I saw an exhibit of an entire room full of Calatrava's models at the Meadows Museum at Southern Methodist University in Dallas. One or two models, or buildings, can be an interesting sculptural and engineering statement, but, when massed together, the models have many of the same placeless qualities and inhuman scale as the International style buildings that the new technology is supplanting. Importantly, however, and typical of the region, the old city is preserved as a psychological anchor, a type of nostalgia trigger, that may facilitate appropriation of the new design by long-time residents, as was discussed in Chapter 1. Another example is shown in Figs. 7.8 and 7.9 where the preserved historic character of Eureka Springs, Arkansas, is juxtaposed with the new Museum of American Art in nearby Bentonville, Arkansas.

The "development community" for any given area will be an important, perhaps the *most* important regional determinant for a landscape architecture project in the United States and around the world. The development community includes various design consultants, developers, clients in the public sector, bankers, city regulators and staff, politicians, an area's plant cultivators and wholesale plant suppliers, quarries and stone yards within a reasonable distance, local craftsman, expectations of quality and skill from the local workforce—the entire technological infrastructure of building most of which is subject to regional biases and, at the very least, a window into the normative practices of any given area. All of

Fig. 7.7. Calatrava's train station and city context in Liege, Belgium. Preserving the old city can help the population appropriate the new parametric forms. Psychological resilience is gained by retaining cultural identity and historic nostalgia triggers (2010).

these players affect the development process in ways that may not necessarily be driven by aesthetics, visual or otherwise. By understanding these practices, a designer has a better chance to be a successful partner in a development process that moves the area towards a creative, culturally integrative, and environmentally future viable (or regenerative) regionalism.

There are many non-visual influences on the evolution of regions that come from the development community. The friction that is caused by restrictive or expensive land-use policies that can force the creation of buildings that must be taller and more densely spaced in order to be economically viable becomes a regional parameter. This has implications, both positive and negative, for an urban district's form, transportation options, mix of uses, and walkability. Another example occurred in Austin, Texas, where a new form-based code was adopted that mandated 18–25-foot-wide sidewalks in all new downtown developments along core transit corridors. The resulting linear sidewalk open space, available for street-level activities, unifies the eclectic architecture into a more cohesive district. This new design

FIG. 7.8 (TOP). The town of Eureka Springs, Arkansas, is well known for its intense vernacular character (2012). The preserved vernacular landscape that attracts both tourists and Arkansans may provide both social and psychological capital to make them more accepting of the new parametric style of the Crystal Bridges Museum of American Art in nearby Bentonville, Arkansas, designed by Moshe Safdie.

FIG. 7.9 (BOTTOM). The model for the Crystal Bridges Museum on display in the museum (2012).

FIG. 7.10. West 2nd Street in Austin, Texas, where diverse architecture is unified by the new non-visually-derived district parameter of wide sidewalks, building setbacks, and building heights dictated by form-based codes (2005).

feature (and constraint) is created by a government edict and not by the overt decisions by a team of designers based on regional conditions. In Fig. 7.10, one sees how the various styles around the Austin City Hall are tied together by wide sidewalks and tree-lined streets. The response by local designers to the spatial constraints created by the codes will, eventually, lead to new opportunities for evolving regionalist expressions. Many facets of regional and district design will be influenced as the city develops in response to the non-visually derived codes that created the wide sidewalks. These include use patterns within the sidewalks by restaurants and shops, the materials used for paving, the type of ornamentation and art that will appear (as with San Antonio and Seattle), the mix of uses with concomitant street-level expressions, transportation options, and many more.

People and Regionalism: A Personal and Cultural History Approach

A personal history or cultural history approach to landscape design takes significant events, or landscape elements with significant meaning for a person or population group, and uses them as form generators or detail elements that add regional meaning to a landscape. To understand the spatial, temporal, and social context, the designer must understand the design aesthetics and the cultural influences that are most significant to the person or regional population group.[17] These cultural rules can be from the immediate area where the project is being developed and/or from the area where the user group originated, if that is more appropriate. Immigrants bring from their former homes a "mental image of what a garden ought to be."[18] An understanding of this mental image will allow the designer to use the story of the client as a generator of regional form extracted from universal civilization that is not derived from creative perception of the existing context. Lewis Mumford reminds us that "the people who came to America did not magically transform their personalities as soon as their feet touched the earth of the new continent: They were Spaniards, Dutchmen, Englishmen, Swedes, Frenchmen."[19] A good example of the persistence of culture is the recognizable speech patterns that stay in a family for generations after they have moved away from the region that produced them.[20] Architect Harwell Hamilton Harris believes that "a region's most important resource is its people and not its climate, its topography, nor the particular kind of sticks and stones it has to build with."[21] As with most regional parameters, this certainly should not be an either/or proposition. The influence of a client's taste and background is usually a feature of design for private spaces in residential landscape architecture. In public projects, whether commercial or government financed, this important regional sociological influence is sometimes placed at a lower priority and requires commitment and effort to consummate. Community involvement facilitates appropriation of a new landscape or building by making the populations served implicit in the physical transformations of where they dwell.[22]

Hastings Park in Vancouver, British Columbia, is an example of a regional expression where the commitment to understanding the local cultural influences of a park project led to a public involvement process. The process ended up as one of the prime determinants of form in addition to the observation and analysis of the existing landscape of the district and region. Hastings Park was designed by the landscape architecture firm Phillips, Farevaag & Smallenberg (now PFS Studio) and completed in 1999. The park includes; an active 'people area' in the form of 'Il Giardino Italiano' (a modern adaptation of a classic Italian garden theme complete with opera walk), as well as sculptures, rain gardens, play-fountains, picnic tables, an *allée* of plane trees, a Japanese garden, a children's area, a skateboard park, bocce ball court, basketball and tennis courts, and other sports fields (Fig. 7.11).

The community's vision for the park was arrived at after an intensive year of public involvement and planning forums. The city and the landscape architects identified user groups and held workshops with local organizations such as schools, community centers, residents' associations, and social services

FIG. 7.11 (TOP). Landscape architect Chris Phillips, FCSLA, in front of the Hastings Park Opera Walk Fountain Sculptures in Vancouver, British Columbia (2006).

FIG. 7.12 (BOTTOM LEFT AND RIGHT). Historic Art Deco structure at Hastings Park, showing board-textured concrete and a decorative form that was repeated throughout the new landscape, including the columns for the park's pedestrian bridge shown here (2006).

agencies. One of the research outcomes of the meetings was the identification of a large Italian population group that had moved into the district surrounding the existing fairgrounds (Hastings Park). The Italian community wanted an expression of its cultural heritage. This became the genesis for one of the signature elements of the park design, the Opera Walk (Fig. 7.12). The Italian theme of the Opera Walk is a new addition to the visual regional and district character of the park. The design for the new park combines existing physical district elements with the "universal civilization" of the opera theme by using the rough, board-textured concrete formwork that is a prominent feature of the Art Deco buildings surrounding the garden. The park also responds to historic site alignments by placing the Italian garden in a prominent location at the terminus of Triumph Street where a building once stood. Even the beautifully designed and executed sculptural forms depicting various opera characters are constructed from cast concrete rather than carved stone, as would be the historic norm in Italy.

An additional regional connection at the park is an alternative vision of water impoundment that is both pictorial and ecologically performative (Fig. 7.13). The ponds and wetlands capture and filter stormwater from the 167-acre site and the surrounding neighborhoods. The constructed verdant natural scene is a very small percentage of the area of the park but has a significant impact on the park's environmental footprint. As Kristina Hill has written, "Designers have new challenges on the ecological side in design, and they also have new challenges on the aesthetic side—specifically, to use design to discover, reapply, or reinvent ways of supporting adaptation as a social and emotional process."[23]

This ecological feature of the project has the additional benefit of contributing to the social cohesiveness of the surrounding community. Volunteers conduct educational tours of the natural features for schoolchildren, and environmental watch groups carefully monitor plant growth, birdlife and overall functioning of the natural area (including garbage, dogwatch, repairs and safety issues).[24] In a very short time, wildlife and birds have returned to the area and have become one of its prominent attractions. The forward-thinking aesthetic elements of the design would probably not have been possible without the non-visual functional imperative to mitigate the environmental footprint of Hastings Park. Understanding the district value of engagement by community groups in both the design and the ongoing maintenance of a local feature has made Hastings Park a successful culturally integrative amenity.

The reconceptualized natural features, blending of universal civilization with regional character using a public involvement process, and defamiliarization of the project through unique and creative regionally inspired design place the Hastings Park redevelopment firmly into the realm of critical regionalism. The park is a good example of how critical regionalism can be relatively conservative stylistically and need not be "cutting edge" from the standpoint of pure abstract form.

Both formal and informal cultural studies are an invaluable addition to critical regionalism. The original premise of critical regionalism—seeking to mediate universal civilization with the particulars of place—is subject to regional calibration. The degree to which an area is cosmopolitan is another

FIG. 7.13. A constructed wetland at Hastings Park in Vancouver, British Columbia (2006).

important region or district defining parameter. Designers should be consciously aware of this in the design process, as they tend to be much more cosmopolitan than most population groups, due to design education and travel. This awareness will facilitate an understanding of the appropriate balance between the local and the universal and will, ultimately, help determine the expressiveness of the new landscape to a local user group.

Conclusion

In this chapter, I demonstrated the importance of non-visual regional elements to a critical regionalism design ideology. Such elements as expanding the "tactile presence" of a project, part of the early description of critical regionalism as defined by Kenneth Frampton, understanding the regional technological network and form-based codes, and design influences from shifting population groups are important to every discipline of creative environmental design. In the next chapter, I shift the focus to a creative area in the development process in which landscape architects have a singular role and a unique understanding of aesthetic, environmental, and practical considerations: planting design.

FIG. 8.1. A dormant prairie at Cedar Hill State Park in a metropolitan area of North Texas near Dallas (2020). This powerfully defamiliarized scene was made possible by an ongoing restoration that brought the prairie back from a woodland choked with exotic and highly invasive Chinese privet (*Ligustrum sinense*).

Chapter 8:

Critical Regionalism, Plants, and Natural Systems

Plants and natural systems are important landscape design elements for which ideas developed by architects for critical regionalism need significant translation and expansion to apply to landscape design. The reconceptualization that is a hallmark of critical regionalism has led to many interesting and instructive approaches to the creative possibilities inherent in plants and natural systems. Some approaches are historic and well resolved, and some are new, experimental, and creative, redefining the way nature is expressed and the role of plants within an increasingly complex cultural context.

Certainly, the idea of making plants "visible" and a focus of our attention is in concert with the idea of defamiliarization, which has been a part of planting design for centuries. As Aldo Leopold wrote, "We can be ethical only in relation to something we can see, feel, understand, love, or otherwise have faith in."[1] Leopold understood that the "death of nature," which began with the Enlightenment and continues to this day with the ethos and professional practice of many design professionals, can be addressed by increasing both ecological and aesthetic appreciation of plants and other biota. Critical regionalism, applied to planting design, is a productive tool in that process.

There are countless examples of plant juxtapositions and planting design arrangements that attract attention and provoke critical thinking. One of the most common terms that designers use is "specimen plant." It is a specimen precisely because it is placed to be noticed and admired. A specimen plant, however, does not reflect the complete design and does not usually rise to the level of a human intervention that would both defamiliarize the environment and provoke critical thinking, as Cedar Hill State Park certainly did for me when I took the photograph (Fig. 8.1). Specimen plants are sculptural objects placed in the landscape and do not by themselves define the landscape, unless the plant is very large and the landscape is very small.

Plants and building materials have the important commonality of requiring designers to understand not just the complexities of using them for design, but also the inherent qualities of the materials themselves. The detail elements of buildings, such as approaches to fenestration and surface materials, can be one of the most expressive regional components of architecture.[2] The details that are the constituent parts of the design *are* the way the design is most immediately understood and experienced by people who dwell in structures. John Dewey applied this concept to a variety of media and arts:

> Even brick and mortar become a part of the house they are employed to build: they are not mere means to its erection. Colors are the painting; tones are the music . . . Sensitivity to a medium is the very heart of all artistic creation and esthetic perception.[3]

In order to understand expressive regional potentialities in landscape design, landscape architects must have a similar level of understanding of the much more complex material of plants. One plant can easily have more geometry in its stems, leaves, flowers, and fruit than an entire building. Additionally, plants are constantly changing through the seasons, growing and dying, and must be addressed as living things that interact with their immediate environment and beyond in complex ways.

Some designers use mostly trained forms of plants, such as hedges and other forms of pruned shrubs, primarily for their ability to define space and to assume the same functions and shapes as elements that are constructed from hardscape materials such as brick or stone. This design approach removes the powerful aesthetic potential created by understanding and celebrating the material itself as part of the expression. Plants lose an essential expressive quality when their inherently complex form, line, and texture are subjugated by training to the simple geometric forms used for many designed landscapes. This debate has been going on for centuries, as trained plant forms are greater or lesser defining components of many regional planting design styles worldwide.

The theory of critical regionalism was developed for rapidly growing areas where imported design styles threaten to overwhelm a natural and cultural context. Therefore, the *inherent* qualities of regional plants in developing areas must be considered when making decisions about the appropriateness of using "architecturally" trained plant forms based on foreign archetypes. The trained forms are often derived from areas where they are well established regional determinants. Our enchantment with the long-held cultural gardening traditions that have evolved in countries such as Italy and France does not mean that a transference to other regions will have the same appropriate regional resonance. Formal elements will always be simpler to use for design because of their ready transferability across biomes and cultures. It is much easier to replicate the form of a trained plant than it is to understand and absorb into design methods both the unique qualities of regional plants and the complex four-dimensional relationships that create successful regional plant communities. Understanding these plants and plant communities becomes another important area of resistance against the highly imageable and facile use of plants as simple formal ordering systems in the design process. As part of critical regionalism, landscape architects are increasingly discovering and appropriating regional plants and plant communities for their creative, environmental, and ecological potentialities as design elements. We discover these potentialities by *experiencing* them in diverse regional landscapes, by *observing* their forms and character throughout a growing season and lifespan, and by continual *testing* and modification of design solutions.

Ecologically Performative Landscapes in Complex Cultural Environments

Performative theory has been applied to many facets of social theory, including economic theory, sexual orientation, and regionalism in architecture. Simply stated, it is the notion that a thing becomes what it purports to be through actions and behaviors.[4] The term is applied here to landscapes in complex cultural environments with environmental and ecological features that are used to enhance the environmental and ecological performance provided by the landscape. These "performative" landscapes are a response to the recognition that, with increasing development, designers can no longer separate environmental and ecological issues in "natural" areas from the places where people actually live and work—in a world with what Richard Weller describes as a "hybridized, denatured, co-evolving ecology of our own making."[5] As William Cronon writes:

> Idealizing a distant wilderness too often means not idealizing the environment in which we actually live, the landscape that for better or for worse we call home. Most of our most serious environmental problems start right here, at home, and if we are to solve those problems, we need an environmental ethic that tells us as much about using nature as about not using it.[6]

In a performative landscape, the designer creates what Kongjian Yu has termed "deep form . . . shaped by the interactions of inner ecological processes and human vision, which makes the underlying order visible and meaningful in human terms."[7] It is an anthropogenic nature that seeks ecological balance but recognizes that any natural ecological system in a complex urban environment is "human centered" and subject to all the decisions involved in its inception.

Weller, Yu, and many other writers agree that the developed realm is where we can have the greatest impact because, in this view, almost all wilderness areas that can be saved have already been saved. Others are pushing back by citing the terrible rise in the rate of extinctions that the current small worldwide percentage of wilderness has caused. The best estimate is that the extinction rate is currently approximately 1,000 times the pre-industrial revolution background rate. E. O. Wilson (1929–2021) wrote a very compelling and readable book on the subject of the current mass extinction called *Half Earth: Our Planet's Fight for Life*.[8] Wilson was a leader as a public intellectual promoting the subject of his most famous book, *Biophilia* (which means "a love of living things"), since the time of Rachel Carlson in the early 1960s. Wilson, like Aldo Leopold, advocated for ecology and ecological education; he understood that we will not grieve for the loss of something that we don't know or understand. In *Half Earth*, Wilson makes the case for raising the approximately 17 percent of Earth's surface that is currently protected (25% if marine areas are included) to approximately 50 percent so that natural ecosystems can survive and evolve in perpetuity.[9] This idea dilutes the more convenient notion, often written about by landscape architects, that people are an intrinsic part of nature. This idea is certainly true for dense cultural environments, but it is not working to sustain global ecological diversity in the current mass-extinction. Landscape architects can help preserve a 50 percent ecological set-aside by developing it very carefully for ecotourism and other rigorously selected human uses. Still, the primary concern of the profession, alongside other design professions, must be the current 83 percent that is developing and is not protected—the portion that has the greatest effect on the ecological crisis that is outlined in Wilson's book. Landscape architects and other design professionals continue to justify exotic species without sufficient regard for the massive human-caused extinction rate that these invasive specifies amplify. The push-back against native plants has even included comparisons between a desire to keep exotic species out and a desire to keep immigrants out.[10] We must be diligent in both practice and in writing to advocate for *both* improved regional ecological function in developed areas and a smaller human footprint in much larger natural areas. The worldwide habitat loss just between 2000 and 2012 was approximately 579,153 square miles—the area equivalent of two entire states of Texas or almost 2,000 New York Cities.[11] A 2019 report by the UN Intergovernmental Science-Policy Platform on Biodiversity and Ecosystem Services (IPBES) found that more than three quarters of the land-based environment on the planet has been significantly altered by human actions.[12] Therefore, it is time to discuss the *details* of transforming the profession of landscape architecture's relationship to bringing ecology into designs and not just the ideology that motivates people to seek solutions. Borrowing from Al Gore, I refer to this imperative as an even *more* inconvenient truth.

Critical regionalism and this research primarily address the human arena. Ian McHarg also prioritized this in his introduction to the 25th anniversary edition of *Design with Nature* by selecting for analysis "arenas of human dominance."[13] McHarg felt strongly that we can't allow the instinct to find nature, as exemplified by the popular desire by many to move out of cities and into sprawling suburban areas, to become the mechanism that destroys nature.[14] The difficult and multivalent arenas of aesthetics and creativity are also included here and not just the more quantifiable aspects of physical sciences to which McHarg purposefully delimited his highly influential work.

The projects presented in this chapter take an approach to environmental benefits with a design of human-created nature that is self-examining and self-questioning of the motives, materials, and effects on regionalism created by plants and natural systems. This parallels, but in many ways is more complex than, the approach of critical regionalism design that focuses on hardscape materials in the landscape, such as brick, stone, and concrete, or in building architecture. Hardscape materials and plants both address environmental effects, including the carbon footprint of the material. Plants, however, have a much more direct impact on the often neglected but increasingly critical area of ecology. The discussion below on reconceptualizing prairies for metropolitan areas demonstrates the level of understanding required for a successful regionalist design *before* aesthetic criteria enter into the design process.

The most important issues in ecologically performative design are "practice and engagement" and not endless theories and debates.[15] While theory may set the parameters, it is the difficult and uncertain realities of practice that determine the outcomes. The examples and principles of performative landscapes in this research are extracted from designs that are on the ground and testing their assumptions every day.

Addressing the actual environmental and ecological conditions where we live and the implications of our professional designs there raises the value of movements toward future viable practices and explains why these environmental and ecological benefits are worth pursuing. Incrementalism should be a guiding principle and a refutation that one's professional practice is immune to consequences, both positive and negative. Incrementalism is relevant to the practice of landscape architecture as designers make small but impactful day-to-day decisions on landscape development that are either part of the problem or part of the solution. Peter Berg refers to the frame of mind necessary to address these actual conditions as "living in place" and "reinhabitation," as was explained in Chapter 5.[16] In aggregate, the design professions have both a tremendous opportunity and a deep responsibility to lead, as in the title of E. O. Wilson's book, *Our Planet's Fight for Life.*

Ecologically Influenced Design

Many landscape architects have difficulty determining the potentialities of regional ecological plant communities that will be most useful for their designs. Even as the public places an ever-higher priority on local ecology, it has become almost a sub-specialty. Reasons for this include:

1. Wide-ranging geographical areas of practice with highly variable plant materials in each area;
2. students who study plant materials and ecology in one region and then move to work in another region;
3. the relatively small proportion of professional services budgets devoted to plants and the resulting lower priority placed on plant knowledge by many principals of firms as well as by their clients; and
4. the green industry, which often lags in innovation related to regional ecology and the environmental footprint of plants as a national arena for sales takes precedence for business reasons.

At the same time, scientists, horticulturists, educators, designers, artists, and writers are expressing and disseminating an ever-increasing understanding of how to bring natural systems into the design process. In Texas, plant hunters such as the late Benny Simpson and the ongoing efforts of Robert J. Okennon, institutions such as the Lady Bird Johnson Wildflower Center and the Botanical Research Institute of Texas, native plant nurseries, and native-plant and environmental societies are creating voluminous amounts of information that is readily accessible through written works, lectures, educational institutions, online, and in public landscapes. There are no longer obstacles to the use of these resources sufficient to justify the environmental and ecological toll that ignoring them extracts. The expediencies of professional practice, however, do not sufficiently reward, either monetarily or with approbation, the research required to use them successfully.

In the Dallas/Fort Worth area, where I live and work, the prairie is the dominant pre-settlement ecosystem. Designing with a special sensitivity to the physical characteristics of the prairie goes back to the work of Jens Jensen and O. C. Simonds, who were leaders of the "Prairie School" of landscape architects beginning in the 1870s.[17] These landscape architects believed that one of the most important roles of designers seeking to undertake a design in the prairie is to sensitize themselves and their clients to its subtle beauty, illustrated in Figures 8.1 and 8.2. Such an education leads to the preservation of existing natural landscapes, a process which was, as stated, "more beautiful and less costly than leveling every hill and filling every ravine."[18]

A second aspect of the Prairie School was the introduction of native species into the built landscape. Jensen, Simonds, and others studied prairie remnants, forests, and transitional zones to discover not just the showiest plants, but also the more common plants that grouped themselves naturally into "communities" that could become the basis for planting design. The plants deemed suitable for cultivation were carefully photographed, both as individual specimens and in their native community associations. By the late 1890s, attention to habitat led to numerous books on gardening with native plants, and information on horticultural practices and propagation of native plants.

A third aspect of the Prairie School was the extraction of form systems from the prairie landscape and an artistic response to those systems. These landscape designers believed that a "unity of repose" and a "rightness of fit" in planting design could be achieved by studying such design elements as the forms of plant groupings in fields and forests, their massing and voids, and the patterns and repetitions they created. They focused on horizontal planes inspired by the wide "endless" horizon of the prairies. These horizontal lines were mirrored in horizontally branching plant material, wide expanses of water, and flat bedding planes of stonework. They also used the huge open spaces of the prairie to experiment with levels of enclosure and perspective effects. The strong sunlight in the prairie landscape was used to create "sun openings" as focal points in wooded areas and to create visual highlights with backlit plants (Fig. 8.2).[19]

The quote that follows was taken from the book, *Art into Landscape: Landscape into Art*, by A. E. Bye, educator and landscape architect. It echoes the attitudes of many designers, particularly in design-build firms, who use the experience of being on the site as a major focus of their design approach:

> To create effectively, the landscape architect must work outdoors to "feel" each rock and stone, the trees and vines, sand and earth, the sky and water, reflecting light and shadow, the mist, the snow and ice, the rain, the wind and the odors and the noises that are all about us.[20]

Fig. 8.2. Sun opening with Lindheimer's muhly grass (*Muhlenbergia lindheimeri*) at the Hopman residence in Dallas, Texas (2004).

In his book, Bye cites numerous specific examples of how the natural forms, ecology, and plants of a particularly beautiful place can be used as form generators for the designed landscape. Bye makes the native landscape a more readily accessible source for design inspiration by showing varied examples of how widely divergent types of native un-designed landscapes can be integrated into the built environment. He closes the book with a photographic montage of "moods" in the landscape. The examples cited of mystery, dazzle, cleanness, complexity-intricacy, delicacy-fragility, elegance, and brittleness help the designer to see, categorize, and later use regional landscape elements in new ways.

These new ways of seeing are the first step towards an environmentally and ecologically influenced ideology—critical regionalism—that uses a region's plants to their full expressive potential (Fig. 8.3).

The written works of the husband and wife team of Sally and Andy Wasowski are examples of more recent counterparts to the work of the Prairie School and the work of Bye. They, along with the poetic and beautifully photographed books by Rick Darke and many others, outline similar possibilities for ecologically based design processes in various areas of the United States.

The Wasowskis and Darke demonstrate how regionally based ideas that are useful to landscape architects have evolved out of related disciplines. The authors are not landscape architects, having come

FIG. 8.3. Brittleness is demonstrated by this dormant cottonwood forest (*bosque*) along the Rio Grande near Albuquerque, New Mexico, on Tamaya Nation land (2022).

from the professions of garden design (Sally Wasowski) and freelance writing and garden photography (Andy Wasowski and Darke). Much of their secondary research comes from the natural sciences of horticulture, botany, ecology, soil science, and range management. The ideas expressed in their books, however, are useful to landscape architects, as evidenced by the many landscape architects with projects featured in their books. As the expectations for the level of understanding by landscape architects of ecological poetics and processes rise, it will become increasingly important for landscape architects everywhere to incorporate an understanding of plants and ecology into a creative regionalist design approach. Aldo Leopold wrote about this eloquently back in 1940:

> Is it not a little pathetic that poets and musicians must paw over shopworn mythologies and folklores as media for art, and ignore the dramas of ecology and evolution?[21]

Reconceptualizing Nature

Reconceptualizing nature as part of critical regionalism's methodology is no trivial matter. It is one thing to address the visual aesthetic forms of nature in a naturalistic planting design, as part of a critical regionalism ideology, and quite another to bring ecological functioning into the design process, particularly in the urban or urbanizing areas where the vast majority of landscape architecture projects are implemented. The level of understanding required to accomplish the latter calls into question the way landscape architecture practice is presently constituted and the skill sets that will be required as the profession moves forward.

The Dallas/Fort Worth/Arlington area of North Texas is instructive for this aspect of critical regionalism in many ways. The dissipated and rapidly developing cultural context makes an understanding of cultural rules complex. The complexity is equally confounding when the use of fixed natural elements, such as individual plants, or continually evolving new ecological systems in human-made areas are considered as design components for this sprawling metropolitan area with more than 8,000,000 people that is larger than the state of Massachusetts. John Wesley Powell (1834–1902), the geologist, surveyor, and explorer, wrote about the problematic carrying capacity regarding precipitation of the DFW region and other areas of the Interior West and High Plains in their very earliest stages of development. Later, during the Depression era of the 1930s, Aldo Leopold was also concerned about the difficulty of understanding Midwestern landscapes: "The incredible intricacies of the plant and animal community . . . were as invisible and incomprehensible to Daniel Boone as they are today."[22] And Patrick Geddes famously promoted the use of biological principles to observe humans in their 'natural environment'.[23] This imperative has now flipped, and design professionals must once again become as adept at observing and appropriating the local natural environment as they have become at observing human behavior in recent years.

The impetus for developing an understanding of the natural systems in arid, semi-arid, and less temperate regions of the United States, in order to develop them more sensitively and effectively, is a key concern of design decisions for Texas, the most rapidly developing state in the United States. The problems and opportunities associated with reconceptualizing nature in North Texas clarify an understanding of the issues in other areas where integrating nature may not seem as complex and problematic.

North Texas is a non-temperate area where plants and other biota have evolved to deal with regularly occurring extreme disturbances. These disturbances include wide, and sometimes rapid, swings in temperature, long periods of drought punctuated with very intense rain events and flooding, herbivory by the largest migrating herds ever recorded (bison), tornados and hurricanes, frequent wildfires, and insect invasions. The evolutionary response to these conditions throughout the Midwest was millions of acres of prairie, ranging from the dry shortgrass upland prairies of the Intermountain West to the tall grass prairies in bottomlands that gradually transform into the great deciduous forests east of the

Mississippi River. Approximately 240,000,000 acres of these prairies were converted to farm and ranch land between 1830 and 1900, and today, less than 1 percent remains.[24]

Scientists representing many disciplines are actively working on issues related to restoring and preserving what is left of the prairies. These include botanists, ecologists, prairie and range restoration and management specialists, the entire panoply of biological scientists, and others. Many of these researchers have concluded that the most viable course of action is to preserve and to restore as many connected patches of prairie as possible in order to return to some semblance of the ecosystem that was in place before settlement by Euro-Americans. This course of action, however, does not usually address the changes that have forever transformed these landscapes, particularly the places that are rapidly evolving into metropolitan areas. Human use and aesthetics are not always part of the discussion when scientists consider landscape design and development. I have personally heard statements by highly accomplished scientists, for example, that trees do not belong in urban areas of North Texas, as they were not a historical feature of the landscape outside of riparian corridors, before Euro-American and other immigrants settled in the region during the nineteenth century.

Using prairies for planting design in metropolitan areas is, however, highly problematic. To begin with, prairies are hazardous to traverse on foot because of insects and are inhospitable to most forms of human activity. For example, there is a microscopic insect called a chigger (*Eutrombicula alfreddugesi*) that appears in the summer months. Chiggers live outdoors and pass through four life stages: egg, larva, nymph, and adult. During the early, warm days of spring, females deposit their eggs in leaf litter and damp soil. The chigger larvae (about 1/100 inch in diameter) are parasitic. Once a larva finds a host, it typically feeds for three days before dropping off to digest its meal and molt into its next life stage.[25] Unprotected people can suffer from hundreds of bites if a particularly dense infestation is encountered. Unfortunately, there is no way to tell if you have been infected until two to four hours after exposure when the itching and swelling on the skin begins. Chiggers can be controlled using an insect repellent with DEET or using sulfur as a repellent, but this requires forethought and constant vigilance and may represent a larger human health problem than the chiggers themselves. Chiggers are not life-threatening, but they are very uncomfortable and one of the elements that add to the general perception of prairies as places that are best avoided. Preference studies using photo elicitation have shown that the grasslands that were once the predominant biome of the Great Plains are one of the least popular types of natural landscapes, compared with the favorability ratings for mountains, rivers, forests, and large water bodies. Wetlands are the only type of natural landscape that is perceived as less attractive and desirable to the general population.[26]

Another problem with prairies is their general incompatibility with most human activities. What can one do in a prairie except experience the prairie by hiking on trails or study the prairie (certainly very worthwhile endeavors) or view it from a distance? There is not a way for people living in metropolitan areas to use the mix of grasses and forbs in a prairie for their day-to-day activities without trampling and defacing them. Prairies are not amenable to the heavy foot traffic encountered in urban parks. Additionally, most prairie plants need full sun; not an ideal condition for human comfort in hot areas with dangerously rising temperatures and urban heat islands. Prairies are also incompatible with the imperative to cover hard paving surfaces in urban areas with biomass for both shade and the low impact development of stormwater.

Many of the more than 200 species of plants typically found in a given mature prairie are annuals that survive the extreme disturbances in the Great Plains as seed. These seeds have strategies for widespread disbursement by gravity, wind and water, attachment to and ingestion by birds and animals, and ballistic dispersal mechanisms (as seen in the seed pods of Impatiens that burst open when touched and Ruellias that shoot their seeds like small darts when it rains). These strategies are very effective for large areas of prairie where there is room for these dispersal mechanisms to be effective. Metropolitan planting areas, however, tend to be in very small patches that are mostly edge conditions, and the edges are where aggressively reseeding exotic invasive species are most likely to take hold. The combination of exotic invasive species pushing in from the edges and the problematic dispersal systems of many of the native annuals makes a historic mix of native prairie plants only suitable for areas of sufficient size. For the smaller patches typically found in metropolitan areas, aggressive exotic annuals can outcompete the native prairie annuals, which will then quickly disappear.

The seed banks of *exotic* species in urban areas are the unfortunate result of not including aggressively reseeding *native* species, called *ruderals,* in urban planting designs. Spontaneous native urban vegetation in urban areas from the urban seed bank can be a valuable addition to urban ecology, if the ruderal native plants are given a fighting chance by including them in metropolitan planting designs.

As a response to these and other problematic attributes of prairies, landscape architects, homeowners and business owners, other types of landowners, and regulators have chosen a different direction for using plants. They are still thinking primarily in terms of aesthetics, cost/maintenance, and environmental issues, particularly water savings. The more forward-thinking apply traditional planting design criteria to new designs with the important difference of using a few Texas native plants in combination with non-native selections and cultivars of native plants, called *nativars,* and well-adapted plants from other areas of the world. The plants are chosen for low water, fertilizer, and pesticide needs, and other environmental and horticultural imperatives. The ecological value is mostly understood as that which is most immediately appealing and visible to users—primarily butterflies, bees, and birds. The native species that have co-evolved complex and perhaps unknowable interactions with the vast panoply of biota that live in and around them are largely absent from consideration. Plants from desert areas in Texas or coastal ecosystems are given the same priority in the plains because of their status as native plants within the political boundaries of Texas as opposed to the bioregions outlined in Chapter 5.

Plants that are *actually* native to a recognized biome in North Texas are sometimes referred to as "indigenous plants" to distinguish them from what are called "native plants" by many landscape architects and by the green industry in general . The idea of indigenous plants, however, is currently largely the purview of a small, relatively sophisticated cadre of native plant specialists and enthusiasts. The public, and most nurseries, still consider the entire state with its many biomes ranging from desert mountains to coastal marshes as fair game for "native" plant status and thus useful for any other part of the state.

Reconciling these two points of view—restoring complete prairie ecosystems and using Texas native and other adapted plants with a more traditional design approach— requires a reconceptualization of the natural systems of the Great Plains within a cultural context, "the very thoughts which lead to . . . design" (from the discussion on the word 'critical' in Chapter 1), that is at the core of critical regionalism thinking.[27] This reconceptualization offers an opportunity for landscape architects to apply their unique understanding of plants and their ability to use both art and science for the design process, elements that define the profession of landscape architecture. This difficult problem must first be addressed at the macro scale by finding the most appropriate native ecosystems, within a specific biome, that are the most practical and useful for the new environment, the "new nature" created by development. It must also be addressed at the micro scale by finding a successful way to constitute the details of this environment, the particular plant species, so they meet the biological, cultural, personal, and environmental goals that are at the heart of critical regionalism in landscape design and the experience of place.

Using Research to Define Aesthetically Qualified "New Urban Nature" in North Texas

Trees are highly desirable for urbanizing areas of North Texas, a state that is warming faster than most in the United States. The average increase in summer temperatures statewide from 1895–2020—a rise of 2.2°F on average for both high and minimum temperatures—is exacerbated by the growing urban heat islands that come with rapid growth.[28] The many benefits of using trees to mitigate heat and a host of other biological, environmental, aesthetic, and even sociological problems are well documented and continue to be extensively studied. Therefore, at the macro scale, a forest biome, with exceptions for sunny places such as green roofs and others, makes sense as an overall model for the cities of North Texas—despite their location in a former prairie. In North Texas, this means studying the mesic (moist) forests in the riparian corridors that surround rivers. This biome will have both canopy trees and shade-tolerant understory plants that will be compatible with building shade, tree shade, and the frequently compromised subsurface drainage that is found in the small patches of soil in urbanizing areas. The decision to use riparian forests as a model does not, however, address the most difficult element of using native ecosystems for a critical regionalism design: the difficult task of choosing which plants will be used and how they will be arranged for aesthetics while still functioning ecologically in meaningful ways as they would in a native biome.

Addressing this problem illustrates the tremendous knowledge required to understand the complexity of natural systems and to bring this type of ecological thinking into the design process. In North Texas and in many other areas of the United States and around the world, the information needed for reliable application in built projects is largely unavailable. Academic practitioners of landscape architecture can have a unique role in developing this information as the following description of a research effort I led demonstrates. The research described below was focused on plants for ecological detention structures (large-scale rain gardens) but can apply to any type of planting design in metropolitan conditions in the Great Plains or other biomes throughout the world.

The impetus for the research was a landscape project at the Botanical Research Institute of Texas (BRIT) where one design was installed and tested in a large ecological detention island between two parking bays in the parking lot of the LEED Platinum BRIT headquarters in Fort Worth, Texas. BRIT and the Fort Worth Botanic Garden share the parking lot and were struggling to find a plant palette that was more ecologically constituted than the typical ornamental native and adapted plant palette featured at the Fort Worth Arboretum. The new plant palette also required more aesthetic appeal for botanic garden visitors than the existing native prairie plants on the BRIT site (Fig. 8.4).

Fig. 8.4. Plant character in an existing parking lot at the BRIT headquarters in Fort Worth (2015).

FIG. 8.5. *Number 7* by Jackson Pollock. Enamel and oil on canvas, 53.25 x 40 inches (1952). Courtesy of the Pollock-Krasner Foundation.

The research began with a few important assumptions regarding the first round of plant selections. First, for aesthetic (regional character), environmental, and ecological reasons, only plants that are indigenous to North Texas would be used. Applying this ecological imperative with the use of indigenous plants requires the greatest commitment, as it can create the most friction with the norms of landscape development. Second, annuals would be avoided to make the plant combinations more resilient and persistent within an urban context. Third, plants must be adaptable to both low water use and to regular inundation. Fourth, and most importantly, aesthetically qualified combinations of plants would be selected that are designed to grow together in compatible but sometimes unpredictable ways in dense intermingled combinations, rather than arranging them as discrete monocultures and maintaining the arrangement over time as the planting matures. I refer to these plant groupings as "aesthetically qualified native urban polycultures." These densely intermingled polycultures can either be a design element, depending on how compellingly they are constituted, or they can be integrated with the shape of the planting beds or other structural plantings to complement or create a critical regionalism design. This approach acknowledges that a true ecological restoration is impossible in an urban condition because the forces of change and succession that develop the native communities in the first place are vastly different.

I like to think of polycultures as slow-motion action painting (see Fig. 8.5) that utilizes a palette of underlying matrix plants (think polyculture groundcovers), accent plants (like "boulders in a stream"), and the important emergent and transparent scatter plants that move your eye through the design, help unify the polyculture and add structure, character, and seasonal interest.[29] They are the planting design manifestation of the twenty-first-century focus on the four dimensional aesthetic potential of indeterminacy, here within an artistic regional framework.[30] The ten polyculture groupings produced for use at BRIT have a range of visual character from relatively subtle, low, and controlled to tall, dramatic, and exuberant (Fig. 8.6).

Fig. 8.6. Aesthetically qualified native urban polyculture at BRIT (2016). A low-edge polyculture acts as the "frame" and the grasses and grass-like native plants used in the center of the polyculture are unified by species with upright to diagonal lines, fine textures, and hummock (dome) shapes.

FIG. 8.7. Tianjin Qiaoyuan Wetland Park designed by Turenscape in association with Peking University's Graduate School of Landscape Architecture (2017).

I usually design a frame for polycultures to provide what Joan Nassauer refers to as a "cue to care."[31] The more formal frame layer that is adjacent to pedestrians prevents the polyculture from becoming too discordant from the aesthetics of people who are either afraid of wilder looking landscapes or who see them as deleterious to the image and economic development of an area. This frame can be a low border, a hedge or other "edge" plant species, or even hardscape as was done in the massive Tianjin Qiaoyuan Wetland Park in China (Fig. 8.7), where a relatively wild looking wetland species was used for phytoremediation of a heavily polluted water body, surrounded by steel, concrete and stone edges that enhance formal attributes of the urban park design.[32] The many elevated paths and other use areas make this critical, but potentially uninhabitable, green infrastructure into a heavily used park space.

The ecological detention plant research started with a list of 734 taxa, identified over a 30-year period by scientists at BRIT, growing around the more than 1,200 cattle ponds (stock tanks) at the Caddo-LBJ National Grasslands, just northwest of Fort Worth, Texas.[33] The Caddo-LBJ National Grasslands comprises 20,250 acres and is the largest publicly accessible undeveloped open space near the Dallas/Fort Worth/Arlington area.

It was a high priority in the native plants selected to have an aesthetic presence that can be subtle but makes a significant aesthetic contribution to the new plant groupings. This is where the judgment of an experienced planting designer, such as a trained landscape architect, is key. We had to be able to assess the aesthetic attributes and document them so that the species can be combined effectively to form an aesthetically qualified native polyculture (Fig. 8.6). We also needed to see good photographs of species in various stages of growth and colonization to get a good idea of their potential for the polycultures. The final consideration is critical to the ultimate success of the polycultures after installation: There must be enough horticultural information available about the indigenous plants to make meaningful decisions about their potential for success in the artificial environment of an ecological detention structure and for maintenance.

Understanding each species' mode of spread and its role as either an aggressively reseeding early successional ruderal, an increaser that spreads vegetatively by root or by air layering, and/or a stress tolerator that bounces back quickly from droughts and floods is another key to the long-term viability and resilience of any evolving synthetic ecosystem.[34] Ecological detention structures have extreme cycles of flooding and inundation, and plants must be chosen that fill in and/or survive after a flood, high winds, and other disturbances or after stress from drought in the fast-draining detention growing media. The resilience built into the native polycultures is both an attribute of regional design aesthetics and a major selling point to clients who may not place as a high a priority on the ecological value of native polycultures.

The 109 native plants selected from the original list of 734 based on the criteria above were then carefully analyzed horticulturally and aesthetically by using the 55 database fields shown in the following multilevel list:

1. Taxonomic information
    a. Family, Latin name and synonyms, common names
2. Horticultural information
    a. Habit, duration, leaf retention, aquatic?, water use, hardiness rating (according to the U.S. Department of Agriculture), preferred climate zones, light requirements, high and low PH, preferred soil description, soil moisture range, CACO3 (calcium carbonate) tolerance, heat tolerance, drought tolerance, tap root?, best installation method (pots, seed, other), mode of spread.

3. Useful aesthetic information for design.
    a. Form, texture, line, height, spread, spacing, months of leaf color and interest, autumn foliage interest/color, conspicuous flowers?, flower color (hue), fragrant flowers, months of flower interest, fruit season, fruit color, winter interest, and pictures.
4. Ecological information.
    a. Wetness index rating (according to the U.S. Fish and Wildlife Service), suitability for four main North Texas biomes, native habitat, succession, uses for wildlife, attracts, larval host, nectar source, deer resistance, RSI balance (ruderal and/or increaser and/or stress tolerator).
5. Use information
    a. Availability, sources, uses, problems/comments
6. Polyculture information
    a. Overall rating for potential polycultures, suitability as matrix, accent, and scatter plants, tested companions, polycultures used for, relative aggressiveness.

At this stage, many books on native Texas plants were used as well as Web-based resources that included university, state, and federal databases, botanical gardens and arboreta Websites, and even plant social media sites. These fields will need to be adjusted for other regions. For example, we did not look intensively at salt tolerance since we are not near a salty body of water and we rarely have ice and snow events in North Texas that result in the streets being salted.

The process of studying the large database of taxa from the Caddo-LBJ National Grasslands was interesting and revealed compelling plant species that were new to me, even though I have used native plants for planting design since the early 1990s and have been teaching native plants in the UT-Arlington MLA program since 2004. It was a wonderful way to dig into some exciting possibilities for regional character that are beyond what is currently offered in the native plant industry.

By extracting plant species from similar biomes (the LBJ Grassland Ponds) and using them in relatively large combinations compared to traditional groundcover planting designs, synthetic communities of indigenous plants are created that provide some, but certainly not all, of the environmental and ecological services provided by a community created through a full-blown restoration process. More benefits will accrue if the idea is scaled up, so that a range of native polycultures in aggregate contain a significant portion of the native plants that would have been in a given biome in a more natural condition. As of this writing, the idea that working designers can understand all of the multivariate interactions between the biota in a system of our design seems as far out of reach as a well-known thought experiment of Ian McHarg's that illustrated the complexity of creating a working system for ecological services on a space capsule more than 50 years ago.[35] Nonetheless, the positive and negative ecological effects of planting designs in dense cultural environments can be addressed, if not entirely controlled, by using indigenous plants for complex polyculture arrangements; that is, plants that come with thousands of years of co-evolved ecological relationships already built in.

Designers are also able to address cultural rules and personal creativity by tailoring the plant communities to the practical and aesthetic goals set for each project, particularly with the accent plants in the polyculture mix and the formal structure planting that may or may not be a part of the design. The expression of a region and other attributes of critical regionalism are under the designer's control without separating the key element of local ecology from other factors that allow cultural landscapes to evolve.

The control of the evolution of a polyculture through maintenance is another shift from traditional horticultural practices. The evolving and sometimes surprising emergence of a micro synthetic ecosystem requires what Piet Oudolf, a well-known designer and writer about intermingled planting design, calls "active maintenance."[36] James Corner calls this "an entrepreneurial and adaptive form of management."[37] As with the evolution of complex cultural modifiers, a creative and artistic sensibility, coupled with critical thinking and experience, will elevate the nurturing of planted spaces beyond the "passive" or purely mechanistic freezing in place of the original design graphic. Polycultures place the designer more in the position of "setting the stage" or curating the development trajectory of the designed plant assemblages. This type of management will also require the designer, or a highly trained and experienced horticulturist, to evaluate periodically the evolving plant mix in the polyculture as the plants increase, die off, move around, and intermingle. New species that enter the community will need to be evaluated and edited based on their contribution to the aesthetic and ecological contributions to the new community. These new synthetic native ecologies tend to get more complex over time with more desirable native species coming in. This is another big change from traditional planting designs in Texas that feature monocultures and exotic plants, where species tend to die out over time and the once rich and varied plant palette can be reduced to just a few species by attrition over a period of years.

The idea of using aesthetically qualified native urban polycultures may, in time, become a cultural rule in the Great Plains and other regions throughout the world. As of this writing, the idea is still emergent, and it remains to be seen if the culture of North Texas will be receptive to it. This approach is the most promising that I have personally encountered for constituting a new urban nature that features a more careful balance between aesthetics, environmental concerns, and ecology. One thing is for certain: The active involvement of landscape architects in research and implementation is the only course that will make this new cultural rule a potential solution for an environmentally and ecologically based critical regionalism in the emerging cities of the Great Plains and elsewhere.

FIG. 8.8. Olympic Sculpture Park in Seattle, Washington, showing major ecological planting typologies from the Seattle area (2018). Design/plan by Weiss/Manfredi architects with planting design by Charles Anderson, FASLA. Courtesy of Google Maps.

Critical Regionalism as a Garden Narrative in Performative Landscapes

A critical regionalism design can both educate the population of an area about the aesthetic potential of its landscape and celebrate a region to create a greater sense of belonging. A notable example that exhibits elements of critical regionalism using plants is the Olympic Sculpture Park in Seattle, Washington. The Seattle firm Charles Anderson Landscape Architecture consulted on the overall design of the park. Landscape architect Charles Anderson, FASLA, was the project's principal planting designer, and the lead designers for the overall project were Weiss/Manfredi architects based in New York City. In Fig. 8.8, the layout of the former industrial site is revealed in an aerial view with the dramatic z-shaped path transitioning down over existing rail lines from downtown Seattle to a newly restored beach on Puget Sound.

The planting scheme is conceived of as a garden narrative that passes through pockets of archetypal Northwest landscapes. These landscapes include:

1. The Valley—inspired by evergreen forests and their associated understory plants;
2. The Grove—landscape based on aspen trees and their seasonal interest;
3. The Meadow—native grasses and wildflowers; and,
4. The Shore—a reconnection to the experience and processes of shoreline in downtown Seattle.

These four areas are connected by a linking greensward of lawn and tree-lined pathways. Anderson has written that the Olympic Sculpture Park is "not intended as a restoration but instead to give people the sense of similar existing places and parks."[38] The dramatic geometry of the site and the separation and clarity of the expression of ecological zones help to both unify and defamiliarize the landscape—even through the strong influence of the sculpture placed in it. The Olympic Sculpture Park will, as it matures, add time to the list of natural form generators. The architect and educator Spyros Amourgis refers to this temporal quality as "stressing the importance of the seasons or by implication through reference to the geographic isolation and ingrained evolution of life" (Figs. 8.9 and 8.10).[39]

The Roxhill Bog in West Seattle, Washington, is another project by Charles Anderson that exhibits characteristics of critical regionalism. Urban infrastructure, the plant palette, and the whole concept of a neighborhood park have been reconceptualized (Fig. 8.11). The Roxhill Bog marks the headwaters of both the Longfellow Creek Legacy Trail and Longfellow Creek in West Seattle. During the renovation of Roxhill Park, peat was discovered under several feet of fill soil. This led to the decision to "daylight" a historic peat bog that had been covered in soil since the 1960s. The restoration of the bog was intended to improve water quality and water flow along Longfellow Creek, restore natural habitat, provide an educational resource, enhance the aesthetics of the creek, contribute to the economic revitalization of the area with an attractive amenity, and improve salmon habitat. The bog accepts untreated stormwater from both the landscape in the park and the surrounding street grid, mitigates extreme swings in flow rates, and removes silt, hydrocarbons, and other pollutants before they enter the headwaters of Longfellow Creek and flow down to Puget Sound. The new urban ecology of the Roxhill Bog has contributed to the economic revitalization of the surrounding neighborhood in a disadvantaged area of West Seattle.

A question then arises: Does a project such as the Roxhill Bog, with its relatively low "design profile," represent critical regionalism? Tsonis and Lefaivre have stated that implicit in critical regionalism is a critical rethinking of "the very thoughts which lead to . . . design and through which people use and appreciate . . . buildings."[40] In this case, the whole idea of the landscape in a neighborhood park has been rethought. Rather than being a traditional park that features mostly passive open space (lawn) and ball fields (more lawn), Roxhill Park reemerges with a natural bog area that cleans the flow into the creek

FIGS. 8.9 AND 8.10. Olympic Sculpture Park in Seattle, featuring the Valley (TOP), with the monumental steel sculpture "Wake" by Richard Serra (2019), and the Shore (BOTTOM), the first publicly accessible water near the Seattle Harbor in many years (2019).

FIG. 8.11. Roxhill Bog in Seattle, with a corner of a new soccer field on the left renovated in 2000 and 2002 (2008).

and brings a natural corridor into an inner city area of West Seattle. The Roxhill Bog in Roxhill Park is a unique response to environment that is a "soft" expression of critical regionalism; soft in the sense that it is relatively subtle and is composed of *softscape,* a term commonly used by landscape architects to refer to plants as opposed to the hardscapes of concrete, stone and other building materials. The bog is only critical regionalism in the sense that it is a *unique* response to environment that can provoke critical thinking as it did for me. If bogs become the norm at creek headwaters in Seattle, the design would no longer be as defamiliarized and the project could rightly be referred to more as environmentally constituted (green) infrastructure or ecologically performative design.

Tanner Springs Park in Portland, Oregon (Fig. 8.12) is an example of a more imageable presentation of nature in the city that is a better fit with the principles of critical regionalism. The park, designed by Atelier Dreiseitl and GreenWorks, PC opened in 2005. The internal juxtapositions of Tanner Springs Park, with their mix of art and man-centered natural features, are unique enough in the context of Portland to provoke critical thinking. The park does not have interpretive signage, which may contribute to the defamiliarization of the park as its complex biological functions intended to mitigate stormwater are easy to miss and, if they are noticed, difficult to understand. Visitors to the park can only use their experience with the design of plants in a naturalistic meadow and in a designed wetland to gain an understanding of the park's aesthetics and function. I personally found my visit to Tanner Springs Park very thought- provoking, as it triggered inquiry into the appropriateness of "boutique" natural features in dense urban areas, the balance of human use and expressions of historic natural systems, and pictorial versus aesthetic experience.[41] Tanner Springs Park has a variety of cultural ties to the Portland

Fig. 8.12. The feature meadow at the Tanner Springs Park "Park Block" in Portland, Oregon (2008).

region that go beyond the use of native plants and natural systems. These include the use of traditional Portland porphyry paving, recycled steel rails used for dramatic and highly imageable fencing material (see Fig. 4.2), and the size and shape of the park in the tradition of the Portland "Park Blocks."

The Olympic Sculpture Park, Roxhill Bog, and Tanner Springs Park illustrate two types of ecological approaches that exhibit elements of critical regionalism. The Olympic Sculpture Park and Tanner Springs Parks have bold hardscape design elements that are likely to always be defamiliarized while The Roxhill Bog will probably fade slowly from notice as it continues to mature. A discussion of how designers can encourage continued critical thinking about subtle natural features in dense cultural areas follows.

Nature/Culture Alternatives

One method to make nature visible is to design a careful and sharp delineation of the boundaries between more natural and more carefully designed areas. These juxtapositions have practical as well as aesthetic benefits for human use. The projects that are most successful in terms of human use in urbanized areas allow people to find their comfort level with natural features through nature/culture alternatives. Just as landscape architects design sun-shade alternatives and prospect-refuge alternatives, it is important to recognize that some people enjoy being immersed in natural settings, some people enjoy proximity to nature as long as they are, what they consider, a comfortable distance away, and some people best enjoy nature in a pictorial way from a distance.

In Fig. 8.13, a hard edge defines Denver Commons Park in downtown Denver, Colorado, designed by Civitas and Jones and Jones. The park is a village green for the rapidly developing LoDo (lower Denver) area. The hard edges of the park, such as the heroically-scaled stairs, will continue to provide a frame for both the naturalistic and the more carefully manicured areas that will help keep both defamiliarized as the project matures.

Fig. 8.13. A hard edge of Denver Commons Park (2006), opened in 2000, separates the lawn area on level ground (above left) from more naturalizing areas in the hillside (below). Design by Civitas and Jones and Jones architects and landscape architects, with the Arbor designed by EDSA.

A project that takes full advantage of both the time-tested idea of the garden narrative and the careful juxtaposition of landscape experiences is The Bloedel Reserve on Bainbridge Island in Washington State. The Bloedel Reserve sits on roughly 150 acres of land, with 80 acres of forest to be preserved in perpetuity. The gardens were developed over a 30-year period beginning in 1954 by Prentice and Virginia Bloedel, with the help of various landscape architects, including Richard Haag and Thomas Church. The mission statement for The Reserve states:

> The Bloedel Reserve should be regarded as a natural reserve that also possesses some of the attributes of an arboretum. Its primary purpose is the creation and maintenance of a place where people enjoy natural beauty as evidenced by plants. It will specialize in the preservation of the wildflowers, shrubs and trees native to this area and of the woods, fields and streams, which are their natural environment. The impression of raw nature is often one of chaos and confusion. Accordingly, the enjoyment of natural beauty may be enhanced by introducing some organization into the primitive confusion, but that organization should not destroy a sense of naturalness. The Reserve as a whole should be an example of man working harmoniously with nature; where his power to manage is used cautiously and wisely.[42]

The Bloedels, and the landscape architects who worked with them, had a profound understanding of the special qualities of the native landscapes of Washington. They used this understanding to manipulate a sequence of experiences that are powerful enough to provoke critical thinking and change the way nature is perceived by the large numbers of people who visit The Reserve each year. The concept of the garden narrative, as exemplified by the seminal English garden designer Lancelot "Capability" Brown (1716–1783) is the overall planning scheme, whereby the itinerary of the garden unfolds over time along a carefully designed and choreographed trail.[43] The region's prototypical archetypes—meadow, pond, and woods—are juxtaposed in a way that intensifies and defamiliarizes the experience of each zone. As Anna Maria Rilke states:

> Perhaps we are here in order to say: house, bridge, fountain, gate, pitcher, fruit tree, window, at most column, tower. But to say them, you must understand them more intensely than the things themselves ever dream of existing.[44]

The visitor sequence begins with an attractive meadow that first appears as a pleasant transitional space from the entrance and parking areas to the interior gardens. The impression of the meadow is completely changed, however, when the visitor re-emerges at the end of the visitor sequence from the deep, dark, moss-covered forest (Figs. 8.14 and 8.15). The reemergence into bright sunlight, the light color of the soft grasses, and the sheer volume of open space are so intensified as to redefine the internal conception of "meadow."

Figs. 8.14 and 8.15. Bloedel Reserve on Bainbridge Island, Washington: (top) the Meadow at Bloedel Reserve (2019) and the heightened expression of this woodland shows the rebirth of an old-growth forest (bottom) as new trees take root among logged stumps (2019).

FIG. 8.16. This reflection garden in Bloedel Reserve (2019) juxtaposes the woodland and formal geometry, provoking insights in both directions. As Laurie Olin writes, "the juxtaposition of wild and chaotic nature with the works and context of human order makes possible the creation of art of high ambition." As quoted in Laurie Olin, "Water, Urban Nature, and the Art of Landscape Design," in Frederick R. Steiner, George F. Thompson, and Armando Carbonell, eds., Nature and Cities: The Ecological Imperative in Urban Design and Planning (Cambridge, MA: Lincoln Institute of Land Policy, 2016), 397.

These kinds of juxtaposition experiences, referred to by Elizabeth Meyer and others as "hypernature", are found throughout the visitor experience at Bloedel Reserve.[45] Meyer, who has a long and distinguished career as an educator, author, and advocate for a comprehensive understanding of landscape aesthetics, wrote in her "*Manifesto for Sustaining Beauty*":

> The experience of beauty, a process between the senses and reason, an unfolding of awareness, is restorative. By extension, the aesthetic experience of hypernature is transformative . . . ; aesthetic experience can result in the appreciation of new forms of beauty that are discovered . . . because they reveal previously unrealized relationships between humans and non-human life processes.[46]

Another example of intensified and defamiliarizing hypernature is the massive natural limestone walls constructed at the Hays Medical Center in Hays, Kansas, as shown in Fig. 1.15.

In the Bloedel Reserve, the rigor with which the glen, the woods, the waterfall overlook, the Japanese garden, the moss garden, the bird refuge, and the reflection garden are executed and maintained, and the careful ordering of the spaces and transitions lead to profound experiential and critical insights into the quality and meaning of each element. The intensification and defamiliarization of the natural archetypes of the region mark The Reserve as a type of critical regionalism that is constituted from both highly naturalistic elements as well as more formal plant and hardscape detail elements that serve to unlock nature's sublime potential.

A designed space that can provoke intense critical thinking at the Bloedel Reserve is the reflection garden (Fig. 8.16). The visitor reaches this garden after a considerable amount of time traversing landscapes that impress themselves deeply by using only naturalistic forms and materials in the low light of the lush and dense canopy of the old-growth forest. Emergence into the perfect rectangular symmetry of the reflection garden's pool and hedge, surrounded by primeval forest, provokes a type of spiritual-sublime aesthetic reaction, as the two elements stimulate critical thinking about man's role within the natural context. The space would not make nearly as powerful an impression if the sequences before the emergence into the space were not as intensely naturalistic or if the juxtaposition of the formal design with naturalistic forms were not as carefully executed. It is another example of how, in critical regionalism, context is paramount: A landscape will only be memorable and provoke critical thinking in relation to the context in which it is placed.

Another element that provokes critical thinking in the reflection garden is the level of the water in the pool. Thomas Church worked with the Bloedel family over a three-year period to determine a water level for the pool that is exactly at the level of the water table at the site. The still water at the level of the water table makes "the invisible visible" and provokes philosophical inquiry and critical thinking into the interactions between soil, water, and human interventions.

Plants as Agrarian Form Generators

> While we in the United States have venerated the agricultural garden and enshrined the American farmstead as part of our heritage, we have systematically erased the agrarian elements of landscapes from our ideas of beauty in the garden. The plowed field, wind-rows, and allees admired by travelers as beautiful entrances to Palladian villas and French estates have been ignored, or derided, by garden theorists. We have gone along with the view that the landscape should be Arcadian scenery.[47]

In this excerpt from *Green Architecture and the Agrarian Garden* (1988), Barbara Solomon proposes a regionalist landscape approach that incorporates and celebrates agrarian prototypes. Solomon advocates for using the forms of crop rows, orchards, irrigation canals, and fence rows as points of departure at both the planning and the smaller site specific scale for a new "agrarian garden." The book is a poetic evocation of research by John Stilgoe at Harvard and others into the powerful cultural rules that evolve from agricultural landscapes. Stilgoe's *Common Landscapes of America: 1580 to 1845* contains prose about, historical photographs, and drawings of many agrarian prototypes that are useful as design elements and form generators, particularly for areas in early stages of development that are closer to their agrarian roots.[48]

The regional agrarian form systems are usually in place long before an area is designed by a landscape architect or other design professional. They are the landscape counterpart to the historical ranch and industrial buildings that have become so popular with regionalist architects such as the Texas firm of Lake/Flato. Agrarian gardens use the geometry of agriculture "with the same utilitarian pride in performance needed in the use of traditional building materials."[49] Solomon provides a compelling comparison between the agricultural forms derived from plants and their transformation into the more evolved forms of cities:

> Furrows deepen into streets, trees become columns, and cleared fields become plazas. Grids of orchards become the ground plans of buildings . . . Green walls reinforce inhabited corridors... Until political romantics sought to free the trees along with the people, this habit of planned order...was a model for avenues and allées, palaces and farms, parks and gardens.[50]

Lon Kaufman took this same approach one step further in his graduate research by using the "pattern language" approach of Christopher Alexander. Alexander defined a pattern as "a definite empirical relationship between a limited context, a set of forces that occur there, and the pattern that resolves those forces."[51] Kaufman traveled throughout his study area of rural Iowa and recorded and observed what he deemed the most compelling agrarian sites. The patterns of "space form" were then recorded in written, graphic, and, finally, three-dimensional model forms. These models were used as mnemonic devices to work with clients to create "new, yet indigenous, environmental possibilities."[52] These agrarian prototypes have a direct relevance to form generation on a variety of scales. The regional agrarian corollaries, developed for a variety of ecological zones and cultural variants associated with a region, are important components for critical regionalism, especially with development in working agricultural areas as opposed to redevelopment in cultural environments with more influences.

The Solana development, introduced in Chapter 5, featured an early creative use of agricultural patterning in North Texas. Rows of weeping lovegrass (*Eragrostis curvula*) were alternated with rows of Bermuda turf the width of a typical riding lawnmower (Fig. 8.17). It should be noted that this expression was more of a generic agricultural expression generated from observing the recently developed

Fig. 8.17 (top). Agricultural patterning at the Texas-Solana project in Southlake and Westlake, Texas, now removed (1996).

Fig. 8.18 (bottom). Preserved fencerow of trees at Austin Ranch, a mixed-use project in The Colony, Texas (2008).

status of the surrounding landscape rather than a response to perceived patterning in the area that was mostly ranchland at the time. Additionally, neither plant species used is native to the United States. Nevertheless, the patterns are both a defamiliarizing element, because of their use in a new formal and "high style" context, and a connection to the surrounding agricultural landscapes that were still present during the 1980s when the project was designed and built.

The example of agricultural patterning in Fig. 8.18 is more typical of the type found in ranch areas and has a more direct tie to the history of North Texas. Paul Shaw and the landscape architects at RTKL, Inc. incorporated the preserved fencerow vegetation at the Austin Ranch development into a park design. This line of trees is the only remnant left of the pre-development site after this phase of the project was almost entirely covered by many feet of fill soil.

The linear geometry of the existing trees and the formal grading that leads from the original level at the trees up to the level of the fill are powerful reminders of both the site's history and contemporary development practices. The preserved remnant can provoke critical thinking about both, especially if interpreted with signage. These types of remnants can be replete in a new landscape, although they are often overlooked and not incorporated into a design. Other examples include surviving long-lived orchard trees, such as pecan trees, as well as "wolf trees" that show their historical and old-growth status by having spreading branches where there once was sunlight, before newer saplings started growing and turned the forest into a more vertical experience. Many more examples of regional agricultural forms will reveal themselves as opportunities to be defamiliarized and used to provoke critical thinking about the cultural plant history of a region if this type of site analysis becomes a normative part of the design process as it was for the Austin Ranch project.

Adapting Garden Styles to Regions

There are myriad planting design styles from every region of the planet and thousands of years of history that can be used as elements of universal civilization for implementing critical regionalism in design. Similarly, any personal style can be used if it is adapted to an area's expressive cultural referents and/or natural, environmental, and ecological features. Horticultural adaptation is especially important in non-temperate areas such as the Southwest United States and northern Mexico.

The Chandler Fashion Center near Phoenix, Arizona, opened in 2001 and is a good example of a creative planting design style that is enhanced by its careful adaptation to the region and the site (Fig. 8.19). The planting design by Alan Franz, ASLA (then with Mesa Design Group, Inc.) features native plants from the Sonoran Desert and other well-adapted species, including more than 2,000 cacti.[53] The planting design for the Fashion Center utilized a formal graphic or patterning approach that was purposefully not naturalistic. This design style, a signature of Mesa Design Group at the time, was tailored

Fig. 8.19. Chandler Fashion Center in Chandler, Arizona, showing a formal patterning of native and adapted desert vegetation (2002).

to the region by taking advantage of the sculptural forms inherent in desert plants. The result is a well-adapted planting design that expresses both the personal style of the designers and the artistic qualities of Sonoran Desert plants. The Chandler Fashion Mall exemplifies how personal garden styles can be adapted to a region and be used to create a type of critical regionalism while still addressing a client's requirements for commercial development. It should be noted that in this chapter, I focus on the *intentions* of the designers and not the current state of the projects as of this writing, which is subject to the vagaries of maintenance, weather, and redevelopment, among other factors.

An earlier and more highly celebrated example of using desert plants for both their potential as formal elements and their expressive regional artistic potential is the South Promontory Cactus Garden at the Getty Museum in Los Angeles, California, designed by Olin Partnership (Fig. 8.20). The vertiginous cliff-like heights of the walkways, juxtaposition of colors and sculptural forms, and spectacular

Fig. 8.20. The South Promontory Cactus Garden by Olin Partnership at the Getty Museum in Los Angeles, California (2011).

distant views of Los Angeles make a visit to this garden a very memorable and thought-provoking endeavor. While the *expression* of the California Desert is enormously powerful, an opportunity to express the ecology of Los Angeles is missing since the plants that are actually native to the Los Angeles area are not used.[54] The plant palette reflected the Olin Partnership's practice of experimenting "with alternative Mediterranean and arid-zone plants from elsewhere" rather than using locally native or near-native species and the opportunity for a more regionalist design.[55]

Fig. 8.21. Glass art by Dale Chihuly at the Desert Botanic Garden in Phoenix, Arizona (2014).

At the Desert Botanic Garden in Phoenix, Arizona, a different technique was used to celebrate and defamiliarize the local flora. The Garden commissioned the glass artist Dale Chihuly to create site- specific and plant-specific glass sculptures that have been carefully placed to draw the visitor into-engagement and reflection with the sculptural forms of the plants and surrounding natural landscape (Fig. 8.21). Chihuly has completed this type of garden exhibit in a variety of locales, ranging from his hometown of Seattle to Chicago, Dallas, and London.[56] The careful integration of regionalism into these exhibits creates an expressive bond that makes them very popular with garden visitors and thus very lucrative for the museums. The defamiliarized artistic interpretation of the regional desert flora is, as Kristina Hill states, a way to share what the designers "have perceived, in its terrifying sublimity, with people who might see a [desert] design or plan as poetic or frightening or ethically unacceptable and embrace that multiplicity of readings."[57]

The Chandler Fashion Center, Getty South Promontory Cactus Garden, and Desert Botanic Garden landscapes are frequently visited public places that helped transform the cultural rules for gardens in the region by taking full advantage of the sculptural forms of desert vegetation. These expressive plants have become a celebrated part of the regionalism of the area and have moved out of "boutique" designs for residential gardens. They are now increasingly in the public realm where people who approve

FIG. 8.22. Thames Barrier Park in London, UK, showing regionally derived trained plant forms and neotechnic beauty in the flood-barrier structures behind them that strongly suggest helmets of a line of Anglo-Saxon warriors protecting the city of London (2025).

large-scale civic and corporate projects no longer see them as controversial (because they once were different). The artistic and defamiliarized planting designs created by the many landscape architects who first perceived and utilized the expressive and creative potential of the plants are helping the public to celebrate the unique qualities of the desert rather than lamenting that the desert does not conform to a lost, idealized, and fondly remembered landscape from another part of the world.

Regional Trained Plant Forms

The final projects presented in this chapter illustrate regional adaptation using trained plant forms. In Fig. 8.22, I show a project that demonstrates how traditional garden plants that would otherwise be non-regional are used to create a unique regionally derived, site-specific form at the famous Thames Barrier Park in London, England. The plants are trained as sculptural elements and used in much the same way that any landscape material, such as wood, concrete, or stone, would be used. The plants are also used for their inherent, traditional gardenesque appeal following in the long tradition of English gardens. Planting designs that have the "universal style" of sculptural forms or inspiration from art can accrue the expressiveness of regionalism by the use of exotic plants that have been absorbed into common use by a local population, sometimes referred to as heritage plants. This design at Thames Barrier Park, by landscape architects Groupes Signes of France

Fig. 8.23. A computer model of a native and adapted planting design at an intersection in the Timarron subdivision in Southlake, Texas. The design and rendering are by David Hopman, ASLA (2011).

and the London office of Patel Taylor architects, celebrates both the former Prince Regent Dock at the site and the poetics of water movement with a creative, defamiliarized, and highly memorable regional design.

In Fig. 8.23, I show a much simpler project, more typical of everyday work by landscape architects, that combines the use of regionally resonant plants with trained forms that make the design intelligible at both the pedestrian and the automobile scale. The design responds to the movement and geometry of the intersection's entrance to a subdivision in Southlake, Texas. It is evocative of the logo of the project (a butterfly) and uses both indigenous plants native to North Texas, "Texas native" plants that are not native to North Texas but are native to the state, and adapted plants from around the world. For example, blue mistflower (*Conoclinium coelestinum*) is featured as an indigenous plant that times its fall bloom so that it coincides with the fall migration through the area of the beloved monarch butterflies (*Danaus plexippus*). This "seasonal interest" draws immediate attention to the landscape and encourages people to stop and experience it in real time.

Trained forms are only briefly touched on here to emphasize their potential relevance to a critical regionalism ideology. The high maintenance budget, compromised ecological value, and the large carbon footprint required to maintain them often lowers their value as a strategy if trained forms are scaled up and applied to an entire region. Additionally, trained forms can easily fall prey to monotonous and placeless functional design, form-based academicism, facile eclectic and otherwise non-regionally integrative designs, and kitsch that literally copies historic precedent.

Conclusion

The Denver Botanic Garden was among the first gardens in the United States to emphasize native plants and to promote environmentally responsible practices. The four key values from its mission statement—"transformation, relevance, diversity, and sustainability"—have resonance with the theory and practice of critical regionalism.[58] Planting design will continue to gain importance as designers combine a culturally and artistically constituted regionalism with a regionalism that also supports both environmental and ecological services, especially in an era when sustainability is an increasing imperative. As Elizabeth Meyer has written:

> We are sustained by reducing, editing, and doing less harmful things. But we are also sustained through abundance, wonder and beauty. The performance of a landscape's appearance and the experience of beauty should have as much currency in debates...as the performance of its ecological systems.[59]

Any style of planting design can be considered for use as an element of universal civilization and/or part of a personal design aesthetic. English, French, Italian, Chinese, Japanese, Minimalist, New American, and many other garden traditions from across the United States and around the world have been successfully adapted for new regions and used as part of a critical regionalism methodology.

Plant materials have a special place in any consideration of landscape architecture and critical regionalism. They are the most complex and most interesting materials that landscape architects can take advantage of to create expressive and creative designs that will be viable into the future. With more than 24,000 documented plant species growing without human intervention in North America alone, the possibilities for unique expressions are almost limitless.[60]

The examples presented in this chapter are but a brief introduction to the many fascinating and complex issues involved in this important area of landscape design. My hope is that landscape architects and designers of the built environment will take ever-increasing advantage of the expressive and environmental potential of plants as the theory of critical regionalism continues to evolve and mature. Due to professional time constraints, designers must take an incremental approach to many important aspects of our work without a full understanding of all the implications of our actions. We may be only marginally aware of environmental psychology or many of the social implications of our designs, and yet that does not stop us from doing the best we can within the scope, time, and resources allocated to a project. Similarly, we must not allow gaps in our knowledge related to the use of plants to become an impediment to our best efforts towards bringing both art *and* nature into developed areas, thereby providing an important new step towards sustainable and inspirational designs expressive of critical regionalism.

Conclusion:
The Enduring Value of Critical Regionalism

> A proposition that intends to be more than a passive materialization refuses to reduce that same reality, analyzing each of its aspects, one by one; that proposition can't find support in a fixed image, can't follow a linear evolution.... Each designer must catch, with the utmost rigor, a precise moment of the flittering image, in all its shades, and the better you can recognize the flittering quality of reality, the clearer your design will be.
>
> —Alvaro Siza y Viera[1]

Richard Ingersoll has written that critical regionalism is not only "difficult to understand (because of its dialectical premises) but nearly impossible to visualize . . . for it is not a style; one cannot unequivocally recognize a critical regionalist work."[2] Whether this is an inherent result of the process of critical regionalism or merely the *zeitgeist* of being too close to a contemporary trend to see the style (as was the case with modernism in its early years) remains to be seen. Nevertheless, if critical regionalism is going to continue its move beyond the bounds of academic writing and architectural criticism and into the mainstream of designed works and design thinking by landscape architects, the practical methods and principles that lead to a critical regionalism design must be explored.

Creating any systematic approach to critical regionalism threatens to undermine its original premise as a landscape architect's *unique* response to region. Kristine Woolsey describes the dangers as threefold.[3] The first danger is pursuing a regionalist design without an ideological position. The Gaylord Texan in Figs. 1.12 and 1.13, for example, evokes an image of Texas without a search for knowledge, a rigorous examination of Texas landscapes, or a universal design ideal that arises from the ideological position of the designer. Therefore, the design is unable to rise above illusion.

The second danger is the generation of a "superficial shared vision." The Gaylord Texan design has not taken into account the unique social patterns of the people in North Texas that could have made the design transcend the level of derivative scenographic images from across the state. The Gaylord Texan will influence the creation of similarly trite landscape expressions that create the illusion of truth. The commercial success of Gaylord properties in Texas, Tennessee, Maryland, and Florida continues to push commercial development in this culturally regressive direction, as Disney has done since the period after World War II. The past is taken as a menu of landscapes to copy rather than as a continually evolving context for new creative works.

The third danger, according to Woolsey, is a regionalism without concern for available contemporary technology. She states that technology creates connections both to the time when the project was constructed and to the popular culture that produced the technology. While the Gaylord Texan uses contemporary technology for construction of the landscape, the technology is not reflected in the forms of the "stage set" of historic structures. Frank Welch has also written about the dangers of ignoring contemporary technology and focusing on "bucolic structures" with the consequent loss of a connection in time. The resulting design may be "sentimental, anachronistic, irrelevant, a pretense concerned with effects, not essences."[4] Good architecture must be responsive to "time, place and context," but it must also transcend "time, place, and context" to deliver an original design that is successful on many levels.[5]

The Italian architect and educator Renzo Bassani expressed his concern regarding the development of a systematic approach by writing that "the search for a common denominator, a super method, could result in the formation of a new 'oppressive universal architectural order' . . . [or] might deteriorate into a mere list of approaches."[6] He believes that, with the demise of Modernism as the paradigm for design, "all the rational, social, and methodological" norms should be replaced by a pervasive eclecticism that draws inspiration from outside of the field of architecture. He is interested in using the social sciences to understand how architecture can be reinterpreted in terms of the usage patterns of a given population, rather than using it to play with "technologies and historic or modern forms."[7] Nonetheless, the utility of pervasive eclecticism for cultural integration and appropriation has been shown to be very problematic in the discussion on postmodern design, unless it is modified by expressive regional content. Additionally, creative regionalist design does not need to be oppressive and restrictive to the educated sensibilities of designers, as the local is always enriched by the universal and personal creativity in critical regionalism.

Keith Eggener has written that any theory that attempts to establish currency throughout the world will necessarily devolve into a "facile and misleading mechanism," due to the evolution and dissemination of the theory from one social milieu to others not complicit in its creation.[8] This view reinforces the value of the resistance and the rigor required to stay aesthetically tuned in to the various regions where professional practice may lead. It also reinforces the value of reconceptualization, lest critical regionalism revert to the universalizing tendencies that were such a strong impetus for the development of the concept in the first place. There has been a well-documented shift in thinking away from the concept of a steady state of nature punctuated by disturbance towards "the notion of ecosystems characterized by flux and change," as Anne Whiston Spirn declares.[9] Similarly, developed areas are culturally in a state of cultural flux and any theory that guides design decisions must both lead and react to this evolution. Eggener also wonders if critical regionalism is so dialectic, personal, and broadly applicable that it no longer has any meaning or can hold together as a theory of process. The contention here is that critical regionalism is not a theory of process but, rather, is an ideology—a philosophical posture and habit of mind—that sets the priorities for a variety of subsequent design processes. To

Fig. C.1. Landscape architect Martha Schwartz, FASLA, is a master at extracting shapes from regional influences and running with them, as she did with the rounded forms of barrel cactus at the Mesa Arts Center in Mesa, Arizona. Also see Figs. C.2 and C.3 on page 262.

hold critical regionalism together as an ideology, designers will need to uncover within themselves the elements described in this research that are the most aesthetically resonant and practical, thereby establishing the continuing relevance of the theory to their professional practice.

Another danger is playing with regional forms or even defamiliarizing them in a facile and superficial way. In such a design, the designer may not have the emotional connection to the regional design element required to achieve a superior result, because it has not manifested in their personal design aesthetic. For example, at the Mesa Arts Center Martha Schwartz successfully brought regional inspiration into her well-developed design method of using repetition and creative transformation of simple forms in an artistic landscape design process (Figs. C.1-C.3). The opposite is also true where a more facile process may lead to an overly individualized design expression.

The critical regionalism designer strives to create landscape designs that are not perceived as merely eccentric and overly dissonant with the aesthetics of the end users; rather, they are just creative *enough* within the context and sensibilities of a given area to be sufficiently interesting to be noticed and then absorbed back into the range of what is understandable and can be appropriated by a population as a part of their regional identity. The local cultural conditions must be "ripe" for both the evolution of the creative act that produced the innovative landscape, and "the culture [that] is poised to accept

Figs. C.2 and C.3. At the Mesa Arts Center in Mesa, Arizona, Martha Schwartz created abstract designs of a desert arroyo typical of the region. Photographs courtesy of Martha Schwartz Partners.

the innovation."[10] At some level, the designs must make sense and mesh with a perceivable, if obscure, context to create a mutuality of acceptance of an idea among the designer, the client, and the people who experience the landscape or building. The native Californian architect Willian Wurster, the acknowledged leader of the regional Bay Area style from the 1920s to the 1940s, declared a simple and practical summation of this mutuality of acceptance from the standpoint of an active regionalist practitioner:

> Use the site, the money, the local materials, the client, the climate to decide what shall be. See with eyes to the front, be appropriate in what you do, do not be barbaric in a conventional neighborhood, or unnecessarily prim in Bohemia.[11]

When design parameters are constantly changing, as they are in today's world, reconceptualization itself must be a constant process.[12] The true meaning of a style is then understood as "meaning of today, which means it will be different tomorrow."[13] Designers enter the scene, develop their talent, and pass it on. What endures is the legacy of their best built works and the underlying theory and ideology they leave behind that endures in our collective memory as designers. The long continuity of design experience always informs and challenges contemporary work. Paul Ricoeur refers to this as the phenomenon of accumulation whereby, for good or for ill, "nothing is lost, and everything accumulates" to develop civilization and our social heritage.[14] The critical regionalism designer celebrates and utilizes this accumulation without ever conceding the imperative to move design aesthetics forward with an individualized response to the best design precedents and regional design inspirations. A contrasting take on moving culture forward is the need to rehabilitate landscapes scarred by history. As the landscape and the culture develop, reinvention will adapt to the new regional realities and not overly celebrate a dysfunctional past in a sentimental way, as would be the case in romantic regionalism or a purely historicist style.[15]

For all the reasons above, critical regionalism is better described as a set of design approaches and priorities, not as a settled style or another formal recognizable "ism." The ideology of critical regionalism as described in Chapter 1 points the designer in creative and culturally integrative directions. The design is then consummated using the personal strategies that the designer finds most compelling at various stages throughout a career. The endlessly complex and fascinating issues involved in the understanding of regions, creative seeing of districts, site elements and ecology, and using the four-part aesthetic to inform the design process are combined with traditional tenets of critical regionalism such as defamiliarization, resistance, and always keeping in mind both the local and the universal. This seems like common sense to many designers, and yet there are far too many examples of designs that ignore many of these key components. As Kristine Woolsey states:

> The existence of a focused architectural Ideology as a point of beginning, modified by factors of people, places, and events, allows customized solutions to become part of a greater artistic discourse. The problem then becomes the reconciliation of high art with popular culture, and this is the real strength of critical regionalism as a theory of process.[16]

Kristine Woolsey also believes that the only constant in the process of critical regionalism is the quality of the ideological position of the architect and that this ideological position will necessarily evolve over time through practice, experience, and the evolution of the international debate of the profession. Woolsey's starting position is high art. However, depending on the type and scale of the project and the personal sensibilities of the designer, the ideological position could also be, for example, political, environmental, behavioral, or historic. The ideology of the designer, as driven by critical regionalism, then becomes a means to facilitate resistance as well as a practical means towards an ideological consummation of the design. Personal ideology is always informed and modified by influences of regional and contemporary culture in a critical regionalism process. The four-part aesthetic is used to ground ideology with human experience, the evolution of culture, and appropriation of the environment as designers are presented with an endless array of fashionable new "isms" throughout their careers.

Some examples of personal ideologies available to garden designers have been listed by Brenda Brown writing in *Landscape Journal*. The personal regionalist ideological priorities are referred to as "intentionality." All of these very practical intentions can be subsumed into critical regionalism as applied to garden design:

> Is he or she trying to sell a myth, reveal a landscape's essence, respond in a unique personal way to the environment, supply a collective emblem, arrive at a stunning image, provide a drama, order a stage set, or a background, or just a project that works? And what difference does this finally make to regional garden design?[17]

The list of intentions above would certainly be revised based on the evolution of regional priorities in the 2020s, when this research was published, as opposed to the 1990s when Brown published her article in *Landscape Journal*. For example, there is no mention of diversity, equity, and inclusion, or specific reference to the environmental and ecological concerns that have become a much higher priority and a focus of the personal ideological position of many designers. This illustrates the importance of continuously adapting intentionality within any ideological position that drives design decisions.

FIG. C.4. The partnership of Studio Outside and Ten Eyck Landscape Architects showed the value of both regional and universalizing influences in a large healing garden for the new Parkland Hospital in Dallas, Texas (2015). The aesthetics of the bland modernist glass and metal facades of the billion-dollar hospital are enhanced with powerful regional pedestrian-scale landscape experiences. The creative use of the universal spiral form, juxtaposed with bands of multicolored paving flowing through the garden, is anchored into the local population by familiar regional limestone and native plants that celebrate the Blackland prairie ecoregion where the hospital resides. Environmental psychology further enhances the utility of social spaces in this highly imageable regional landscape. Courtesy of Arland Kennedy. Also see Figs. C.5 and C.6 on page 266.

Keeping the Design Process Fresh

Overcoming the unfamiliarity of regional modifiers in diverse areas leads to completely new patterns of design thinking and creative responses that encourage designers to continually reinvent themselves in surprising ways. The work of design becomes a continually unfolding creative story for both the designer and end user. Obstacles become opportunities, and stale and routine ideas are given new life. An example is Parkland Hospital (Figs. C.4.–C.6.) where the universal and iconic form of a spiral is transformed into a large therapeutic garden by using regional elements. This new vision may capture the public imagination precisely because they "get" the creative use of familiar elements. It may, alternatively, lead to a design that transcends the regional elements and becomes accessible

Figs. C.5 and C.6. The enormous mechanistic and largely featureless buildings in the Parkland Hospital complex have been transformed for both outside users and for people viewing the gardens from inside the buildings (2015). The therapeutic benefits of the landscape for patients, workers, and visitors would be greatly diminished if Parkland Hospital was surrounded by parking lots or by a simple, forgettable landscape of lawns and simple non-native shrubs and trees as other buildings in the large medical complex are. Courtesy of Arland Kennedy.

as an artistic statement to people from outside the area. This can then lead to the design becoming part of the universal design language (referred to here as universal civilization) appropriated by both visitors and local inhabitants and subsequently used as a point of departure for other creative transformations.

Many cultural expressions can be enumerated that started out decidedly regional and were subsequently adopted by diverse areas. For example, early forms of American jazz, which is "part Congo tom-tom, part missionary revival hymn, part French folk song, and part Spanish dance music," was a unique product of the polyglot culture of New Orleans at the turn of the twentieth century.[18] This highly region-specific expression, created using international elements, has subsequently spawned music ranging from Tin Pan Alley to rock-and-roll, to Brazilian Samba. These regional adaptations are themselves mixtures of jazz (now a part of universal musical civilization) and regional folkloric musical elements. Samba started as a blend of the African percussion ensembles known as the "Batucada" with American jazz. A similar process was at work in regional classical music of the early twentieth century. Many of the best-known composers of the period traveled to Paris to study the latest techniques of musical composition and harmony. They then applied those theories to the national folkloric traditions of their home countries. These composers include such musical luminaries as Igor Stravinsky (Russia), Astor Piazzolla (Brazil), Zoltán Kodály (Hungary), George Gershwin (United States), and Manuel Defalla (Spain). The examples of regional jazz and classical musical traditions reinforce the value of *both* the education and skill required to create something meaningful and lasting and the immense creative potential made possible by using regional influences to enrich the existing established conventions.

The Promise of Critical Regionalism

Critical regionalism is a celebration of place—of the history, values, and sensibilities of a particular period and the capabilities and vision of a designer. It promotes the development of local culture, ecological balance and, ultimately, the quality of life for the end users. Critical regionalism enhances "the practical, the social, and the educative."[19] The expressive quality of critical regionalism design transcends both the prosaic and art for art's sake.

A critical regionalist bent puts a high value on individual places. Without this value, the places are much more likely to be used destructively from an environmental and ecological standpoint. Without this the designs may also exhibit a lack of meaning that research has shown is associated with psychopathology or fall prey to a superficial, academic, commercial, or purely decorative design styles. As John Dewey stated:

> It represents the memories, hopes, fears, purposes, and sacred values of those who build . . . Apart from cerebral reveries, it is self-evident that every important structure is a treasury of storied memories and a monumental registering of cherished expectancies for the future"[20]

Fig. C.7. Thorncrown Chapel near Eureka Springs, Arkansas (2012).

Thorncrown Chapel near Eureka Springs, Arkansas (Fig. C.7), is a powerful example of Dewey's "sacred values" and a masterful juxtaposition in architecture of formal design with the experience of regional natural elements. It is one of the most successful and celebrated works by E. Faye Jones, the Arkansas regionalist architect and disciple of Frank Lloyd Wright.[21] The natural materials, vertical forms, complex decorative wooden beams and rafters, and 425 windows trigger powerful, immersive, emotional and spiritual reflections on our relationship to architecture and the natural world. Since 1980, when the chapel opened, more than seven million people have visited this sanctuary, which is surrounded by a woodland setting and sits atop more than 100 tons of native stone and colored flagstone. Those visitation numbers speak volumes to the lure and influence of creative regional design.

Critical regionalism is a very versatile ideology, as the examples in this book show. It is a way forward in its own right and not just a critique of the wide variety of ills that can be summed up as "bad design." Critical regionalism, if it is to be a vibrant and ongoing cultural enterprise, is not a facile use of the most easily available local materials or the simple copying of regional styles of design that were appropriate for their day; rather, it is resilient, continuously adaptive, and open to continuing influences from other parts of the world and to the creativity of individual designers that anchor it in the present. Critical regionalism is a framework for designers that maximizes what Nina-Marie E. Lister refers to as the *transformative capacity* of regions as the regions undergo ever-accelerating waves of cultural, environmental, and ecological changes: a lifelong quest to design landscapes that are "contextual, legible, nuanced, and responsive."[22]

In this book I have endeavored to show the value of the theory of critical regionalism in positioning landscape architecture to embrace a wide range of regional and aesthetic issues that apply at a variety of scales. I have shown the value of *expressive* as opposed to merely creative design both to the development of personal design aesthetics and to the evolution of regions and the inhabitants who dwell in them. The new presentation of critical regionalism set forth in this book is a product of contemporary thinking, as it applies to landscape architecture and not the historical theory as it was originally set forth. My expanded definition, however, is in concert with the reconceptualization that is a key element of the writing on the subject.

As a landscape architect and as a professor, I have personally found critical regionalism to be the most helpful framework I have encountered to understand our purpose as designers in society at large. It is the most useful and flexible "ism" to begin to resolve the myriad claims on the design process beyond the purely utilitarian. Just as practitioners have economic pressures and personal proclivities that can work against a critical regionalism ideology, academics have career pressures to reinvent new design theory in order to establish their academic bona fides. The contention here is that critical regionalism is a practical ideology that can inform these new 'isms' and should, therefore, be an important component of design thinking going forward. The critical regionalism theory presented here reinforces the importance of the concept and raises important issues that need further research. It would certainly be naïve to believe that *any* design theory would have universal applicability for all time and in all places without continuing research and renewal. The theory will continue to evolve with the changing priorities of the designers who put the theory into practice and the writers who experience and critique their work. I look forward to a dialogue about the ideas in this book and to its expansion and combination with other regionalist design theories.

Notes

List of Acronyms

ASLA	American Society of Landscape Architecture
CELA	Council of Educators in Landscape Architecture
FASLA	Fellow of the ASLA
FCSLA	Fellow of the Canadian Society of Landscape Architects
PE	Professional Engineer

The epigraphs on page 5 are from (top to bottom) Elizabeth Meyer, "Sustaining Beauty: The Performance of Appearance," in Frederick R. Steiner, George F. Thompson, and Armando Carbonell, eds., *Nature and Cities: The Ecological Imperative in Urban Design and Planning* (Cambridge, MA: Lincoln Institute of Land Policy, 2016), 119–47, as quoted on 130; Juhani Pallasmaa, "Tradition and Modernity: The Feasibility of Regional Architecture in Post-Modern Society," in Vincent B. Canizaro, ed., *Architectural Regionalism: Collected Writings on Place, Identity, Modernity, and Tradition* (New York, NY: Princeton Architectural Press, 2007), 128–39, as quoted on 133; and John Fraser Hart, "The Highest Form of the Geographer's Art," *Annals of the Association of American Geographers*, Vol. 72, No. 1 (March 1982): 1–29, as quoted on 1.

FOREWORD

1. Aldo Leopold, *A Sand County Almanac and Sketches Here and There* (New York, NY: Oxford University Press, 1949), 197.
2. Lady Bird Johnson, Wildflower Center Board of Directors Meeting (May 9, 2003).
3. Paul Sears, "Ecology—A Subversive Subject," *BioScience*, Vol. 14, No. 7 (July 1964): 11–13, as quoted on 11.
4. Kurt Lewin, "Psychology and the Process of Group Living," *Journal of Social Psychology*, Vol. 17, No. 1 (1943): 113–31.
5. Aldo Leopold, "The Farmer as a Conservationist," *American Forests*, Vol. 45, No. 6 (June 1939): 294–99, 316, and 332.
6. See Nina-Marie Lister, "Resilience Beyond Rhetoric in Urban Planning and Design," in Frederick R. Steiner, George F. Thompson, and Armando Carbonell, eds., *Nature and Cities: The Ecological Imperative in Urban Design and Planning* (Cambridge, MA: Lincoln Institute of Land Policy, 2016), 303–25.
7. J. B. [John Brinkerhoff] Jackson, "The Need to be Versed in Country Things," *Landscape*, Vol. 1, No. 1 (Spring 1951): 1–5.

PREFACE

1. Kenneth Frampton, "Ten Points on an Architecture of Regionalism: A Provisional Polemic," in Vincent B. Canizaro, ed., *Architectural Regionalism: Collected Writings on Place, Identity, Modernity, and Tradition* (New York, NY: Princeton Architectural Press, 2007; originally published in 1987 in *Center 3: New Regionalism*, 20–27), 374–85, as quoted on 380.
2. I offer the following terms to mentally swap out for anyone who can't abide the term critical regionalism: aesthetic regionalism, comprehensive regionalism, cosmopolitan regionalism, creative regionalism, experiential regionalism, ideological regionalism, inclusive regionalism, informed regionalism, knowing regionalism, perceptive regionalism, receptive

regionalism, reflective regionalism, thoughtful regionalism, and universal regionalism.

INTRODUCTION

1. Steven C. Bourassa, *The Aesthetics of Landscape* (London, UK: Belhaven Press, 1991).
2. Christopher Wilson, *The Myth of Santa Fe: Creating a Modern Regional Tradition* (Albuquerque: University of New Mexico Press, 1997).
3. Spyros Amourgis, *Critical Regionalism: The Pomona Meeting Proceedings*, edited by Spyros Amourgis (Pomona: The College of Environmental Design, California State Polytechnic University, 1991).
4. David D. Hopman, "Toward a Critical Regionalism for Rapidly Developing Areas of Texas" (Master's thesis, University of Texas at Arlington, 1998).
5. John Dewey, *Art as Experience* (New York, NY: Perigree Books, 1980; originally delivered as the first William James Lecturer at Harvard in 1934 and first published in 1952 by Minton, Balch and Company of New York City), 242.
6. Ibid.

CHAPTER 1

1. Patrick Geddes, as quoted in Volker M. Welter, *Biopolis: Patrick Geddes and the City of Life* (Cambridge, MA: The MIT Press, 2002), 82.
2. Steven C. Bourassa, *The Aesthetics of Landscape* (London, UK: Belhaven Press, 1991); and Kenneth Frampton, "Prospects for a Critical Regionalism," *Perspecta*, Vol. 20 (1983): 147–62.
3. Alexander Tzonis and Liane Lefaivre, "The Grid and the Pathway: An Introduction to the Work of Dimitris and Suzana Antonakakis, with Prolegomena to a History of the Culture of Modern Architecture," *Architecture in Greece*, Vol. 15 (1981), 164–78.
4. Frampton, "Prospects for a Critical Regionalism."
5. Ben Wescott, "Beijing's population falls for first time in 20 years," *CNN* (January 24, 2018); online at https://www.cnn.com/2018/01/24/asia/beijing-shanghai-population-drop-intl/index.html.
6. Melvin Webber, as quoted in Kenneth Frampton, "Ten Points on an Architecture of Regionalism: A Provisional Polemic," in Vincent B. Canizaro, ed., *Architectural Regionalism: Collected Writings on Place, Identity, Modernity, and Tradition* (New York, NY: Princeton Architectural Press, 2007; originally published in 1987 in Center 3: *New Regionalism*, 20–27), 374–85, as quoted on 382.
7. Paul Ricoeur, "Universal Civilization and National Cultures," in Canizaro, *Architectural Regionalism*, 42–55, as quoted on 47. Originally published in Paul Ricouer, *History and Truth* (Evanston, IL: Northwestern University Press, 1965), 271–84.
8. These permanent exhibitions are contemporary manifestations of the celebrated "Cities and Town Planning" exhibition, curated and presented by Patrick Geddes at Crosby Hall in the Chelsea area of London in 1911. The museum of Chinese Gardens and Landscape Architecture in Beijing features large models of such diverse gardens as New York City's Central Park, Villa Lante in Italy, and the Versailles landscape near Paris, as well as many traditional Chinese gardens and city models. See Welter, *Biopolis*, 124–31, 132, and 133.
9. Paul Ricoeur, as quoted in Frampton, "Prospects for a Critical Regionalism," 148.

10. The term "romantic regionalism" is associated with "kitschy" (overly sentimental and in poor taste) regional elements tied to the tourist industry and other commercial activities such as regionally themed districts.

11. Frampton, "Ten Points on an Architecture of Regionalism," 377.

12. Liane Lefaivre and Alexander Tzonis, *Critical Regionalism: Architecture and Identity in a Globalized World* (New York, NY: Prestel, 2003); and Liane Lefaivre and Alexander Tzonis, *Architecture of Regionalism in the Age of Globalization: Peaks and Valleys in the Flat World* (London, UK: Routledge, 2012).

13. Lefaivre and Tzonis, *Critical Regionalism*, 29.

14. Ibid., 20. See, also, John Brinckerhoff Jackson, *Discovering the Vernacular Landscape* (New Haven, CT: Yale University Press, 1986), and Janet Mendelsohn and Chris Wilson, eds., *Drawn to Landscape: The Pioneering Work of J. B. Jackson* (Staunton, VA: George F. Thompson Publishing, 2015).

15. J. B. Jackson, as quoted in Laurie Olin, "Water, Urban Nature, and the Art of Landscape Design," in Frederick R. Steiner, George F. Thompson, and Armando Carbonell, eds., *Nature and Cities: The Ecological Imperative in Urban Design and Planning* (Cambridge, MA: Lincoln Institute of Land Policy, 2016), 361–405, as quoted on 405.

16. Lefaivre and Tzonis, *Critical Regionalism*, 21.

17. Ibid., 3.

18. Ibid., 20.

19. Ricoeur, "Universal Civilization and National Cultures," 52.

20. Ibid., 53.

21. Richard Ingersoll, "Critical Regionalism in Houston: A Case for the Menil Collection," in Spyros Amourgis, ed., *Critical Regionalism: The Pomona Meeting Proceedings* (Pomona: The College of Environmental Design, California State Polytechnic University, 1991), 237.

22. Kenneth Frampton, as quoted in Alexander Tzonis and Liane Lefaivre, "Critical Regionalism," in Amourgis, *Critical Regionalism*, 9.

23. Ricoeur, "Universal Civilization and National Cultures," 43.

24. Ibid., 47.

25. Lewis Mumford, "Excerpts from *The South in Architecture*," in Canizaro, *Architectural Regionalism* (originally published in 1947 in *The South in Architecture*), 97–101, as quoted on 101.

26. Ibid.

27. Lewis Mumford, as quoted in Anthony Alofsin, "Constructive Regionalism," in Canizaro, *Architectural Regionalism* (originally published in 1980 and revised in 2005), 369–73, as quoted on 371.

28. Technological innovation diffuses much more rapidly than in the past when it was a stronger regional parameter. Therefore, it is increasingly a universalizing influence subject to regional modification.

29. Nikos Kalogeras, as quoted in Spyros Amourgis, "Paradigms in Praxis," in Amourgis, ed., *Critical Regionalism*, 69.

30. Kenza Boussora, "Regionalism: Lessons from Algeria and the Middle East," in Canizaro, *Architectural Regionalism* (originally published in 1990), 121–27.

31. Judith Chafee, as quoted in Amourgis, *Critical Regionalism*, 55.

32. David Woodruff Smith, "Phenomenology," in Edward N. Zalta, ed., *The Stanford Encyclopedia of Philosophy* (Winter 2013 Edition); online at http://plato.stanford.edu/archives/win2013/entries/phenomenology/; accessed in December 2017.

33. John Dewey, *Art as Experience* (New York, NY: Perigree Books, 1980; originally delivered as the first William James Lecturer at Harvard in 1934 and first published in 1952 by Minton, Balch and Company of New York City), 173.

34. David Seamon, "Body-Subject, Time-Space Routines, and Place Ballets," in Anne Buttimer and David Seamon, eds., *The Human Experience of Space and Place* (London, UK: Croom Helm, 1980).

35. Frederic Jameson, as quoted in Ricardo Castro, "The Work of Rogelio Salmona: The President's Guest House in Cartagena, Colombia," in Amourgis, ed., *Critical Regionalism*, 208.

36. Georges Descombes, "Shifting Sites: The Swiss Way, Geneva," in James Corner, ed., *Recovering Landscape: Essays in Contemporary Landscape Architecture* (New York, NY: Princeton Architectural Press, 1999), 79–86.

37. Ricardo Castro, "The Work of Rogelio Salmona," 208.

38. Colin Rowe and Fred Koetter, *Collage City* (Cambridge, MA: The MIT Press, 1978), 49.

39. Peter Walker and Melanie Simo, *Invisible Gardens: The Search for Modernism in the American Landscape* (Cambridge, MA: The MIT Press, 1994), 252.

40. Laurie Olin "Form, Meaning, and Expression in Landscape Architecture," in Marc Treib, ed., *Meaning in Landscape Architecture & Gardens: Four Essays, Four Commentaries* (New York, NY: Routledge, 2011; originally published in 1988 by Routledge), 22–71.

41. Charlie Albright, "'Classical' music is dying . . . and that's the best thing for classical music," *CNN* (May 29, 2015); online at https://www.cnn.com/2016/05/29/opinions/classical-music-dying-and-being-reborn-opinion-albright/index.html.

42. As of this writing (April 2025), Todd Johnson is Associate Professor of Landscape Architecture and Environmental Planning and Professional Practice at Utah State University in addition to Principal and Chief Design Officer at the Denver office of Design Workshop.

43. Martin Lockley, Professor of Geology, as quoted on signage.

44. "About Islandwood," http://www.islandwood.org/about/default.php.

45. Timothy Beatley, "New Directions in Urban Nature: The Power and Promise of Biophilic Cities and Blue Urbanism," in Steiner, Thompson, and Carbonell, *Nature and Cities*, 272.

46. Jennifer Senior, "Some Dark Thoughts on Happiness," *New York Magazine* (July 16, 2006); online at https://nymag.com/news/features/17573/.

47. Diane Rehm, interview of Tal Ben Shahar, *The Diane Rehm Show* (June 21, 2007).

48. Daniel Kahneman, "A Survey Method for Characterizing Daily Life Experience: The Day Reconstruction Method," *Science*, Vol. 306, No. 5702 (December 2004): 1776–80.

49. Ibid.

50. John Evans, This song is unpublished and has not been recorded. John and I worked together as a singer-songwriter team in Memphis during the mid-1970s and recorded demos together at the famous Sun Studio in Memphis.

51. *Iconoclasts* (television series), Sundance Channel (2005–2012), see https://www.imdb.com/title/tt0472004/.

52. See the heading titled "Architecture for Thinkers" in Nietzsche's *The Joyful Wisdom*; referenced in Welter, *Biopolis*, 221.

53. Lizzie Widdicombe, "The Higher Life: A Mindfulness Guru for the Tech Set," *The New Yorker* (July 6 and 13, 2015): 40–47. Kathleen Chaykowski, "Meet Headspace, The App That Made Meditation A $250 Million Business," *Forbes* (January 8, 2017); https://www.forbes.com/sites/kathleenchaykowski/2017/01/08/meet-headspace-the-app-that-made-meditation-a-250-million-business/.

54. Jacqueline M. Stavros, and Cheri B. Torres, *Dynamic Relationships: Unleashing the Power of Appreciative Inquiry in Daily Living* (Chagrin Falls, OH: Taos Institute, 2005).

55. Richard Weller, "The City Is Not an Egg: Western Urbanization in Relation to Changing Perceptions of Nature," in Steiner, Thompson, and Carbonell, *Nature and Cities*, 45.

56. Dewey, *Art as Experience*, 290.

57. Chris Reed, "Projective Ecologies in Design and Planning" in Steiner, Thompson, and Carbonell, *Nature and Cities*, 341.

58. Dewey, *Art as Experience*, 324.

59. Frederic Jameson, as quoted in Castro, "The Work of Rogelio Salmona," 209.

60. Ricoeur, "Universal Civilization and National Cultures," in Canizaro, *Architectural Regionalism*, 51.

61. Dewey, *Art as Experience*, 142.

62. Sanford Kwinter, "Combustible Landscape," in Chris Reed and Nina-Marie Lister, eds., *Projective Ecologies* (New York, NY: Actar Publishers, 2014), 338.

63. Martin Scorsese, *No Direction Home: Bob Dylan*, a documentary film (208 minutes) that premiered on PBS television on September 27, 2005.

64. See Chapter 2, page 76.

65. See the discussion of Castells in Robert L. Thayer, *Lifeplace: Bioregional Thought and Practice* (Berkley: University of California Press, 2003), 62.

66. Timothy Cassidy, "Becoming Regional Over Time: Toward a Reflexive Regionalism," in Canizaro, *Architectural Regionalism*, 410–19. (This essay was from Cassidy's unpublished dissertation.)

67. Doug Kelbaugh, "Towards an Architecture of Place: Design Principles For Critical Regionalism," in Amourgis, *Critical Regionalism*, 182.

68. The Cultural Landscape Foundation is a high-profile NGO (non-governmental organization) that actively preserves valuable regional exemplars. See https://tclf.org/threat-weyerhaeuser-campus-increases.

69. Frampton, "Ten Points on an Architecture of Regionalism," 385.

70. Chris Wilson, *The Myth of Santa Fe: Creating a Modern Regional Tradition* (Albuquerque: University of New Mexico Press, 1997).

71. LeFaivre and Tzonis, *Critical Regionalism*, 10.

72. Michel Desvigne and Christine Dalnoky, as quoted in Sebastien Marot, "The Reclaiming of Sites," in James Corner, ed., *Recovering Landscape: Essays in Contemporary Landscape Architecture* (New York, NY: Princeton Architectural Press, 1999), 55.

73. Lawrence W. Speck, "Regionalism and Invention," in Canizaro, *Architectural Regionalism*, 70–79, as quoted on 71. Originally published in *Center: New Regionalism 3* (1987): 8–19.

74. Rexford Newcomb, "Regionalism in American Architecture," in Canizaro, *Architectural Regionalism*, 80–95. Originally published in Merrill Jensen, ed., *Regionalism in America* (Madison: University of Wisconsin Press, 1951): 273–95.

75. Jim Dodge, "Living by Life: Some Bioregional Theory and Practice," in Canizaro, *Architectural Regionalism*, 341–49, as quoted on 347. Originally published in *Co-Evolution Quarterly* (Winter 1981): 6–12.

76. Boussora, "Regionalism," 127.

77. Brian Walker, as quoted in Nina-Marie E. Lister, "Resilience Beyond Rhetoric in Urban Planning and Design," in Steiner, Thompson, and Carbonell, *Nature and Cities*, 314.

78. William C. Welch and Greg Gant, *The Southern Heirloom Garden* (Dallas, TX: Taylor Publishing Company, 1995).

79. Doug Kelbaugh, "Towards an Architecture of Place: Design Principles for Critical Regionalism," in Amourgis, *Critical Regionalism*, 186.

80. Bruce G. Sharky, "Strong Attitudes on Regionalism . . . but No Consensus," *Landscape Architecture*, Vol. 75, No. 2 (March/April 1985):78–81.

81. Keith L Eggener, "Placing Resistance: A Critique of Critical Regionalism," in Canizaro, *Architectural Regionalism*, 394–409. Originally published in *Journal of Architectural Education*, Vol. 55, No. 4 (May 2002): 228–37.

82. Lewis Mumford, as quoted in Vincent B. Canizaro, "Situating Architectural Regionalism," in Canizaro, *Architectural Regionalism*, 16.

83. Kelbaugh, "Towards an Architecture of Place."

84. Wendell Berry, "The Regional Motive," in Canizaro, *Architectural Regionalism*, 39. Originally published in *A Continuous Harmony; Essays Cultural and Agricultural* (New York, NY: Harcourt Brace Janovitch, 1972), 63–70.
85. Frank Welch, "Regionalism as Renewable Resource," *Texas Architect*, Vol. 39, No. 3 (May/June 1989): 38–41, as quoted on 41.
86. Juhani Pallasmaa, "Tradition and Modernity: The Feasibility of Regional Architecture in Post-Modern Society," in Canizaro, *Architectural Regionalism*, 128–39, as quoted on 133. Originally published in *The Architectural Review*, Vol. 184, No. 1095 (May 1988): 26–34.
87. For an interactive 360-degree video of the Spanish Steps context, see: https://www.360cities.net/video/20160629-300005stepsvr-mp4.
88. Kenneth Frampton, as quoted in Kelbaugh, "Towards an Architecture of Place," 182.
89. Frampton, "Ten Points on an Architecture of Regionalism," 374.
90. Michael Sorkin, *Variations on a Theme Park: The New American City and the End of Public Space* (New York, NY: The Noonday Press, 1992).
91. A copy of something that never existed as in Disney's mythical "main streets."
92. Dewey, *Art as Experience*, 177.
93. Suha Ozkan, "Regionalism Within Modernism," in Canizaro, *Architectural Regionalism*, 103–09, as quoted on 108. Originally published in Robert Powell, ed., *Regionalism in Architecture* (Singapore: Concept Media, 1985), 8–15.
94. C. Routledge, T. Wildschut, C. Sedikides, and J. Juhl, "Nostalgia as a Resource for Psychological Health and Well-Being," *Social and Personality Psychology Compass*, Vol. 7, No. 11 (November 2013): 808–18.
95. T. Wildschut, C. Sedikides, J. Arndt, and C. D. Routledge, "Nostalgia: Content, Triggers, Functions," *Journal of Personality and Social Psychology*, Vol. 91, No. 5 (November 2006): 975–93.
96. Colin Rowe and Fred Koetter, *Collage City* (Cambridge, MA: The MIT Press, 1978), 49.
97. Routledge, "Nostalgia as a Resource for Psychological Health and Well-Being," 813.
98. Alva D. Logsdon, *Westminster Promenade;* http://www.landscapeonline.com/research/article.php?id=1863.
99. Ibid.
100. For the complete text of the plaque, see: https://www.waymarking.com/waymarks/WMDRA9_Chief_Little_Raven_Westminster_CO.
101. This expands on the idea that beauty is only arrived at through an intellectual process, a critical analysis, as promoted by art critic and philosopher Arthur Danto, landscape architect Elizabeth Meyer, and others. Environmental psychology shows us that we are capable of experiencing beauty in a subconscious or pre-conscious way, before critical analysis or moral judgement. See Elizabeth Meyer, "Sustaining Beauty: The Performance of Appearance," in Steiner, Thompson, and Carbonell, *Nature and Cities*, 136–37.
102. Dewey, *Art as Experience*, 258.
103. Anne Whiston Spirn, "The Poetics of City and Nature: Towards a New Aesthetic for Urban Design," *Landscape Journal,* Vol. 7, No. 2 (Fall 1988): 108–26.

CHAPTER 2

1. Ellen H. Makowski, *Landscape and Place Research: Concepts and Methods* (Arlington: University of Texas at Arlington, School of Architecture, 1994).
2. Eleftherios Pavlides, "Four Approaches to Regionalism in Architecture," in Spyros Amourgis, ed., *Critical Regionalism: The Pomona Meeting Proceedings* (Pomona: College of Environmental Design, California State Polytechnic University, 1991).

3. Louis Mumford, *Art and Technics* (New York, NY: Columbia University Press, 1952), 86.

4. Kimberly Dovey, "The Quest for Authenticity and the Replication of Environmental Meaning," in David Seaman and Robert Mugerauer, eds., *Dwelling, Place, and Environment* (Dordrecht, Netherlands: Kluwer, 1985).

5. Steven A. Moore, "Technology, Place, and Nonmodern Regionalism," in Vincent B. Canizaro, ed., *Architectural Regionalism: Collected Writings on Place, Identity, Modernity, and Tradition* (New York, NY: Princeton Architectural Press, 2007), 433–42.

6. Juhani Pallasmaa, "Tradition and Modernity: The Feasibility of Regional Architecture in Post-Modern Society," in Canizaro, *Architectural Regionalism*, 128–39.

7. Moore, "Technology, Place, and Nonmodern Regionalism."

8. Steven C. Bourassa, *The Aesthetics of Landscape* (London, UK: Belhaven Press, 1991), 77.

9. Lewis Mumford, as quoted in Liane Lefaivre and Alexander Tzonis, *Critical Regionalism: Architecture and Identity in a Globalized World* (New York, NY: Prestel, 2012), 20.

10. Doug Kelbaugh, "Towards an Architecture of Place: Design Principles For Critical Regionalism," in Amourgis, *Critical Regionalism*, 185.

11. McHarg's chapter on "The Naturalists" outlines his rationalist philosophy and scientific approach. See Ian L. McHarg, *Design with Nature* (New York, NY: John Wiley, 1992), 117–26. Originally published in 1969 by the Natural History Press of Garden City, NY, for the American Museum of Natural History.

12. James Corner, "The Ecological Imagination: Life in the City and the Public Realm," in Frederick R. Steiner, George F. Thompson, and Armando Carbonell, eds., *Nature and Cities: The Ecological Imperative in Urban Design and Planning* (Cambridge, MA: Lincoln Institute of Land Policy, 2016), 3.

13. Lefaivre and Tzonis, *Critical Regionalism*, 13.

14. Alfred H. Barr, et al., "What is Happening to Modern Architecture," in *The Bulletin of the Museum of Modern Art*, Vol. XV, No. 3 (Spring 1948): 4–20; reprinted in Canizaro, *Architectural Regionalism*, 303.

15. Lewis Mumford, "The Sky Line: Status Quo," in *Architectural Regionalism*, 289–91.

16. Balkrishna V. Doshi, "Cultural Continuum and Regional Identity in Architecture," in Canizaro, *Architectural Regionalism*, 111–18, as quoted on 113. Originally published in Robert Powell, ed., *Regionalism in Architecture* (Singapore: Concept Media, 1985), 87–91.

17. Ibid, 113.

18. For more information, see: https://tclf.org/landscapes/illinois-institute-technology; accessed in January 2019.

19. Norman Mailer, as quoted in Suzy Banks, "25 Things I love About Dallas" (December 2017); https://www.texasmonthly.com/travel/25-things-i-love-about-dallas/.

20. Suha Ozkan, "Regionalism within Modernism," in Canizaro, *Architectural Regionalism*, 103–09, as quoted on 107.

21. See Chapter 6 for my discussion on styles of modernism.

22. Lefaivre and Tzonis, *Critical Regionalism*, 150–57.

23. Le Corbusier, as quoted in Alan Colquhoun, "Critique of Regionalism," in Canizaro, *Architectural Regionalism*, 141–45, as quoted on 144.

24. *Skogskyrkogården*, UNESCO (December 2017); http://whc.unesco.org/en/list/558; and Harriet Atkinson, *Woodland Cemetery, Stockholm* (December 2017); http://www.c20society.org.uk/botm/woodland-cemetery-stockholm/.

25. *The World Heritage Convention* (online at https://whc.unesco.org/en/convention/; accessed in August 2014).

26. Hugh S. Morrison, "After the International Style—What?," in Canizaro, *Architectural Regionalism*, 281–87.

27. Pallasmaa, "Tradition and Modernity," 137.

28. Charles Correa, as quoted in Ozkan, "Regionalism Within Modernism," 109.

29. Kenza Boussora, "Regionalism: Lessons from Algeria and the Middle East," in Canizaro, *Architectural Regionalism*, 121–27, as quoted on 123.

30. Ibid., 123.

31. Patrick Geddes, as quoted in Volker M. Welter, *Biopolis: Patrick Geddes and the City of Life* (Cambridge, MA: The MIT Press, 2002), 47.

32. See Chris Wilson, *The Myth of Santa Fe: Creating a Modern Regional Tradition* (Albuquerque: University of New Mexico Press, 1997).

33. Luis Fernandez-Gallano, "Ten Aphorisms on Regionalism," in Amourgis, *Critical Regionalism*, 32.

34. Pallasmaa, "Tradition and Modernity," 129.

35. Robert Venturi, *Complexity and Contradiction in Architecture* (New York, NY: Museum of Modern Art, 1966), 16.

36. Roger Trancik, *Finding Lost Space* (New York, NY: Van Nostrand Reinhold, 1986).

37. Bourassa, *Aesthetics of Landscape*, 136.

38. Pallasmaa, "Tradition and Modernity," 136.

39. Ann Cline, "Bounded Domains and Tactile Presences: The 'Little Houses' of Cannaregio, the Teahouses of Japan, and Critical Regionalism," in Amourgis, *Critical Regionalism*, 290–304.

40. Ibid.

41. William J. Thompson, "Metamorphosis: What's more desirable in a corporate plaza: avant-garde aesthetics or a comfortable place to sit," *Landscape Architecture*, Vol. 89, No. 9 (September 1999): 95–101.

42. Kenneth Frampton, "Ten Points on an Architecture of Regionalism: A Provisional Polemic," in Canizaro, *Architectural Regionalism*, 374–85. Originally published in 1987 in Center 3: *New Regionalism*, 20–27.

43. Bourassa, *Aesthetics of Landscape*, 136.

44. Michael Collins and Andreas Papadakis, *Postmodern Design* (New York, NY: Rizzoli International Publications, 1989), 128.

45. John Dewey, *Art as Experience* (New York, NY: Perigree Books, 1980; originally delivered as the first William James Lecturer at Harvard in 1934 and first published in 1952 by Minton, Balch and Company of New York City), 162.

46. All quotes are from Bourassa, *Aesthetics of Landscape*, 136–37: Hal Foster, "Postmodernism: A Preface," in Hal Foster, ed., *Postmodern Culture* (London, UK: Pluto Press London, 1985), 20–27; Hilton Kramer, "The Idea of Tradition in American Art Criticism," *The American Scholar*, Vol. 56, No. 3 (Summer 1987): 327; Ada Louise Huxtable, "The Troubled State of Modern Architecture," *The New York Review of Books* (May 1, 1980): 26; and Kenneth Frampton, *Modern Architecture and the Critical Present* (New York, NY: Architectural Design and Academy Editions, 1982), 76.

47. Pallasmaa, "Tradition and Modernity," 130.

48. Siegfried Gideon, "The New Regionalism," in Canizaro, *Architectural Regionalism*, 310–19, as quoted on 311.

49. See Figs. 7.7 and 7.8: fishbone and canoe bridges.

50. Ada Louise Huxtable, as quoted in Bourassa, *Aesthetics of Landscape*, 13.

51. Morrison, "After the International Style—What?," 286.

52. Wilson, *The Myth of Santa Fe*, 110–45.

53. Ibid., 111.

54. Ibid.

55. Lefaivre and Tzonis, *Critical Regionalism*, 18.

56. Wendell Berry, "The Regional Motive," in Canizaro, *Architectural Regionalism*, 37–40, as quoted on 37.

57. Paul Ricoeur, "Universal Civilization and National Cultures," in Canizaro, *Architectural Regionalism*, 42–55, as quoted on 48. Originally published in Paul Ricouer, *History and Truth* (Evanston, IL: Northwestern University Press, 1965), 271–84.

58. Pallasmaa, "Tradition and Modernity," 130.

59. Harwell Hamilton Harris, "Regionalism and Nationalism in Architecture," in Canizaro, *Architectural Regionalism*, 57. Originally published in *Texas Quarterly*, Vol. 1, No. 1 (February 1958): 115–24.

60. Moore, "Technology, Place, and Nonmodern Regionalism."

CHAPTER 3

1. "Vitruvius," *Encyclopedia Britannica Online*; http:// www.britannica.com/topic/architecture/Commodity-firmness-and-delight-the-ultimate-synthesis; accessed in December 2017.

2. For a critical review of Geddes's contributions to the evolution of regional thinking and city and regional planning, see Volker M. Welter, *Biopolis: Patrick Geddes and the City of Life* (Cambridge, MA: The MIT Press, 2002).

3. Lewis Mumford's introduction to Ian L. McHarg, *Design with Nature* (New York, NY: John Wiley, 1992), vii.

4. Steven C. Bourassa, *The Aesthetics of Landscape* (London, UK: Belhaven Press, 1991), xv.

5. For a comprehensive overview of Leopold's 50-year career of writing and speaking, see Susan L. Flader and J. Baird Callicot, eds., *The River of the Mother of God and other Essays by Aldo Leopold* (Madison: University of Wisconsin Press, 1991), 10.

6. Bourassa, *The Aesthetics of Landscape*, 16.

7. John Agnew, as quoted in Steven A. Moore, "Technology, Place, and Nonmodern Regionalism," in Vincent B. Canizaro, ed., *Architectural Regionalism: Collected Writings on Place, Identity, Modernity, and Tradition* (New York, NY: Princeton Architectural Press, 2007), 435.

8. Ibid.

9. Ibid.

10. For a broad and comprehensive exposition on the topic of environmental imperatives across many disciplines, including aesthetics and philosophy, see Michael Charles Tobias and Jane Gray Morrison, *On the Nature of Ecological Paradox* (Cham, Switzerland: Springer, 2021). The focus here is on how designers can practically adopt the results of these philosophical debates into how they perceive and respond to landscapes as part of a creative regional design process..

11. For a discussion of specific experiments, see Bourassa, *The Aesthetics of Landscape*, 55–64.

12. Ibid., 88.

13. Ibid., 91.

14. Jay Appleton, *The Experience of Landscape* (New York, NY: John Wiley, 1975), 196.

15. Rachel Kaplan and Eugene J. Herbert, "Cultural and Subcultural Comparisons in Preferences for Natural Settings," in *Landscape and Urban Planning*, Vol. 14 (January 1987): 281–93.

16. J. Juhl, C. Routledge, J. Arndt, C. Sedikides and Tim Wildschut, "Fighting the Future with the Past: Nostalgia Buffers Existential Threat," *Journal of Research in Personality*, Vol. 44, No. 3 (June 2010): 309–314, as quoted on 314.

17. Haptics is the study of touching behavior.

18. Clare Cooper Marcus and Carolyn Francis, *People Places: Design Guidelines for Urban Open Space* (New York, NY: John Wiley, 1998); and Clare Cooper Marcus and Naomi A. Sachs, *Therapeutic Gardens: An Evidence-Based Approach to Designing Healing Gardens and Restorative Outdoor Spaces* (New York, NY: John Wiley, 2014).

19. Cooper Marcus, *People Places*, 107.

20. Walter Gropius, transcript of a panel discussion, "What Is Happening to Modern Architecture?," in Canizaro, *Architectural Regionalism*, 300–01. Originally published in *The Bulletin of the Museum of Modern Art*, Vol. XV, No. 3 (Spring 1948): 20–27.

21. David Hume, as quoted in Bourassa, *The Aesthetics of Landscape*, 66.

22. Ibid., 90.

23. Albert Meyer, "Regional Development: The Architects Role," in Canizaro, *Architectural Regionalism*, 256. Originally published in *AIA Journal*, Vol. 60, No. 10 (October 1971): 17–19 and 20–27.

24. Siegfried Gideon, "The New Regionalism," in Canizaro, *Architectural Regionalism*, 312. The original, slightly abridged version was published in his book, *Architecture You and Me: The Diary of a Development* (Cambridge, MA: Harvard University Press, 1958), 138–51.

25. Aldo van Eyck, as quoted in Kenneth Frampton, "Critical Regionalism Revisited," in Spyros Amourgis, ed., *Critical Regionalism: The Pomona Meeting Proceedings* (Pomona: College of Environmental Design, California State Polytechnic University, 1991), 375.

26. Kenneth Rowntree, as quoted in Bourassa, The Aesthetics of Landscape, 94.

27. Lewis Mumford, "Skyline," *The New Yorker* (October 11, 1947), as quoted in Alexander Tzonis and Liane Lefaivre, "Critical Regionalism," in Amourgis, *Critical Regionalism*, 14–15.

28. Luis Ferandez-Gallano, "Ten Aphorisms on Regionalism," in Amourgis, *Critical Regionalism*, 33.

29. Ibid.

30. Kimberly Dovey, "The Quest for Authenticity and the Replication of Environmental Meaning," in David Seaman and Robert Mugerauer, eds., *Dwelling, Place, and Environment* (Dordrecht, The Netherlands: Kluwer, 1985).

31. Robert L. Thayer, *Lifeplace: Bioregional Thought and Practice* (Berkeley: University of California Press, 2003), 1.

32. Juhani Pallasmaa, "Tradition and Modernity: The Feasibility of Regional Architecture in Post-Modern Society" (1988), in Canizaro, *Architectural Regionalism*, 128–39. Originally published in *The Architectural Review*, Vol. 176, No. 6 (May 1988): 26–34.

33. Aldo van Eyck, as quoted in Pallasmaa, "Tradition and Modernity," 130.

34. Arthur Koestler, *The Act of Creation* (New York, NY: Macmillan, 1964), 96.

35. These themes are discussed repeatedly and in detail in Koestler, ibid.

36. The idea of "reading a landscape" resides with J. B. Jackson, a principal founder of landscape studies, who famously wrote in the inaugural issue of *Landscape* in 1951, which he founded:

> "Whenever we go, whatever the nature of our work, we adorn the face of the earth with a living design which changes and is eventually replaced by that of a future generation. How can one tire of looking at this variety, or of marveling at the forces within man and nature that brought it about?
>
> "The city is an essential part of this shifting and growing design, but only a part of it. Beyond the last street light, out where the familiar asphalt ends, a whole country waits to be discovered: villages, farmsteads and highways, half-hidden valleys of irrigated gardens, and wide landscapes reaching to the horizon. A rich and beautiful book is always open before us. We have but to learn to read it."

John Brinckerhoff Jackson, "The Need to be Versed in Country Things," *Landscape*, Vol. 1, No 1 (Spring 1951): 1–5, as quoted on 5.

37. Michael Speaks, "After Theory," *Architectural Record* (June 2005): 72–77; quoted on 77.

38. Pallasmaa, "Tradition and Modernity," 132.

39. John Dewey, *Art as Experience* (New York, NY: Perigree Books, 1980; originally delivered as the first William James Lecturer at Harvard in 1934 and first published in 1952 by Minton, Balch and Company of New York City), 326.

40. See Simon Elias Bibri, "The Eco-city and its Core Environmental Dimension of Sustainability: Green Energy Technologies and their Integration with Data-driven Smart Solutions," *Energy Informatics* (June 15, 2020); https://energyinformatics.springeropen.com/articles/10.1186/s42162-020-00107-7.

41. Aldo Leopold, *A Sand County Almanac: With Essays on Conservation from Round River* (New York, NY: Ballantine, 1986).
42. Edward O. Wilson, *Biophilia* (Cambridge, MA: Harvard University Press, 1984).
43. Timothy Beatley, "New Directions in Urban Nature: The Power and Promise of Biophilic Cities and Blue Urbanism," in Frederick R. Steiner, George F. Thompson, and Armando Carbonell, eds., *Nature and Cities: The Ecological Imperative in Urban Design and Planning* (Cambridge, MA: Lincoln Institute of Land Policy, 2016), 265–85, as quoted on 267.
44. Lucy R. Lippard, *The Lure of the Local: Senses of Place in a Multicentered Society* (New York, NY: The New Press, 1997).
45. Leopold wrote in 1947 about the connection between environmental psychology and cultural rules. He interpreted it as "animal instincts" (what is now called environmental psychology), evolving into a "community instinct" (referred to in my book as cultural rules), in the development of a land ethic. See his book, *A Sand County Almanac*, 239.
46. Moore, "Technology, Place, and Nonmodern Regionalism," 441.
47. Patrick Geddes divided products that are required to maintain a society into "necessaries" and "super necessaries." Super necessaries are placed above ordinary functional products as aesthetic objects that stimulate the sense organs of higher forms of life. He believed that the proliferation of short-lived necessaries waste matter and energy and robs a society of the resources needed to create super necessaries with lasting social value. See Welter, *Biopolis*, 15.

CHAPTER 4

1. Paul Ricoeur, "Universal Civilization and National Cultures," in Vincent B. Canizaro, ed., *Architectural Regionalism: Collected Writings on Place, Identity, Modernity, and Tradition* (New York, NY: Princeton Architectural Press, 2007), 51. Originally published in Paul Ricouer, *History and Truth* (Evanston, IL: Northwestern University Press, 1965), 271–84.
2. Timothy Cassidy, "Becoming Regional Over Time: Toward a Reflexive Regionalism," in Canizaro, *Architectural Regionalism*, 414.
3. Juhani Pallasmaa, "Tradition and Modernity: The Feasibility of Regional Architecture in Post-Modern Society," in Canizaro, *Architectural Regionalism*, 139.
4. Lewis Mumford, as quoted in Lawrence W. Speck, "Regionalism and Invention," in Canizaro, *Architectural Regionalism*, 79. Originally published in Center: New Regionalism 3 (1987): 8–19.
5. Lawrence Speck, ibid., 79.
6. Romaldo Giurgola, "Architecture: More than a Building," *Architecture Australia*, Vol. 76. No. 3 (April 1987): 44.
7. *American Beauty Mill Lofts,* http://search.reel-scout.com/Slideshow.aspx?lid=048-10058059&id=1847949; accessed in December 2017.
8. Charlie Chaplin, as quoted in Liane Lefaivre and Alexander Tzonis, *Critical Regionalism: Architecture and Identity in a Globalized World* (New York, NY: Prestel, 2003), 45.
9. John Dewey, *Art as Experience* (New York, NY: Perigree Books, 1980; originally delivered as the first William James Lecturer at Harvard in 1934 and first published in 1952 by Minton, Balch and Company of New York City), 341–44.
10. See *Island Heritage*, http://granvilleisland.com/discover-island/island-heritage; accessed in December 2017.
11. Dean Cardasis, "Imaginary Gardens with Real Frogs: Space in the Work of Martha Schwartz," *GSD News* (Winter/Spring 1996): 1–4.
12. William H. Whyte, *The Social Life of Small Urban Spaces* (Washington, DC: The Conservation Foundation, 1980), 19.
13. Bing Thom, as quoted in Jared Green, *Bing Thom: Social Architect*; online at http://dirt.asla.org/2011/07/28/bing-thom-social-architect/; accessed in December 2017.

14. Kenneth Frampton, "Ten Points on an Architecture of Regionalism: A Provisional Polemic," in Canizaro, *Architectural Regionalism*, 374–85.

15. Susan Harrington, "Framed Again: The Picturesque Aesthetics of Contemporary Landscapes," *Landscape Journal*, Vol. 25, No. 1 (March 2006): 22–37.

16. Steven C. Bourassa, *The Aesthetics of Landscape* (London, UK: Belhaven Press, 1991).

17. See http://web2.uwindsor.ca/hrg/amckay/Claudemirror.com/Claudemirror.com/Archived_Tintern_Abbey_Images.html; accessed in December 2017..

18. Alex McKay and C. Suzanne Matheson, "The Transient Glance: The Claude Mirror and the Picturesque"; online at http://web2.uwindsor.ca/hrg/amckay/Claudemirror.com/Claudemirror.com/Claude_Mirror_Introduction.html; accessed in June 2014; and Arnold Berleant, *Living in the Landscape: Towards an Aesthetics of Environment* (Lawrence: University Press of Kansas, 1997), 26.

19. Rick Darke, *The American Woodland Garden: Capturing the Spirit of the Deciduous Forrest* (Portland, OR: Timber Press, 2002).

20. Donald MacKenzie and Judith Wajcman, as quoted in Steven A. Moore, "Technology, Place, and Nonmodern Regionalism," in Canizaro, *Architectural Regionalism*, 433–42.

21. Ibid., 442.

22. Craig Campbell, "Seattle's Gas Plant Park," *Landscape Architecture*, Vol. 63, No. 4 (July 1973): 338–42.

23. Ibid., 342.

24. Elizabeth K. Meyer, "Seized by Sublime Sentiments: Between Terra Firma and Terra Incognita," in William Saunders, ed., *Richard Haag: Bloedel Reserve and Gas Works Park* (New York, NY: Princeton Architectural Press, in association with the Harvard University Graduate School of Design, 1998), 9.

25. Author's unpublished interview with Bill Wenk, FASLA (2006).

26. For more information on Northside Park, including drawings by Bill Wenk, plans, and more images, see William E. Wenk, *Working Water: Reinventing the Storm Drain* (Novato, CA: Oro Editions, 2021), 34–41.

27. Americans with Disabilities Act (ADA) and Crime Prevention through Environmental Design (CPTED).

28. James Corner, "Eidetic Operations and New Landscapes," in James Corner, ed., *Recovering Landscape: Essays in Contemporary Landscape Architecture* (New York, NY: Princeton Architectural Press, 1999), 153–69.

CHAPTER 5

1. Albert Mayer, "Regional Development: The Architects Role," in Vincent B. Canizaro, ed., *Architectural Regionalism: Collected Writings on Place, Identity, Modernity, and Tradition* (New York, NY: Princeton Architectural Press, 2007), 252–57.

2. For an image of the valley section, see Volker M. Welter, *Biopolis: Patrick Geddes and the City of Life* (Cambridge, MA: The MIT Press, 2002), 60.

3. Forster Ndubisi, "Adaptation and Regeneration: A Pathway to Urban Spaces," in Frederick R. Steiner, George F. Thompson, and Armando Carbonell, eds., *Nature and Cities: The Ecological Imperative in Urban Design and Planning* (Cambridge, MA: Lincoln Institute of Land Policy, 2016), 203.

4. Doug Kelbaugh, "Towards an Architecture of Place: Design Principles for Critical Regionalism," in Spyros Amourgis, ed., *Critical Regionalism: The Pomona Meeting Proceedings* (Pomona: College of Environmental Design, California State Polytechnic University, 1991), 186.

5. Steven C. Bourassa, *The Aesthetics of Landscape* (London, UK: Belhaven Press, 1991).

6. Mayer, "Regional Development," 257.
7. Jeffrey Cook, "A Post-Industrial Culture of Regionalism," in Amourgis, *Critical Regionalism*, 164–80.
8. Edward Relph, *Rational Landscapes and Humanistic Geography* (London, UK: Billings and Sons, 1981).
9. Ibid., 189.
10. Ibid.
11. Leo Marx, *The Machine in the Garden: Technology and the Pastoral Ideal in America* (London, UK: Oxford University Press, 1964).
12. Erich Fromm, *Marx's Concept of Man* (New York, NY: Frederick Ungar Publishing, 1961), as quoted in Marx, *The Machine in the Garden*, 177.
13. George Santayana, as quoted in John Dewey, *Art as Experience* (New York, NY: Perigree Books, 1980; originally delivered as the first William James Lecturer at Harvard in 1934 and first published in 1952 by Minton, Balch and Company of New York City), 18.
14. Aldo Leopold, *A Sand County Almanac: With Essays on Conservation from Round River* (New York, NY: Ballantine, 1986), 279.
15. Ibid., 118.
16. Charles Baudelaire, *The Painter of Modern Life*, translated by P. E. Charvet (London, UK: Penguin Books, 1972).
17. Siegfried Gideon, "The New Regionalism," in Canizaro, *Architectural Regionalism*, 310–19.
18. Charles W. Moore, William J. Mitchell, and William Turnbull, Jr., *The Poetics of Gardens* (Cambridge, MA: The MIT Press, 1988).
19. North Central Texas Council of Governments, "What is NCTCOG?"; online at http://www.nctcog.org/pa/WhatIsNCTCOG.pdf; accessed in August 2014.
20. Lewis Mumford, "Regional Planning," in Canizaro, *Architectural Regionalism*, 237–43.
21. Christopher Alexander, "Excerpts from *A Pattern Language*," in Canizaro, Architectural Regionalism, 247.
22. Peter Berg, "Bioregionalism" (defined and updated 2002); http://www.planetdrum.org/shadow/bioregion_bioregionalism_defined.htm; accessed in August 2021.
23. Lewis Mumford, "Regional Planning," in Canizaro, *Architectural Regionalism*, 237–43, as quoted on 237.
24. Jim Dodge, "Living by Life: Some Bioregional Theory and Practice," in Canizaro, *Architectural Regionalism*, 341–49.
25. Ibid.
26. Gary J. Coates, "Biotechnology and Regional Integration," in Canizaro, *Architectural Regionalism*, 350–61.
27. Ibid., 352
28. Peter Berg and Raymond Dasmann, "Reinhabiting California," in Canizaro, *Architectural Regionalism*, 335–39.
29. Ibid, 336.
30. Aldo Leopold wrote in 1944: "In short, a land ethic changes the role of *homo sapiens*, from conqueror of the land-community to plain member and citizen of it. It implies respect for his fellow members, and also respect for the community as such." From his book, *A Sand County Almanac*, 240 and 263.
31. Robert, L. Thayer, *Lifeplace: Bioregional Thought and Practice* (Berkeley: University of California Press, 2003).
32. See https://www.epa.gov/eco-research/level-iii-and-iv-ecoregions-continental-united-states for the latest Level III ecoregion map.
33. Leopold studied the movement patterns of birds and mammals at the Shack on his farm in Wisconsin and wrote about it in the elegiac *A Sand County Almanac*, 263.
34. Thayer, *Lifeplace*, 5.

35. Timothy Cassidy, "Becoming Regional Over Time: Toward a Reflexive Regionalism," in Canizaro, *Architectural Regionalism*, 410–19.

36. Judith Butler, as quoted in Barbara L. Allen, "On Performative Regionalism," in Canizaro, *Architectural Regionalism*, 423.

37. Allen, "On Performative Regionalism," 423.

38. Ibid., 426.

39. Cook, "A Post-Industrial Culture of Regionalism," 168.

40. Gabriel Arboleda, "What is Vernacular Architecture?"; online at http://www.vernaculararchitecture.com; accessed in July 2014.

41. See Ian L. McHarg, *Design with Nature* (New York, NY: John Wiley, 1992), 29.

42. Amos Rapoport, *House, Form, and Culture* (Englewood Cliffs, NJ: Prentice Hall, 1969), 4, 27, and 47

43. Eleftherios Pavlides, "Four Approaches to Regionalism in Architecture," in Amougis, *Critical Regionalism*, 184.

44. William Bechhoefer, "Aspects of Regionalism as a Tool for Teaching," in Amougis, *Critical Regionalism*, 279–89.

45. Kristina Hill, "Form Follows Flows: Systems, Design, and the Aesthetic Experience of Change," in Steiner, Thompson, and Carbonell, *Nature and Cities*, 346.

46. Labelle Prussin, as quoted and discussed in Eleftherios Pavlides, "Four Approaches to Regionalism in Architecture," in Amougis, *Critical Regionalism*, 312–13.

47. Ibid., 307.

48. Balkrishna V. Doshi, "Cultural Continuum and Regional Identity in Architecture," in Canizaro, *Architectural Regionalism*, 111–18.

49. For a discussion of adobe in Texas vernacular architecture; see https://www.tshaonline.org/handbook/entries/texas-mexican-vernacular-architecture; accessed in August 2021.

50. Lewis Mumford, "Excerpts from *The South in Architecture*," in Canizaro, Architectural Regionalism, 98.

51. David R. Williams, "Toward a Southwestern Architecture," in Canizaro, *Architectural Regionalism*, 170–77, as quoted on 174.

52. See Anthony Alofsin, "In Defense of the Suburbs," *The Atlantic* (June 6, 2018); online at https://www.theatlantic.com/technology/archive/2018/06/a-defense-of-the-suburbs/562136/.

53. Alexander Tzonis and Liane Lefaivre, "Critical Regionalism," in Amourgis, *Critical Regionalism*, 1991.

54. See http://barefootartists.org/projects/village/; accessed in December 2017.

55. "Lily Yeh Biography"; online at http://www.udel.edu/art/artassocialactivism/content/lilyyeh_bio.html; accessed in March 2008..

56. This idea has now become a national phenomenon. For a more recent example in California, see Alisha Ebrahimji, "San Francisco neighbors erect boulders to keep the homeless away," *CNN* (September 25, 2019); online at https://www.cnn.com/2019/09/25/us/san-francisco-homeless-boulders-trnd/.

57. Steve Brown, "1980s landmark Solana campus gets reboot for modern businesses," *The Dallas Morning News* (April 3, 2015); online at https://www.dallasnews.com/business/real-estate/2015/04/02/1980s-landmark-solana-campus-gets-reboot-for-modern-businesses.

58. Maguire Thomas, as quoted in Joel Warren Barna, "Solana in the Sun," *Progressive Architecture*, Vol. 70, No. 4 (April 1989): 68.

59. Peter Walker, as quoted in Peter Walker, "Dal Parco al Giardino, From the Park to the Garden," *Lotus International*, No. 87 (1995): 41.

60. Murotani Bunji, "Peter Walker: Landscape as Art," *Process Architecture*, No. 85 (October 1989): 106.

61. Ibid., 106.

62. Marta Carvello, "Peter Walker: A Contribution to Landscape Architecture," *Quaderns d'arquitectura i Urbanisme*, No. 185 (April–June 1990): 92–93.

63. See https://popestimates.nctcog.org; accessed in September 2021.

64. Kimberly Dovey, "The Quest for Authenticity and the Replication of Environmental Meaning," in David Seaman and Robert Mugerauer, eds., *Dwelling, Place, and Environment* (Dordrecht, The Netherlands: Kluwer, 1985), 38.

65. Harwell Hamilton Harris, "Regionalism and Nationalism in Architecture," in Canizaro, *Architectural Regionalism*, 57–64. Originally published in Texas Quarterly, Vol. 1, No. 1 (February 1958): 115–24.

66. For an encyclopedic discussion of historical regionalism trends in architecture, see Liane Lefaivre and Alexander Tzonis, *Architecture of Regionalism in the Age of Globalization: Peaks and Valleys in the Flat World* (London, UK: Routledge, 2012).

67. Dodge, "Living by Life," 346.

CHAPTER 6

1. Juhani Pallasmaa, "Tradition and Modernity: The Feasibility of Regional Architecture in Post-Modern Society," in Vincent Canizaro, ed., Architectural Regionalism: *Collected Writings on Place, Identity, Modernity, and Tradition* (New York, NY: Princeton Architectural Press, 2007), 128–39. Originally published in *The Architectural Review*, Vol. 176, No. 6 (May 1988): 26–34.

2. Patrick Geddes, as quoted in Volker M. Welter, *Biopolis: Patrick Geddes and the City of Life* (Cambridge, MA: The MIT Press, 2002), 40.

3. William Bechhoefer, "Aspects of Regionalism as a Tool for Teaching," in Spyros Amourgis, ed., *Critical Regionalism: The Pomona Meeting Proceedings* (Pomona: College of Environmental Design, California State Polytechnic University, 1991), 283.

4. William James, "Pragmatism and Humanism," Lecture 7 in his book, *Pragmatism: A New Name for Some Old Ways of Thinking* (New York, NY: Longman Green and Co, 1907), 245.

5. See James Corner, "The Ecological Imagination: Life in the City and the Public Realm," in Frederick R. Steiner, George F. Thompson, and Armando Carbonell, eds., *Nature and Cities: The Ecological Imperative in Urban Design and Planning* (Cambridge , MA: Lincoln Institute of Land Policy, 2016), 7.

6. See John Dewey, *Art as Experience* (New York, NY: Perigree Books, 1980; originally delivered as the first William James Lecturer at Harvard in 1934 and first published in 1952 by Minton, Balch and Company of New York City), 1952.

7. Ibid., 88.

8. For the summation of Andropogon Associates, Ltd.'s strategies and tools that have guided its practice, see Jose Albinana and Carol Franklin, "Creative Fitting: Toward Designing the City as Nature," in Steiner, Thompson, and Carbonell, *Nature and Cities*, 168–69..

9. Elizabeth Meyer, "Sustaining Beauty: the Performance of Appearance," in Steiner, Thompson, and Carbonell, *Nature and Cities*, 140.

10. Known independent of any experience. See http://www.iep.utm.edu/apriori/.

11. Dewey, *Art as Experience*, 282.

12. Freeway Park is one of the most written about landscapes of the twentieth century. For more details on the project, see Susan Hines, "Contested Terrain," *Landscape Architecture Magazine* (May 2005); http://www.asla.org/lamag/lam05/may/feature2.html.

13. Lawrence W. Speck, "Regionalism and Invention," in Canizaro, *Architectural Regionalism*, 70–79, as quoted on 71. Originally published in Center: *New Regionalism 3* (1987): 8–19. This also follows Leopold's famous dictum that can be equally applied to natural and cultural capital: "The first law of intelligent tinkering is to save all the parts."

14. Aldo Leopold, *Round River* (New York, NY: Oxford University Press, 1993), 145–46.

15. Lewis Mumford, "Excerpts from *The South in Architecture*," in Canizaro, Architectural Regionalism, 97–101, as quoted on 98.

16. Rexford Newcomb, "Regionalism in American Architecture," in Canizaro, *Architectural Regionalism*, 80–95, as quoted on 81.

17. For examples of the programming at Klyde Warren Park, see *Klyde Warren Park* at http://www.klydewarrenpark.org/Things-To-Do/index.html.

18. Newcomb, "Regionalism in American Architecture," 82.

19. Sanford Kwinter, "Combustible Landscape," in Chris Reed and Nina-Marie Lister, eds., *Projective Ecologies,* (New York, NY: Harvard University Press and Actar Publishers, 2014), 336–53.

20. Adapted from a discussion of ecological change and resilience. See Nina-Marie E. Lister, "Resilience Beyond Rhetoric in Urban Planning and Design," in Steiner, Thompson, and Carbonell, *Nature and Cities*, 308.

21. Pallasmaa, "Tradition and Modernity."

22. Mumford, "Excerpts from *The South in Architecture*," 100.

23. Kristine D. Woolsey, "Critical Regionalism: A Theory of Process," in Amourgis, *Critical Regionalism*, 325.

24. Kenneth Frampton, "Ten Points on an Architecture of Regionalism: A Provisional Polemic," in Canizaro, *Architectural Regionalism*, 374–85.

25. Geddes, as quoted in Welter, *Biopolis*, 34.

26. Kongjian Yu, "Creating Deep Forms in Urban Nature: The Peasant's Approach to Urban Design," in Steiner, Thompson, and Carbonell, *Nature and Cities*, 95.

27. See *Millenium Water: The Southeast False Creek Olympic Village-Vancouver, Canada*; online at http://www.thechallengeseries.ca/chapter-03/parks-waterfront/.

28. For an image of a racing shell, see http://www.nauticexpo.com/prod/salani-costruzioni-nautiche-snc/product-34529-378643.html and http://www.lavocedellabellezza.it/wp-content/uploads/2012/10/filippi4.jpg.

29. Robert L. Thayer, *Lifeplace: Bioregional Thought and Practice* (Berkeley: University of California Press, 2003), 93.

30. Ibid.

31. Paul D. Spreiregen, "Perspectives on Regional Design," in Canizaro, *Architectural Regionalism*, 258–67.

32. Frampton, "Ten Points on an Architecture of Regionalism."

33. James Stevens Curl and Susan Wilson, *The Oxford Dictionary of Architecture* (New York, NY: Oxford University Press, 2015), 124.

34. Don Luymes, "Reinventing Suburban Identity: A city hall in British Columbia aspires to urbanity," *Landscape Architecture Magazine*, Vol. 92, No. 7 (July 2002): 60–65 and 93.

35. See Ed Fuentes, "California Scenario: Isamu Noguchi's Hidden Public Sculpture Garden in Orange County" (August 27, 2013); online at https://www.kcet.org/history-society/california-scenario-isamu-noguchis-hidden-public-sculpture-garden-in-orange-county.

36. Steven Fox, "Regionalism and Texas Architecture," in Canizaro, *Architectural Regionalism*, 204–13, as quoted on 206.

37. Ibid.

38. As quoted in Fox, ibid., 211.

39. Speck, "Regionalism and Invention," 70–79.

40. Chris Abel, *Architecture and Identity* (Oxford, UK: Oxford Architectural Press, 2000), Chapter 5.

41. For a discussion of both the architectural and the graphic influences of *Townscape*, see Mira Engler, *Cut and Paste Urban Landscape: The Work of Gordon Cullen* (New York, NY: Routledge, 2016), 164–219.

42. Dewey, *Art as Experience*, 299.

43. Ibid., 312.

44. Paul Ricoeur, "Universal Civilization and National Cultures," in Canizaro, *Architectural Regionalism*, 52. Originally published in Paul Ricouer, *History and Truth* (Evanston, IL: Northwestern University Press, 1965), 271–84.

45. Pallasmaa, "Tradition and Modernity."

46. Don P. McAdams, "The Psychology of Life Stories," *Review of General Psychology*, Vol. 5, No. 2 (June 2001): 100–22.

47. Edward Relph, *Rational Landscapes and Humanistic Geography* (London, UK: Billings and Sons, 1981), 179.

48. Aldo Leopold, "Ecology and Politics" (1941), in Susan L. Flader and J. Baird Callicot, eds., *The River of the Mother of God and Other Essays by Aldo Leopold*, (Madison: University of Wisconsin Press, 1991), 286. From notes written in Spring 1941 for the introduction to the course, "Wildlife Ecology 118," offered to liberal arts majors starting in 1939 at the University of Wisconsin. Leopold continued to work on the lecture and never published it, although Russel Lord, editor of *The Land*, offered to publish a slightly revised version in 1941 (see Flader and Callicot, 281).

49. Ian McHarg echoes this thinking in his essay "The Rationalists" with a discussion of genetic diversity and adaptation to "exigency." He attempts to conflate natural systems and ethics into a new rationalist cosmology. See Ian L. McHarg, *Design with Nature* (New York, NY: John Wiley, 1992), 120–25.

50. Steven C. Bourassa, *The Aesthetics of Landscape* (London, UK: Belhaven Press, 1991), 107.

51. Ibid., 108.

52. Ibid.

53. Romaldo Giurgola, "Architecture: More than a Building," *Architecture Australia*, Vol. 76, No. 3 (May 1987): 43–46, as quoted on 44.

54. Doug Kelbaugh, "Towards an Architecture of Place: Design Principles For Critical Regionalism," in Amourgis, *Critical Regionalism*, 184.

55. Ibid.

56. Ann Cline, "Bounded Domains and Tactile Presences: The 'Little Houses' of Cannaregio, the Teahouses of Japan, and Critical Regionalism," in Amourgis, *Critical Regionalism*, 299.

57. George Santayana, as quoted in Dewey, *Art as Experience*, 156.

58. Donald Schon, as quoted in Abel *Architecture and Identity*, 103.

59. S. J. Brown, as quoted in ibid., 102.

60. Ibid., 97.

61. For a thorough exposition of metaphor in Japanese gardens, see Charles W. Moore, William J. Mitchell, and William Turnbull, Jr., *The Poetics of Gardens* (Cambridge, MA: The MIT Press, 1988).

62. For a compelling and comprehensive discussion of semiotics related to landscape, see Anne Whiston Spirn, *The Language of Landscape* (New Haven, CT: Yale University Press, 1998). Metonymy is defined on page 227.

63. For an introduction to semiotics as they apply to landscape architecture and a bibliography with many more resources, see Chia Yin Wu, "Semiotics and New Urbanism in North Texas: Comparing Designer Intention and User Perception" (The University of Texas at Arlington, ProQuest, UMI Dissertations Publishing, 2012).

64. "The Acequias of San Antonio"; online at http://www.tamu.edu/ccbn/dewitt/adp/archives/glossary/glossary.html.

65. John Haldane, "Form, Meaning and Value: A History of the Philosophy of Architecture," *The Journal of Architecture*, Vol. 4, No. 1 (Spring 1999): 9–20.

66. Ian L. McHarg, Design with Nature (New York, NY: John Wiley, 1991), 5.

67. Lewis Mumford, as quoted in Gary J. Coates, "Biotechnology and Regional Integration," in Canizaro, *Architectural Regionalism*, 354.

68. Michael Polanyi, *The Tacit Dimension* (Garden City, NY: Doubleday, 1966).

69. Denis Donoghue, as quoted in Laurie Olin, "Water, Urban Nature, and the Art of Landscape Design," in Steiner, Thompson, and Carbonell, *Nature and Cities*, 404.

CHAPTER 7

1. Architecture for the Blind, http://arch4blind.com/.

2. Excerpt from Aldo Leopold, "Ho! Compadres Piñoneros" (1929), in Susan L. Flader and J. Baird Callicot, eds., *The River of the Mother of God and other Essays by Aldo Leopold* (Madison: University of Wisconsin Press, 1991), 148–49. This celebration of the sounds of the pinyon jay appeared originally in *Forest Fire and other Verse*, edited by John D. Guthrie (Portland, OR: Dunham Printing Company, 1929).

3. See https://en.wikipedia.org/wiki/Suikinkutsu.

4. Connie X. Wang, Isaac A. Hilburn, Daw-An Wu, Yuki Mizuhara, Christopher P. Cousté, Jacob N. H. Abrahams, Sam E. Bernstein, Ayumu Matani, Shinsuke Shimojo, and Joseph L. Kirschvink, "Transduction of the Geomagnetic Field as Evidenced from 94 Alpha-band Activity in the Human Brain," *eNeuro* (18 March 2019); online at http://www.eneuro.org/content/eneuro/early/2019/03/18/ENEURO.0483-18.2019.full.pdf.

5. Volker M. Welter, *Biopolis: Patrick Geddes and the City of Life* (Cambridge, MA: The MIT Press, 2002), 39.

6. "Mexican Oregano, Oregano Cimarrón, Hierba Dulce," http://www.texasbeyondhistory.net/ethnobot/images/mexican-oregano.html.

7. For specific locations in Africa, see http://loessground.blogspot.com/2019/01/adobe-as-loess-why-not.html.

8. Panos Koulermos, as quoted in Spyros Amourgis, "Paradigms in Praxis," in Spyros Amourgis, ed., *Critical Regionalism: The Pomona Meeting Proceedings* (Pomona: The College of Environmental Design, California State Polytechnic University, 1991), 75.

9. Steven A. Moore, "Technology, Place, and Nonmodern Regionalism," in Vincent B. Canizaro, ed., *Architectural Regionalism: Collected Writings on Place, Identity, Modernity, and Tradition* (New York, NY: Princeton Architectural Press, 2007), 436.

10. Panos Koulermos, as quoted in Amourgis, *Critical Regionalism*, 75.

11. See Chapter 7 of this book, "Shops at La Cantera."

12. Welter, *Biopolis*, 12.

13. "Henry C. Beck Jr." Obituary; http://forum.dallasmetropolis.com/showthread.php/7332-Henry-C-Beck-Jr?s=86ff5106508f7c6ed05d348491932918.

14. "Henry C. Beck, Jr. Park, Dallas, Texas," http://asla.org/awards/2006/06winners/521.html.

15. Daniel Levitin, as quoted in Ann Whiston Spurn, "The Granite Garden: Where Do We Stand Today," in Frederick R. Steiner, George F. Thompson, and Armando Carbonell, eds., *Nature and Cities: The Ecological Imperative in Urban Design and Planning* (Cambridge, MA: Lincoln Institute of Land Policy, 2016), 66.

16. For a video, see Andrew Gipe, "VIDEO: *Elegance in Motion at Calatrava's Liège-Guillemins Railway Station in Belgium*," ArchDaily (February 15, 2014); http://www.archdaily.com/?p=476994.

17. For a thorough exposition of techniques and case studies for public involvement in landscape architecture, see David De la Pena, Diane Jones Allen, Randolph T. Hester Jr., Jeffrey Hou, Laura J. Lawson, and Marcia J. McNally, eds. *Design as Democracy: Techniques for Collective Creativity* (Washington, DC: Island Press, 2017).

18. William C. Welch and Greg Gant, *The Southern Heirloom Garden* (Dallas, TX: Taylor Publishing, 1995).

19. Lewis Mumford, "Excerpts from *The South in Architecture*," in Canizaro, Architectural Regionalism, 97.

20. Juhani Pallasmaa, "Tradition and Modernity: The Feasibility of Regional Architecture in Post-Modern Society," in Canizaro, *Architectural Regionalism*, 128–39. Originally published in The Architectural Review, Vol. 176, No. 6 (May 1988): 26–34.

21. Harwell Hamilton Harris, "Regionalism and Nationalism in Architecture," in Canizaro, *Architectural Regionalism*, 57–64. Originally published in *Texas Quarterly*, Vol. 1, No. 1 (February 1958): 115–24.

22. A key source for community involvement in landscape design and planning is Randolf T. Hester, Jr. and Amber D. Nelson, *Inhabiting the Sacred in Everyday Life: How to Design a Place that Touches Your Heart, Stirs You to Consecrate and Cultivate It as Home, Dwell Intentionally within It, Slay Monsters for It, and Let It Loose in Your Democracy* (Staunton, VA: George F. Thompson Publishing, 2019).

23. Kristina Hill, "Form Follows Flows: Systems, Design, and the Aesthetic Experience of Change," in Steiner, Thompson, and Carbonell, *Nature and Cities*, 354.

24. Mariken van Nimwegen, "Hastings Park"; http://www.pps.org/great_public_spaces/one?public_place_id=517.

CHAPTER 8

1. Aldo Leopold, *A Sand County Almanac and Sketches Here and There* (New York, NY: Oxford University Press, 1949), xxvi.

2. Fenestrations are openings in the walls of a structure.

3. John Dewey, *Art as Experience* (New York, NY: Perigree Books, 1980; originally delivered as the first William James Lecturer at Harvard in 1934 and first published in 1952 by Minton, Balch and Company of New York City).

4. Judith Butler, *Gender Trouble: Feminism and the Subversion of Identity* (New York, NY: Routledge, 1990).

5. Richard Weller, "The City Is Not an Egg: Western Urbanization in Relation to Changing Perceptions of Nature," in Frederick R. Steiner, George F. Thompson, and Armando Carbonell, eds. *Nature and Cities: The Ecological Imperative in Urban Design and Planning* (Cambridge, MA: Lincoln Institute of Land Policy, 2016), 48.

6. William Cronon, *Uncommon Ground: Toward Reinventing Nature* (New York, NY: W.W. Norton, 1995), 83.

7. Kongjian Yu, "Creating Deep Forms in Urban Nature: The Peasant's Approach to Urban Design," in Steiner, Thompson, and Carbonell, *Nature and Cities*, 95.

8. Edward O. Wilson, *Half Earth: Our Planet's Fight for Life* (New York, NY: Liveright, 2016).

9. In December 2022, at the UN 2022 biodiversity conference in Montreal, Canada, roughly 190 countries approved a United Nations agreement to protect 30 percent of Earth's land and oceans by 2030 and to take a variety of other actions to mitigate the loss of biodiversity. See https://www.nytimes.com/2022/12/19/climate/biodiversity-cop15-montreal-30x30.html.

10. See Steph Wong Ken, *The Line Between 'Invasive' and 'Native' Blurs*; https://thelocal.to/invasive-tree-species/.

11. Weller, "The City Is Not an Egg," 43.

12. *UN Report: Nature's Dangerous Decline 'Unprecedented'; Species Extinction Rates 'Accelerating'*; online at https://www.un.org/sustainabledevelopment/blog/2019/05/nature-decline-unprecedented-report/.

13. Ian L. McHarg, *Design with Nature* (New York, NY: John Wiley and Sons, 1992), 154.

14. Ibid., iv.

15. Jim Dodge, "Living by Life: Some Bioregional Theory and Practice," in Vincent B. Canizaro, ed., *Architectural Regionalism: Collected Writings on Place, Identity, Modernity, and Tradition* (New York, NY: Princeton Architectural Press, 2007), 341–49.

16. Peter Berg, "Bioregionalism" (defined and updated 2002); online at http://www.planetdrum.org/shadow/bioregion_bioregionalism_defined.htm; accessed in August 2021.

17. A thorough discussion of the Prairie School can be found in Robert E. Grese, *Jens Jensen: Maker of Natural Parks and Garden* (Baltimore, MD: The Johns Hopkins University Press, in association with the Center for American Places, 1992).

18. Wilhelm Miller, as quoted in Grese, *Jens Jensen*, 50. Miller wrote about Jensen in *Architectural Record, Country Life in America* and other publications and, according to Grese, was likely the first person to write about Jensen's design work as a "distinctive American style of landscape architecture" (Grese, *Jens Jensen*, 45).

19. Ibid.

20. Arthur E. Bye, *Art into Landscape: Landscape into Art* (Mesa, AZ: PDA Publishers, 1983).

21. Aldo Leopold, "The State of the Profession" (1940), in Susan L. Flader and J. Baird Callicot, eds., *The River of the Mother of God and Other Essays by Aldo Leopold* (Madison: University of Wisconsin Press, 1991), 277.

22. Leopold, *The Conservation Ethic*, 291.

23. Volker M. Welter, *Biopolis: Patrick Geddes and the City of Life* (Cambridge, MA, The MIT Press, 2002), 37.

24. "Northern Tallgrass Prairie National Wildlife Refuge," HPA Environmental Impact Statement Summary. Online at http://www.fws.gov/midwest/planning/northerntallgrass/.

25. Glen C. Moore, and M. E. Merchant, *Chiggers*; https://insects.tamu.edu/extension/publications/epubs/e-365.cfm.

26. For a discussion on landscape preferences, see Steven C. Bourassa, *The Aesthetics of Landscape* (London, UK: Belhaven Press, 1991), 121–32.

27. Liane Lefaivre and Alexander Tzonis, *Critical Regionalism: Architecture and Identity in a Globalized World* (New York, NY: Prestel, 2003), 20.

28. Erin Douglas, "Climate change is making Texas hotter, threatening public health, water supply and the state's infrastructure, *Texas Tribune* (October 7, 2021)"; online at https://www.texastribune.org/2021/10/07/texas-climate-change-heat-water/.

29. To learn about both the practical concerns and the aesthetics of intermingled planting combinations, see Piet Oudolf and Noel Kingsbury, *Planting: A New Perspective* (Portland, OR: Timber Press, 2013).

30. See the discussion on indeterminacy and postmodernism in Weller, "The City Is Not an Egg," 41–42.

31. See Joan. I. Nassauer, "Messy ecosystems, orderly frames," in *Landscape Journal*, Vol. 14, No. 2 (Fall 1995): 161–70.

32. See "Tianjin Qiaoyuan Park: The Adaptation Palettes, Tianjin City, China"; https://www.asla.org/2010awards/033.html.

33. I am very fortunate and grateful to have received access, with the help of Robert O'Kennon, to the plant database of BRIT for this purpose.

34. For a thorough discussion of plant growth strategies from what Grime refers to as CSR theory (Competitors, Stress Tolerators, and Ruderals), see Phillip J. Grime, *Plant Strategies, Vegetation Processes, and Ecosystem Properties, 2nd Edition* (New York, NY: John Wiley, 2006).

35. For an early discussion in the 1960s of the complexity of creating what later became known as "biospheres," see the chapter, "The World is a Capsule," in McHarg, *Design with Nature*, 95–115.
36. Oudolf provides a detailed description of the contrast between passive and active maintenance in intermingled planting designs in Oudolf and Kingsbury, *Planting*.
37. See the discussion of Fresh Kills Lifescape in James Corner, "The Ecological Imagination: Life in the City and the Public Realm," in Steiner, Thompson, and Carbonell, *Nature and Cities*, 20.
38. Clair Enlow and Charles Anderson, "Art in the Open," *Landscape Architecture*, Vol. 97, No. 8 (August 2007): 107.
39. Spyros Amourgis, "Paradigms in Praxis," in Spyros Amourgis, ed., *Critical Regionalism: The Pomona Meeting Proceedings* (Pomona: The College of Environmental Design, California State Polytechnic University, 1991), 43–143, as quoted on 118.
40. Lefaivre and Tzonis, *Critical Regionalism*, 20.
41. J. William "Bill" Thompson, from "Land Matters," *Landscape Architecture*, Vol. 96, No. 4 (April 2006): 11.
42. "Bloedel Reserve Self-Guided Tour" brochure (2011).
43. "Lancelot 'Capability' Brown," http://www.capabilitybrown.org/lancelot-capability-brown.
44. Anna Maria Rilke, as quoted in Amourgis, "Paradigms in Praxis," 62.
45. Elizabeth Meyer wrote a manifesto on the imperative to include aesthetics in ecological design that includes a detailed discussion of hypernature as a defamiliarizing and psychologically transformative experience. See Elizabeth Meyer, "Sustaining Beauty: the Performance of Appearance," in Steiner, Thompson, and Carbonell, *Nature and Cities*, 119–45.
46. Ibid., 137.
47. Barbara Stauffacher Solomon, *Green Architecture and the Agrarian Garden* (New York, NY: Rizolli International Publications, 1988).
48. John R. Stilgoe, *Common Landscapes of America, 1580 to 1845* (New Haven, CT: Yale University Press, 1982).
49. Solomon, *Green Architecture and the Agrarian Garden.*
50. Ibid., 95.
51. Christopher Alexander, *The Timeless Way of Building* (New York, NY: Oxford University Press, 1979), 254.
52. Lon D. Kaufman, "The Design of an Architectural Design Process: Implementing Critical Regionalism in Eastern Iowa" (Master's thesis, University of Iowa, 1985), 12.
53. "About Chandler," http://www.visitchandler.com/static/index.cfm?contentID=43.
54. Gail Feigenbaum, "Radical Cactus: The Other Garden at the Getty Center," *Australian Humanities Review* (July 1, 2005); online at https://australianhumanitiesreview.org/2005/07/01/radical-cactus-the-other-garden-at-the-getty-center/.
55. Laurie Olin, "Water, Urban Nature, and the Art of Landscape Design," in Steiner, Thompson, and Carbonell, *Nature and Cities*, 381.
56. "Chihuly," http://www.chihuly.com/biography.aspx.
57. Kristina Hill, "Form Follows Flows: Systems, Design, and the Aesthetic Experience of Change," in Steiner, Thompson, and Carbonell, *Nature and Cities*, 355.
58. "Denver Botanic Gardens' Core Values," https://www.botanicgardens.org/mission-values.
59. Meyer, "Sustaining Beauty," 147.
60. Shirley L. Maina and Jane Villa-Lobos, "North America: A Regional Overview," *Smithsonian National Museum of Natural History*; online at http://botany.si.edu/projects/cpd/na/na.htm.

CONCLUSION

1. Alvaro Siza y Viera, as quoted in Kenneth Frampton, "Prospects for a Critical Regionalism," *Perspecta*, Vol. 20 (1983): 150.
2. Richard Ingersoll, "Critical Regionalism in Houston: A Case for the Menil Collection," in Spyros Amourgis, ed., *Critical Regionalism: The Pomona Meeting Proceedings* (Pomona: The College of Environmental Design, California State Polytechnic University, 1991), 233.
3. Kristine D. Woolsey, "Critical Regionalism: A Theory of Process," in Amourgis, *Critical Regionalism*, 322–30.
4. Frank Welch, "Regionalism as Renewable Resource," *Texas Architect*, Vo. 39, No. 3 (May–June 1989): 38–41.
5. Woolsey, "Critical Regionalism."
6. Renzo Bassani, "Historic Continuity: Building and Urban Typological Studies in Architectural Education," in Amourgis, *Critical Regionalism*, 269.
7. Ibid., 269–70.
8. Keith L. Eggener, "Placing Resistance: A Critique of Critical Regionalism," in Vincent B. Canizaro, ed., *Architectural Regionalism: Collected Writings on Place, Identity, Modernity, and Tradition* (New York, NY: Princeton Architectural Press, 2007), 400.
9. Ann Whiston Spirn, "The Granite Garden: Where Do We Stand Today?," in Frederick R. Steiner, George F. Thompson, and Armando Carbonell, eds., *Nature and Cities: The Ecological Imperative in Urban Design and Planning* (Cambridge, MA: Lincoln Institute of Land Policy, 2016), 54.
10. Steven C. Bourassa, *The Aesthetics of Landscape* (London, UK: Belhaven Press, 1991), 114.
11. William Wurster, as quoted in Welch, "Regionalism as Renewable Resource," 39.
12. See Spyros Amourgis, "Paradigms in Praxis," in Amourgis, *Critical Regionalism*, 43–143.
13. William Wurster, as quoted in Welch, "Regionalism as Renewable Resource," 39.
14. Paul Ricoeur, "Universal Civilization and National Cultures," in Canizaro, *Architectural Regionalism*, 46. Originally published in Paul Ricouer, *History and Truth* (Evanston, IL: Northwestern University Press, 1965), 271–84.
15. Wendell Berry, "The Regional Motive," in Canizaro, *Architectural Regionalism*, 37–40.
16. Woolsey, "Critical Regionalism."
17. Kile D. Brown, Nicholas T. Dines, and Charles W. Harris, eds., *Time-saver Standards for Landscape Architecture* (New York, NY: McGraw-Hill, 1998).
18. Lawrence W. Speck, "Regionalism and Invention," in Canizaro, *Architectural Regionalism*, 70–79, as quoted on 72. Originally published in *Center: New Regionalism 3* (1987): 8–19.
19. John Dewey, *Art as Experience* (New York, NY: Perigree Books, 1980; originally delivered as the first William James Lecturer at Harvard in 1934 and first published in 1952 in New York City, NY, by Minton, Balch and Company).
20. Ibid., 222.
21. Critics have called Thorncrown Chapel "one of the finest religious spaces of modern times," and it has received numerous honors and awards, including the American Institute of Architects (AIA) Design of the Year Award in 1981 and AIA's prestigious 25 Year Award. AIA members also ranked Thorncrown Chapel fourth on an AIA list of top buildings of the twentieth century. See www.thorncrown.com.
22. See Nina-Marie E. Lister, "Resilience Beyond Rhetoric in Urban Planning and Design," in Steiner, Thompson, and Carbonell, *Nature and Cities*, 303–25.

Index

Note: Illustrations appear in *italics*.

Acknowledgments

This book is the culmination of a long journey of regional and aesthetic exploration. It began with the help of Richard Rome, then a professor at the University of Texas at Arlington who incited this journey with his summer classes on landscape aesthetics and later served as the chair of my thesis committee when I undertook my early research on critical regionalism. Other academic practitioners who assisted the evolution of the manuscript through discussions, encouragement, and funding include Dr. Pat Taylor, Dr. Diane Jones Allen, Dr. Richard Francaviglia, Gary O. Robinette, and Don Gatzke. Financial support was provided by the University of Texas at Arlington in the form of a research grant, funding for travel and participation at numerous conferences, and a faculty development leave that facilitated completion of the manuscript.

Many of the ideas in this book were originally proposed during lectures at conferences of the Council of Educators in Landscape Architect (CELA). These conferences were an invaluable source of carefully curated tours where I captured many of the images in this book and were also a source of travel funds that facilitated visits to the built projects featured here throughout the United States, and in Europe and Asia.

One of the goals for this book is to bridge academic theory with landscape architecture practice. Many working landscape architects generously gave of their time to present their projects and to outline their design thinking with formal interviews, unstructured informal conversations on regional topics, and tours of their built projects. Special thanks go to Bill Wenk, FASLA, Charles Anderson, FASLA, Chris Phillips, FCSLA, and Kelty McKinnon. Special mention is also given to Rosa Finsley, ASLA, who was my first mentor as an employer, a committed regionalist designer, and the person who first introduced me to the work of the architecture firm Lake/Flato, as we designed and constructed landscapes for several Lake/Flato projects. Other landscape architects, architects, and artists who made important contributions include: The landscape architects J. Robert Anderson, David Andrews, Stuart Appel, Roger Burhart, Stan Cowan, James David, Topher Delaney, Angela Danadjieva, Colin Franklin, Jennifer Guthrie, Theodore Hare, Todd Johnson, Mark Kopatz, Peter Latz, Eleanor H. McKinney, Mark Naylor, Jim Richards, William S. Seaman, Bob Smith, Barbara Swift, and Oliver Windham. The architects Holly Arthur, Ted Flato, Kenneth Frampton, Bob Harris, and Bing Thom were also very helpful. The environmental artists and sculptors Lorna Jordan and Stacy Levy contributed to the book with their ideas and their projects. I am forever indebted to all of them and to all the designers and educators who offered ideas and suggested built examples for this book.

This book would not have been possible without the tireless efforts of George Thompson to keep the fires burning for book publishing, in general, and for the study of places, in particular. The current incarnation of the award-winning George F. Thompson Publishing Company and its affiliation with the Center for the Study of Place is the ideal vehicle for this work, and I am very fortunate to have landed there in the company of so many distinguished authors and the book designers, Ann Lowe and David Skolkin. I also wish to acknowledge Dr. Frederick R. "Fritz" Steiner, who started his involvement in this project with a very productive and supportive peer review of the manuscript and continued his support by composing the foreword to this book.

Many thanks are due to the people who have helped to edit the text including George F. Thompson, Dr. Tracey Daniels Lerberg, Dr. Cole Ryberg, Mikki Soroczak, and Sonja Ryberg, my life partner who has been an enormous source of support through every step of the publishing process.

About the Essayist

Frederick R. Steiner has been the Dean and Paley Professor for the University of Pennsylvania School of Design since 2016. He previously taught at the University of Pennsylvania; Washington State University; Arizona State University, where he served as the Director of the School of Planning and Landscape Architecture in the College of Architecture and Environmental Design; and most recently at the University of Texas, Austin, where he has served as Dean of the School of Architecture from 2001 to 2016 and held the Harry M. Rockwell Chair in Architecture. He has written, edited, or co-edited 22 books, including *Design with Nature Now* (Lincoln Institute of Land Policy, 2019), which was named a Best Book of 2019 by the American Society of Landscape Architects, *Design for a Vulnerable Planet* (University of Texas Press, 2011), *The Living Landscape* (Island Press, 2008), and *Human Ecology: How Nature and Culture Shape Our World* (Island Press, 2002; paperback edition, 2016). He is a Fellow of both the American Academy in Rome and American Society of Landscape Architects who has also served as President of the Hill Country Conservancy and as Chair of Envision Central Texas.

About the Author

David Hopman, ASLA, PLA was born in Salzburg, Austria, while his father, a U.S. foreign service officer, was stationed there. The Hopman family moved regularly, and he experienced both the adventure and the dislocation of being continually uprooted from place to place. He attended a German school in Bilbao, Spain, for early grade school, then back to Washington, D.C., for grades five through eight before attending high school in Stuttgart, Germany. He has remained in the United States since returning after high school, living in Washington, D.C., Maryland, Connecticut, Tennessee, and in North Texas, where he currently resides. Professor Hopman holds a Master of Music in classical guitar performance from Southern Methodist University and a Master of Landscape Architecture from the University of Texas at Arlington.

One of the most powerful memories from his childhood was the experience of returning to Spain for a summer trip from his home in Germany in the summer between the 9th and 10th grades. Waves of emotion engulfed him and he wept uncontrollably upon seeing his childhood home in Neguri, near Bilbao. This unforgettable experience demonstrated to him in a visceral way the psychological hold that place can have on us and how we dismiss the importance of place at our peril.

Ironically, the place where he made his home and practiced three careers—as a professional classical guitarist, as a landscape architect, and, since 2004, as an educator at the University of Texas at Arlington's MLA program—is famous for its dissipated physical and cultural regional character. His longstanding interest in regionalism that culminated with this book reflects his effort to make sense of and to nurture regionalism in his home of North Texas and also far beyond.

Early in his career as a landscape architect he discovered that critical regionalism is a vessel deep and broad enough to hold his regional design thinking and his evolution as both a designer and as an educator. He has broadly shared his ideas as an advocate for regionalism at academic conferences and public venues throughout the United States and in Asia and Europe. He has also taught a graduate studio based on critical regionalism for the landscape architecture program at the University of Texas at Arlington since 2004, bringing regionalist thinking to new generations. Most of the chapters in this book received their first readings by both landscape and architecture students in his studios and design theory classes.

David Hopman has also been very active in promoting environmental and ecological sustainability in the profession of landscape architecture. He designed and installed the first extensive green roof in North Texas on the campus of UT-Arlington. He was also in charge of Sustainable Sites Initiative

(SITES) Certification for one of the first three landscapes certified worldwide during the pilot project phase in 2012. He subsequently participated in a subject matter expert group formed for development of the first SITES AP test in Washington DC., sponsored by the Green Building Council, owner of LEED and SITES.

Since 2014, Professor Hopman has written and lectured extensively on his ideas for developing a new urban ecology using synthetic communities of indigenous plants he calls "aesthetically qualified native urban polycultures." A short introduction to the topic is presented here in Chapter 8. For more information, essays and videos search for Hopman PPN, or Hopman polyculture.

ABOUT THE BOOK

Creative Regionalism: Renewing the Aesthetic Experience of Landscape in Environmental Design and Planning was brought to publication in an edition of 800 softcover copies with gatefold flaps. The text was set in Minion, the paper is Moorim–Neostar matte, 150 gsm weight, and the book was professionally printed and bound by P. Chan & Edward, Inc., in Korea.

Publisher and Project Director: George F. Thompson
Editorial and Research Assistant: Mikki Soroczak
Manuscript Editor: Purna Makaram
Book Design: Ann Lowe and David Skolkin
Book Production: David Skolkin

Published in 2025. First hardcover edition.
Printed in Korea on acid-free paper.

George F. Thompson Publishing, L.L.C.
217 Oak Ridge Circle
Staunton, VA 24401–3511, U.S.A.
www.gftbooks.com

33 32 31 30 29 28 27 26 25   1 2 3 4 5

The Library of Congress Preassigned Control Number is 2025941729.

ISBN: 978-1-938086-54-0